REVIEWS

"The law of gravity and the Holy Spirit are ultimately part of one and the same divine energy. But for far too long we have not believed that. As believers we felt threatened by science and were mostly defensive towards it. That is a false tension and a false dichotomy. God, as scripture assures us, is the origin of all that is good and true, in both science and religion.

"In *Faith and Science*, Deacon Robert Hesse, speaking competently from both science and theology, shows us how faith and science can be happily married, to the enrichment of both. Hesse brings together perspectives from physics, chemistry, biology, and psychology and weds them with Christian revelation and Christian spirituality in a synthesis that is solid and trustworthy.

"This is a needed book, both for those of us who still fear science and for those of us who have long made peace with it. It will help dispel the fears of the fearful and bring some rich new perspectives to those whose faith has already befriended science."

Ronald Rolheiser, O.M.I., M.A., M.R.Sc., Ph.D., S.T.D., Author & Faculty member in the Institute for Contemporary Spirituality at Oblate School of Theology, San Antonio, Texas

"Dr. Robert Hesse, Ph.D., introduced me and our Institute to the Conference on Medicine and Religion, the Near-Death Experience, and his powerful affirmation of the spiritual and mystical dimensions of the human experience. This book puts all that and more in your hands and convincingly brings together science and faith that for too long have been separated. Read this book and your mind, heart, and soul will say, 'Thank you!'"

John K. Graham, M.Sc., M.D., D.Min., President and CEO, Institute for Spirituality and Health at the Texas Medical Center and author

"If you desire to rediscover enchantment in our disenchanted world, read this book. Let Robert Hesse help you look through a new window to see the beauty of the human spirit, the human mind, of nature and the universe. By doing so, you will discover new depth in understanding Jesus' prayer, 'May they all be one. . . .' Hesse shows that what we often presume to be contradictions are really relationships of opposites: whether the messiness and beauty of life, the oneness of the Divine and human, faith and science, chaos and Providence, matter and spirit, mind and body, the conscious and the unconscious. He has the uncanny art of leading the reader to experience joy in the simplicity and beauty inherent in what might, for the unscholarly, seem like intimidating scientific and theological realities. Take the book in hand and let yourself be enchanted."

  Donald Nesti, C.S.Sp., M.A., S.T.L., S.T.D., Founder and Professor Emeritus, The Nesti Center for Faith and Culture, The University of St. Thomas; Former President of Duquesne University

"Reading this book, Deacon Robert Hesse gave me a seat on his journey of faith and science, garlanded with his spiritual love. His amazing voyage came across theology, classical and quantum physics, chemistry and finally coming to a crucial, enigmatic and controversial neuroscientific subject: consciousness. I am honored to be his companion in his foldaway researching the mystery of the dying brain. But I am more privileged to be the friend of a man, with plenty of humility, a commonality with those who suffer and always ready to help. Let's accompany Bob on his astonishing and inspiring journey."

  Calixto Machado M.D., Ph.D., Neuroscientist; Discoverer, new state of disordered consciousness; Fellow, American Academy of Neurology; President, International Symposia and Author of book, both titled, *Brain Death and Disorders of Consciousness*; and Cuban Society of Clinical Neurophysiology

"Robert Hesse dares to undertake such a daunting task in writing this book. For the secular mind, it is not easy to maintain two seemingly contradictory realities of science and faith, physics and metaphysics, nature and the Supernature. The author testifies how he manages to reconcile these two worlds through a personal journey. The reader will discover in here an adventure characterized by child-like awe, deep yearning for the Truth, and surprising encounters with Love."

> **Joseph Tham, L.C., S.T.L., M.D., Ph.D.**, Former Dean of the School of Bioethics, Pontifical University Regina Apostolorum; Author and editor of numerous articles and books, including *Interreligious Perspectives on Mind, Genes and the Self*

"It is not uncommon for scientists to 'flip,' that is, for them to transcend, often quite suddenly, their hard-won secular rationalism and materialism in surprising moments of ecstasy and extraordinary experience. They often then understand, with something of a shock, that their materialism was just an interpretation of the science, not the science itself. The present book is a deeply autobiographical story of a similar transformation, but one spread out over many years and decades. Bob is transparent, blunt, and honest about his birth Catholicism, about his falling away and its good reasons, and about his eventual return and its good reasons. He is just as open and vulnerable about his ecstatic rapture in a chapel, about the teachings of the Christian mystics, and about the gorgeous details of physics, cosmology, mathematics, biology, and neuroscience that can work with and through all of this. The result is a vision of God and the cosmos that does not unduly separate them, that sees religion and science as two sides of the same human coin."

> **Jeffrey J. Kripal, M.A., Ph.D.**, J. Newton Rayzor Professor of Religion and Associate Dean of the School of Humanities, Rice University and author of *The Flip: Epiphanies of Mind and the Future of Knowledge*

"Secularism, materialism, scientism and individualism have attempted to silence the mystical, religious and contemplative voice. More than ever contemporary society needs to rediscover and restore our contemplative and mystical consciousness.

"Deacon Robert Hesse, with his utter openness and simplicity of a man searching for the path leading to deep intimacy with the unconditional and unrestricted source of life and light, enables us sojourners of life to restore awe, beauty and poetry. His willingness to move from hurt and suffering to the encounter with unconditional love, truth and beauty provides us a guide to move through difficult situations in life by letting go of dualistic assumptions and surrendering to the Love of God.

"The insights of *Faith & Science: A Journey into God's Mystical Love* help us cultivate a vital relationship with the transcendent-immanent God, an openness to life and everything that implies and a contemplative consciousness which connects us with all creation."

Binh Quach, C.S.Sp., Ph.D., Director of The Nesti Center for Faith and Culture at the University of St. Thomas, and author

"Not many theological works on science begin with the concept of love; that is because not many see as clearly as Deacon Hesse does here. The triune love of God is the foundation of all reality, as He is both Love and Lover, both *esse* and *ens*. Modern scientific inquiry will advance correctly only when rooted in this reality, in a God who creates, conserves, and crowns all things in a supreme act of charity."

David Meconi, S.J., Lic. Theol., D.Phil. (Oxford), Director of Catholic Studies Centre, St. Louis University, and author of *On Self-Harm, Narcissism, Atonement, and the Vulnerable Christ*

"In our secular world it is so refreshing to hear how a personal journey was transfigured by science into a return to faith and God. I highly recommend this book to both the scientist and theologian dwelling within all of us."

    Harold Koenig, M.D., editor, *Handbook of Religion and Health*, and author

"This is an amazing book. It lays out the author's journey from what many assume to be a duality of science and faith and it ends with the convergence of all science and faith in love. This provides guidance to anyone who is frustrated by duality and is looking for a synthesis."

    Kimball Kehoe, M.Div., D.B.A. (Harvard), Chairman, Contemplative Network; Retired Professor, Rice University; Retired Board Member, Institute for Spirituality and Health

"I have had the honor and privilege to be walking the spiritual path with Bob Hesse for a number of years. We have both listened in awe as Fr. Thomas Keating taught us how to surrender to the Divine Therapy and let the transformative process work on our false selves.

"Dr. Hesse has one foot firmly planted in the world of neuroscience and the other foot in the mystical realm of Spirit. This grounding in both worlds uniquely qualifies him to serve as a guide to all who experience the scientific and the spiritual as a both-and phenomenon. Prepare to be charmed, challenged, and educated by this courageous journey into the mysteries of faith and science."

    Nicholas G. Cole, M.D., Former Board Chairman of Contemplative Outreach Ltd., Presenter of Centering Prayer Workshops, and Facilitator of Contemplative Retreats since 1993

"On the long journey to find his truth Robert Hesse searched intently in all the eight directions of the natural and social sciences only to find his successful studies did not bring him peace.

"Enhancing his Catholic faith Hesse turned to Trappist monks and Zen masters and with their guidance he discovered the inner pattern of the mind.

"On the last page of his book Hesse extols the serenity of interreligious dialogue where, instead of an answer, he found his peace in service of others in accord with quiet mystery."

 Robert Kennedy, S.J., M.A., Th.M., Ph.D., S.T.D., D.Min., Professor Emeritus (Retired), St. Peter's University; Zen Buddhist Roshi, Jesuit Priest, Psychotherapist, and author of *Zen Gifts to Christians* and *Zen Spirit, Christian Spirit*

"This reviewer has been most drawn to the memoir chapters, placed at the beginning and the end of *Faith & Science*, by my long-time Centering Prayer friend Robert Hesse. I found them to be very moving—authentic, courageous vulnerability. Which is also present in the other chapters, where I made brief forays.

"Getting to know Bob better in this way has been a privilege. It has also been a journey for me—God speaking to me. Grace.

"Since we are all connected, which was shown in numerous ways throughout the book, I invite other readers to explore what might be the grace for them in *Faith & Science: A Journey into God's Mystical Love*. It is a book to read SLOWLY. And to savor . . . To trust . . ."

 Carole G. Pentony, Ph.D., Clinical Psychologist and Contemplative Network board member; Former Faculty, Baylor College of Medicine and the University of St. Thomas; Published on Psychology of Community, Therapists and Children.

"Deacon Robert Hesse writes, 'With further study and my diaconate ordination approaching and continued serious illnesses in the family, I more than ever needed a prayer life that would allow me to surrender to God's will.' How many of us need a prayer life, an ongoing, intimate dialogue with God, to help us surrender to some of the life-long heartaches life can bring? We search for meaning, comfort, and strength in scripture, from religious writers, through prayer. Deacon Hesse searched science or, as he more accurately writes, was led by the Spirit to explore what science reveals about the eternal presence, the unfailing purpose, and the love of God for us and all creation.

"For those of us minimally schooled in the world of scientific discoveries, Hesse takes us on a somewhat challenging journey through some of the basics in physics, chemistry, and biology, all of which help expand our appreciation and consciousness of God's compassionate design in the ever-expanding universe. His clear and concise descriptions will take you beyond simplistic or domesticated images of God and God's will towards a renewed, awe-filled respect for our Creator who continues to create and who still so loves the world. Finally, Hesse describes well how the spiritual practice of contemplative prayer can free us to respect, surrender, and even participate in God's ongoing creative work. It is this deeper consciousness that can become for us a new source of meaning, comfort, and strength as we are 'distracted' by the truly extraordinary beauty and mystery of God's love and ways."

Maureen Bacchi, M.S.W., L.S.C.W., Psychotherapist and Certified Spiritual Director; Adjunct Professor, University of St. Thomas, Center for Faith and Culture, teaching the Art and Asceticism of Dialogue

FAITH AND SCIENCE

FAITH AND SCIENCE

A Journey into God's Mystical Love

Robert J. Hesse, Ph.D.

Foreword by Robert J. Spitzer, S.J., Ph.D.

A Crossroad Book
The Crossroad Publishing Company
New York

ROYALTY DONATONS—All author royalties are donated to Contemplative Network Inc. (www.contemplative.net), a nonprofit 501(c)(3), interdenominational Christian organization. Its mission is to teach centering and contemplative prayer, participate in prayer-related scientific research, and promote interfaith dialogue. Its governing board has interfaith representation.

The Crossroad Publishing Company
1 Blue Hill Plaza Lobby Level, Suite 1509
Pearl River, New York 10965

Copyright © 2022 Contemplative Network

All Rights Reserved. No part of this book may be reproduced, stored in a retrieval system, or transmitted, in any form or by any means, electronic, mechanical, photocopying, recording, or otherwise, without the written permission of The Crossroad Publishing Company.

Printed in the United States of America

No copyright infringement is intended, ref. figure credits in endnotes

Figures without endnotes are by author © 2022 Contemplative Network

Library of Congress Cataloging-in-Publication Data available from the Library of Congress.
hard cover   ISBN: 9780824595074
tradepaper   ISBN: 9780824595081
epub   ISBN: 9780824595098

Cover Photo: Penguins, Half Moon Island, Antarctic - Photo
Front Cover by Author
Text design by Tim Holtz
Editing by Jan Masterson

To my blessed wife, Linda, who taught me how to love.

Contents

Foreword xix
Preface xxi

1 MOTIVATED TO LOVE 1
   SECULARISM & SCIENCE – I had all the answers 2
   RELINQUISHING CONTROL – Letting go & letting God 3
   MYSTICISM TO LOVE – God is relationship 6

2 REVELATION TO PRINCIPLES 11
   GOD'S REVELATION – God manifested in everything 13
      Scripture – God's Word became flesh 14
      Tradition – Holy Spirit's truth dwells within everyone 14
      Nature – God is manifested in all His creation 15
   FAITH PRINCIPLES – Love others as God loves us 16
      Faith & Reason – Use God's gift of reason to love 17
      Body & Soul – Jesus always heals physically and spiritually ... 17
      God & Man – God and man seek mutual union 18
   SCIENCE PRINCIPLES – Always seek truth 18
      Definition of Terms – Know God's manifestations in nature 19
      Deduction & Induction – Reason is God's gift 19
      Concepts & Tools – Build a strong foundation for truth ... 21

3 PHYSICS TO CREATION 23
   UNIVERSE'S MAGNITUDE – God is Awe 25
      Solar System – Warmed by God's love 27
      Stars & Galaxies – Light to true light 28
      Visible & Invisible – God's love outnumbers the sands ... 31
   MATTER & ENERGY – Jesus the Man energized us 32
      Newton's Gravity – God and man mutually attracted 33
      General Relativity – Eternity free of space and time 35

    Special Relativity – God visible and invisible 38
  BIG BANG – God's creative love is explosive 43
    Expanding Universe – Growing with God 43
    Unified Theory – United in God's love 45
    Singularity & Anthropic – Universe to Heaven transcendence .. 49

4 CHEMISTRY TO LIFE 53
  SUBATOMIC TO ATOMS – The smallest among us loves 55
    God Particle – God is the core of all things 55
    Uncertainty & Chaos – Knowing God by unknowing God 58
    Non-Local Universe – God is everywhere 63
  DNA TO CELLS – God imprints His love in us 65
    Amino Acids – God is the cornerstone of our being 65
    Primordial Soup – God's loving embrace 67
    DNA in Cells – Total Body of Christ interstitially in each cell ... 67
  MICROBES TO HUMANS – God's ongoing creation 70
    Cambrian & Pangea – God's love is timelessly non-linear 70
    Evolutionary Theory – God and man continuously co-create ... 71
    Migration & Races – Love is relational with all humans 73

5 BIOLOGY TO CONSCIOUSNESS 79
  BRAIN & FUNCTIONS – Seeing God dwelling within 80
    Biology & Scans – We see God in our true self 80
    Competing Dualities – Spiritual growth through choice 84
    Conscious & Unconscious – God protects us from false self 86
  CONSCIENCE & FREE WILL – Free choice to love 89
    Brain Disorders – God teaches us not to condemn others 90
    Informed Conscience – Faith and reason are God's gifts 94
    Ethics & Bioethics – God gives us principles to live by 98
  HEALING RESEARCH – Divine Healer within 104
    Faith & Liturgy – Knowing and visiting God 106
    Frequent Prayer – God's thoughts not my thoughts 108
    Confirmation Bias – Holy fault of Original Sin 110

6 PSYCHOLOGY TO MYSTICISM 113
MEDITATION & CONTEMPLATION – Indwelling God 114
Theology & History – God deeply rooted in past & present.. 117
Methodology & Thoughts – God guides us by the right paths 119
Unloading Unconscious – God's presence unconsciously there 124
ALTERED CONSCIOUSNESS – States of God's presence 128
Contemplative Experiences – God's infused love 128
Near-Death Experiences – God at the gate for us 130
Transcendent Events – Nature is giving us its map to God 131
NEUROSCIENCE & NEUROTHEOLOGY – Earth & Heaven ... 134
Neuroplasticity Scans – God looks at us from within 135
Ecstasy Proposition – Taste of the Divine Presence 136
Collective Oneness – The relational Body of Christ 137

7 CALLED TO SERVE 143
RUMINATING THOUGHTS – The Devil made me do it 144
LOVING ECSTASY – God brings me home 145
RECOVERY & EVALUATION – Love is what it's about 146

EPILOGUE 149
MINISTRIES & SEMINARIES – Relational love 150
CONFERENCES & RESEARCH – Meeting with God 156
INTERRELIGIOUS DIALOGUE – God within everyone 165

Acknowledgments 167
About the Author 169
Glossary 171
Figures 173
Timeline 175
Bibliography 179
Index 193
Endnotes 207

Foreword

Deacon Robert Hesse is uniquely qualified to write this scientifically accurate and inspirational gateway into the mind and heart of God through the interrelationship between faith and science. Drawing upon his Ph.D. in Physical Chemistry, his background in Trappist mystical theology, and years of leadership in interreligious dialogue, he provides a glimpse into the unrestricted consciousness from which springs the equations of physics, the space-time continuum, molecular structures, the biophysical leap into life, and the biospiritual leap into human consciousness, free choice, loving relationships, and mystical ecstasy. He has accessibly described some of the most remarkable biophysical phenomena to reveal the loving consciousness that is at once the origin and finality of both the universal and eternal order—the loving consciousness who invites us into relationship with him. Though the book aims at bringing a diverse audience to belief in God and religion, Deacon Hesse illustrates his own personal journey with images of Christ, the Holy Spirit, the body of Christ, and the Catholic Church. In that way, he communicates to an interreligious audience how God's love manifest in science, relationships, and mysticism points to Jesus' revelation of the unconditional love of God in the Trinity. This book will prove very helpful to those caught between naturalism and faith as well as those synthesizing the mind and heart of God through the love that animates the natural world, human consciousness, and mystical prayer.

> Robert Spitzer, S.J., Ph.D.
> President of the Magis Center of Reason and Faith
> Former President of Gonzaga University and author of
> *New Proofs for the Existence of God: Contributions of Contemporary Physics and Philosophy*

Preface

Figure 2 Michelangelo's Sistine Chapel, Vatican – Painting/Photo[1]

"The Christian does not think God will love us because we are good, but that God will make us good because He loves us."

C. S. Lewis

The purpose of this book is to share how God used science to lead me back to the Catholic Church after 23 years of absence. How being spiritual, but not religious, adequately launched me, but was not enough. What started with anger toward the Church culminated in becoming a deacon and lecturer on faith and science (F&S) at the Pontifical University in Rome. That others without technical background, but with intellectual scientific curiosity, might lessen their time for a return to faith than it took me to return.

I had a growing awareness in my journey of the asymptotic — my mathematical understanding of the infinitely approaching without touching — convergence between F&S. My understanding was due to the exponential growth in scientific knowledge over the past 100+ years, which also precipitated a trend in the world's seminaries to include F&S courses in their curricula. My Catholic faith recognizes God continues to reveal Himself chronologically through nature, tradition, and scripture.

It is important for me to note F&S answer different questions, which is why they will never totally converge. My faith addresses the question *why*, my science answers the question *how*. Ultimately the language of my faith is silence; the language of my science is mathematics.

There were many ways I could have mapped my journey from science to faith. I recognize over the years F&S has been addressed in one or more of four ways:[2] 1) *Conflict*, which arises out of extreme positions; 2) *Independence*, focusing on differing languages and functions; 3) *Dialogue*, which addresses presuppositions, limitations on questions, as well as methodological and conceptual parallels; and 4) *Integration*, which focuses on the convergence between F&S and systematic synthesis. As I share my spiritual journey, I naturally use the last approach, integration. I don't delve much into philosophy, though others have discussed that intellectual aspect at length.[3]

My journey was too immediate and personal to have it involve historical F&S issues. That is why I don't discuss historical disagreements between F&S, except where necessary to give my journey context. I have no reason to relitigate old conflicts, when scientists were right, like Galileo[4] and Darwin,[5] or when those of faith were right, like Lemaitre[6] and Mendel.[7] Such disagreements have long been resolved. I focus on present-day F&S convergences. For those interested in F&S history[8] there are other sources,[9,10] and a timeline in the Appendix,[11] which demonstrate the exponential growth of scientific knowledge over the past 100 years.

Fortunately I have lived during much of that time. I am blessed to have had brilliant F&S contemporaries such as Albert Einstein, St. Pope John Paul II, and many others. My work contains many quotes of those who influenced me. Most were concurrent with my journey, but some, like St. Pope John Paul II's quotes, were added after as spice to the meal I already cooked, especially in the first chapter. I realized later his influence was sometimes direct and other times subliminal.

I also could have focused on older historical figures, such as perhaps the greatest scientist of all time, Leonardo da Vinci.[12] Instead I wanted to share my perspective of the awe of more current scientists: When they made their discoveries. How those discoveries affected my return to my Catholic faith beliefs. I found those "awe moments" of God's presence, which are best described by modifying a worn-out phrase, "God, and not the devil, is in the details." At times, I thought my journey was leading me into too much detail, getting me lost in the weeds. But when I forged a little further, there was a precious nugget of spiritual insight that made following the details worth it. Through my personal stories, I hope the readers will be encouraged to draw their own informed conclusions about F&S, which don't have to match mine.

I tried to make this book about my faith and science journey accessible in language non-scientists can understand. My purpose and excitement are to enable the reader to gain, as I had, a better understanding of how F&S have come to be mutually affirming over a broad range of disciplines. They include physics to creation, chemistry to life, biology to consciousness and psychology to mysticism. In addition to the scientific titles of each chapter, there is a faith paraphrase, which I hope encourages the reader to forge on and read past the technical title and content.

My conclusion examines the science of the brain and my experience of mysticism. This is a story of my life's spiritual journey, even though originally it was intended as a possible text for continuing education or graduate course for both ordained clergy and interested laity. My experience has shown such courses can have a positive impact on youth and adult formation, homiletics, chaplaincy, spiritual direction, interfaith dialogue, apologetics,[13] and other ministries. The reason? People, including those of faith and even clergy, are not used to hearing a fresh perspective of God revealing Himself via the science of nature.

My personal stories better explain many of the scientific subjects. I recognize the technical aspects of these subjects have been covered in greater detail by more learned authors. Since I cover a broad array of subjects, I acknowledge I am not an expert in every area. Hence my composition required me to be "a Jack of all trades and master of none," or better put, a "Jack of a few trades." When I co-taught a graduate course on F&S, I availed myself of guest lecturers. Their wisdom and other authors have informed the chapters in this book as footnoted.[14]

I offer these reflections with humility. The first and last chapters are bookends to my personal journey. In the intermediate chapters, I share how F&S became healing and inspirational. They are the backstory, the meat of my spiritual journey. My struggles were with betrayal, anger, sin, suffering, grief, forgiveness, and an ultimate awareness of God's love revealed in nature. I pray sharing my journey will do the same for you.

EDITOR'S NOTE

An editor rarely comments on a manuscript she helped shepherd to publication, but *Faith & Science: A Journey into God's Mystical Love* is no ordinary book.

This is not a review, nor an endorsement. It is a thank-you for the privilege of being part of the book's winding road to your hands, dear reader. The story was integral to my return to active participation in the Catholic Church after being away 40-plus years. Bob's story, combined with many spirited discussions, encouraged me to let go of negative experiences with church representatives. I was never at odds with God; I was disillusioned with the humans who were unable to be all they could and should be. Working on the manuscript helped me find my way back to my religious roots. Thank you, Bob, for being an inspiration. Thank you, Holy Spirit, for putting us together. God surely does work in mysterious ways.

Jan Masterson
May 2021

1
MOTIVATED TO LOVE

Figure 3 My Young Family, Norway – Photo

"My Lord God, I have no idea where I am going. I do not see the road ahead of me. I cannot know for certain where it will end. Nor do I really know myself, and the fact that I think I am following your will does not mean that I am actually doing so. But I believe that the desire to please you does in fact please you. And I hope I have that desire in all that I am doing. I hope that I will never do anything apart from that desire. And I know that if I do this you will lead me by the right road, though I may know nothing about it. Therefore I will trust you always though I may seem to be lost and in the shadow of death. I will not fear, for you are ever with me, and you will never leave me to face my perils alone."

Fr. Thomas Merton

A priest, I'll call Fr. Tom, inspired me to enter the seminary; later he sexually molested me. Fortunately, I was 15 years old, old enough to fight him off and had wisdom enough to report him to the Archdiocese within a couple of weeks. The psychological betrayal was immense. But once I reported the incident to the Church authorities, I took great relief in "washing my hands" of further responsibility. I later left the seminary where I had spent 6 years; after marriage, I left the Catholic Church for 23 years.

SECULARISM & SCIENCE – I had all the answers

If someone asked me if I were Catholic I would say "yes," but for all practical purposes I was not, since I was not practicing. I was the poster child for the loaded phrase we have all heard, "I was raised Catholic." Indeed, my parents were good and religious Catholics who sent me to Catholic schools to be taught by dedicated nuns. Perhaps problems ahead should have been expected when my mother gave me the middle name Jude, the patron saint of hopeless cases. I always lovingly teased her about that, but it was chosen because my parents tried for ten years to have me, their first child.

Moving forward, I mentally rationalized I had forgiven the priest, but my reaction of fight then flight belied that self-gratuitous conclusion.

I married a beautiful and loving woman, Linda, and together we had two beautiful children, a boy and a girl. We naturally expected life, at our young age, to continue to be good and thought we both were in control as we moved forward. I had gotten my doctorate in physical chemistry three years after my bachelor's degree in chemistry. I was selling and negotiating major international capital projects. We had planned carefully, traveled extensively, and had all the answers for our future. Oh, the naiveté of youth! I was full of pride, the granddaddy of all sins. I was steeped in sin and shunned the sacraments. Though I thought I had security, ultimately, I did not.

Then illnesses intruded! My wife was diagnosed with a bipolar condition, from which she suffered for 40 of our 45 years of marriage. With no moral rudder, I was lost to understand and deal with the roller coaster of irrational euphoria followed by anger and depression, only to cycle back again. I had to hospitalize her four times. Nothing worked. She endured more suffering than I could possibly imagine. After many years of trying to self-medicate with alcohol, she courageously began to address her illness. She willingly endured dozens of medications over many years, each requiring six to eight weeks of trial and detox before the next could be tried. She tried electroconvulsive therapy (ECT), in lay terms "shock treatments," which peaked at seventeen, the maximum number before permanent memory loss occurs. She willingly tried the latest technologies: vagus nerve stimulation implant and finally ketamine infusions. None of the treatments worked except ketamine, but cruelly the relief, like her joyful manic or alcoholic highs, was short lived, lasting only about a day.

When I thought I was in charge and things went well, of course I could take the credit. But when they didn't go well, I had to face the troubling corollary, I must also take the blame. Suddenly, I was not as smart as I thought. I was no longer in control! I had no morally grounded community for support, since I was deluding myself I was independent. Between Linda's suffering and my sinfulness, I was lost. I had entered my own self-constructed prison, a place without love.

RELINQUISHING CONTROL – Letting go & letting God

I was backed into a corner with no other choice; I finally started searching for a way to relinquish control. When I was young, I prayed mainly to God the Father in Heaven, since I had an earthly father and could relate. But as with my earthly father, there was some fear of retribution if I did wrong. Certainly, a simple image in my spiritual youth. When older I prayed to Jesus, whom I envisioned on my level since He was human and I could relate to Him as a fellow human being. But now I was starting to turn control over to the Holy Spirit. He was an unfamiliar character in my arsenal, but intimately closer, dwelling within me. He confronted my pride at its core, which also dwelt within me.

My craving for God increased as the Spirit showed me His love on numerous occasions. He did it with synchronicity, that is, through independent sources. Initially I craved the tactile touch of God. My first move was to receive the Eucharist, which I craved so much. Though I was in a state of serious sin and it was sinful to receive in that state, I even rationalized my way around that. After all, it was because I loved Him so much. Though my return to Him was out-of-order, my next move was reconciliation. I had to confess my sins to someone who represented God and the community I missed so much.

I knocked on the door of a nearby rectory and asked for Fr. Joe. He was actually a monsignor, but too humble to want to be called that. He was a convert. That seemed appropriate since I was a revert. I asked if he would hear my confession. He said confessions would be heard in the church in three hours. I said it would probably take me too long and would hold up other people. So, blessed soul that he was, he invited me in. I haltingly started: "Bless me father for I have sinned. It has been 23 years since my last confession." With his wonderful sense of humor, he smiled and said, "You weren't kidding about taking a long time." I could only remember sins that are the biggies, of which there were a number. Fr. Joe recommended Fr. Henri Nouwen's book[15] *The Return of the Prodigal Son*, which also helped me. I became the flesh of that book. I was cleansed and started to attend daily Mass with gusto in receiving Christ in the Eucharist.

Then years later, after I was married, out of nowhere comes an invitation to attend my 25-year seminary high school reunion. Prior to Vatican II, seminary began right out of grade school. Though we know now, and as my personal experience confirmed, that is not a healthy beginning, it was the way it was done. Several of my seminary classmates went on to be ordained. One became the Archdiocesan Director of Priest Personnel who recommended assignments for priests in the Archdiocese of St. Louis. When I saw him, I asked how Fr. Tom was doing. He said, "He is having problems." I responded, "I knew he was an alcoholic." He said, "Yes, but his problems are more serious than just that." I said, "Yes, I know. He likes young boys." His jaw dropped. He said, "How did you know?" I responded, "I was one of them." We had the traditional group picture and said farewell.

A few weeks later I discovered Fr. Tom had been assigned to children. While at the class reunion, I learned the Archdiocese knew of his problem and still assigned him to children. What I had "washed my hands" of many years ago, by reporting Fr. Tom to the Archdiocese, had not been dealt with. I was really angry! One of the benefits of international negotiating experience in the business world is I don't put up with dishonest bullshit. And being an engineer, I am trained to fix things. I immediately made an appointment with my classmate priest with whom I had reconnected at the reunion and who was responsible for the assignment of Fr. Tom.

I flew to St. Louis and had lunch with him. After some initial pleasantries, I cut to the chase.

> Father, I know you have assigned Fr. Tom to children and you know he has problems abusing children. So here is how we are going to handle this. You can either immediately remove him from working with children or I will handle it. And I can assure you, you will not like how I will handle it.

The veiled yet real threat was I would go public. This would have been historic, since this was years before the sexual abuse of children by priests became public knowledge. I was not used to making empty threats in negotiations. I was prepared to do it.

Thankfully, a couple of weeks later, Fr. Tom was sent to a retirement home. I sighed with relief. I didn't have to take action. I had this time successfully "washed my hands" of the problem. Or had I?

A few weeks later I got a letter from Fr. Tom. It was innocuous, as if nothing had happened. Now I was really pissed. How did he get my home address? Obviously my classmate Director of Priest Personnel gave it to him. How dare he! I circular filed the letter. Weeks went by. I couldn't sleep. Finally, I called my classmate. Though I had a perfect right to be angry, I realized the Holy Spirit was calling me to something else.

The priest answered the phone and I said: "I got this letter from Fr. Tom." After a long silent pause, I asked, "Was he reaching out to me?" My classmate answered, "Yes." Suddenly my forgiveness of him years ago was being brought to the present. I was forced to face the possibility my previous mental forgiveness was just a rationalization and not a tangible forgiveness. Only by the grace of the Holy Spirit did I know I was now being called to really forgive him — in person!

Another flight to St. Louis. What the hell, or perhaps Heaven, am I doing now? What was I going to say? Why was I going? Deep down I knew it was for selfish reasons. I needed healing through forgiveness. I was not going in order to make him feel good. I was returning 32 years after the incident to find closure.

Ironically the retirement home was on the seminary grounds. God has a strange sense of humor. I knocked. Fr. Tom answered. He was shorter than I remembered and, of course, much older. He presented me with a wooden pen he had made for me. The pleasantries lasted longer than my usual in-your-face approach. Finally, the time arrived.

"I want to let you know, Fr. Tom, I forgive you for what you did to me." He looked gaunt and whispered he was drunk at the time and didn't remember. I knew better and went on. "I had forgiven you within a couple of weeks afterwards, but now wanted to do it in person. I was not really angry at you, but at Church authorities." He suddenly perked up and looked happy. He said, "Oh really?" He was excited to learn why I was angry at the Church authorities. He was also obviously angry at them. He asked why I was angry. "Because they allowed you to continue to minister to children." Suddenly he slumped in his chair. This was not what he wanted or expected to hear. Then his confession began. He almost approached it as a third-party observer talking about someone else. I was the first of many. It turns out all were younger than I was and defenseless. One in particular was abused by a family member and came to him for help, only to be abused by him. I was sick to my stomach. I felt like throwing up. I sat there with a mixture of loathing and sadness. He was clearly mentally ill. I left stupefied. He died a year later.

MYSTICISM TO LOVE – God is relationship

My best friend and classmate in the seminary, Ernie Sanazaro, died in Vietnam. It was a harsh reality right before I got married. Years later after marriage and Fr. Tom's death, while attending Mass, I met the associate pastor of my parish, Fr. Daokim Nguyen. On the Fourth of July, he gave a wonderful homily about his journey to the US from war-torn Vietnam. We became friends. Seeing me at Mass every day, he was not surprised when I told him I was interested in being more active in the Church. He suggested I become a deacon. I essentially told him I thought he was crazy. "Hey, how about just the choir?" I did try out and couldn't sing worth a lick. I went to the first seminary class out of curiosity to learn, not necessarily to be ordained. I was ordained four years later. I am sure my friend Ernie had something to do with it. While in the seminary the first time, Ernie and I talked by phone every night about homework assignments due the next day. Ernie died in Vietnam and Fr. Nguyen came from Vietnam encouraging me. I saw Ernie in Fr. Nguyen calling me for my next life assignment. Ernie was a vehicle of the Holy Spirit.

Meanwhile, the illnesses in my family were not only persisting, but spreading. I continued to pray. God seemed to answer, but in some sort of off-beat way. I don't mean disrespect for God, but He never seems to do things the easy way. In the midst of my wife's serious illness, I was having sexual thoughts that were driving me crazy. As usual, I prayed for His help. I got prostate cancer and had a prostatectomy. I tell people if a man is going shopping for the best buy in cancer, it should be prostate cancer because the cure rate, if caught early, is almost 100%. There are only two side effects. One is incontinence, which fortunately I did not experience. The other is erectile dysfunction. God had answered my prayer! From then on with some humor, I joked with Him I didn't think His solution was very funny. But I always thanked Him for solving the problem.

With further study and my diaconate ordination approaching and continued serious illnesses in the family, I more than ever needed a prayer life that would allow me to surrender to God's will. I depended more and more on prayer. I was stuck on God. I couldn't function without Him. But my prayer life sucked. I found myself telling God what I needed, how I needed it, even when I needed it. Certainly He is smart enough to know all that before I even ask. What in the world was I doing? My prayer life was putting me back in control: the very prison I had put myself into earlier in life. Yet I needed a serious prayer life now more than ever.

When I was originally in the seminary studying for the priesthood, I took a retreat at the Trappist Monastery in Gethsemani, Kentucky, where Fr. Thomas Merton was located at the time. He was considered one of the top spiritual writers of the 20th century. Unfortunately, he was a hermit and I didn't see him. But I knew he was a famous spiritual writer and was writing books while I was there.

So now, remembering that retreat, in desperation, I went back and read his autobiography *The Seven Storey Mountain*,[16] a *New York Times* bestseller. In it he devotes only one sentence to silent prayer; letting go of your thoughts and focusing on God alone. This sounded exactly like what I needed in my spiritual journey: Letting go of my false sense of control. Without any instruction, I tried it while in front of the Eucharist in the adoration chapel. It was a knock-down, drag-out battle with my thoughts. I didn't know how to do it gently, the correct way. Instead, I was rather violent in my approach. Then it happened! For the next three days I was at total peace. I had never experienced that before. I had never been on illicit drugs, but I thought maybe this is addictive. I didn't understand it.

I launched myself into reading as many of the mystics[17] throughout the centuries as I could get my hands on. I was seeking insight into my experience. Then I stumbled on *Open Mind, Open Heart* by Fr. Thomas Keating.[18] This was what I was looking for. It spoke to me in a way that simultaneously embraced many of the mystic giants of the Catholic Church, like doctors of the Church, St. Teresa of Avila[19] and St. John of the Cross.[20] I had come full circle with contemporary mystics, Trappist Monk Fr. Thomas Merton to Trappist Monk Fr. Thomas Keating. I was on fire! I needed to meet this Fr. Keating. I immediately scheduled a ten-day intensive retreat at his monastery in Snowmass, Colorado, to learn more about what Merton called Centering Prayer.

I was completely unprepared for what happened there. It changed my life forever. It was a profound mystical experience. The result was I knew, with absolute certainty, God loved me beyond my wildest imagination. God was preparing me for what I needed in my future life's struggles and joys.

Linda's problems persisted and multiplied. Later in life she developed moderate dementia, then ovarian cancer with a serious blood clot. After chemotherapy and mass-reducing, complicated surgery, she returned from the hospital and died 48 hours later. What has followed is incredible grief. My newfound prayer life sustained me through that difficult and painful journey and continues to sustain me.

Prayer has inspired me to be open to God's challenges to use the gifts He gave me to give greater glory to Him. I can only hope what follows in the subsequent chapters shows how God wove together all those gifts of the experiences described in this chapter to show His love for me and others. I pray I am able to share them faithfully with you. Even though, as Merton says in the initial quote in this chapter, I do not see the road ahead of me.

2
REVELATION TO PRINCIPLES

Figure 4 Mandelbrot Fractal Mathematics of Chaos – Image[21]

"Science can purify religion from error and superstition. Religion can purify science from . . . false absolutes."

St. Pope John Paul II

"Science without religion is lame, religion without science is blind."

Albert Einstein

My 6th grade teacher sadistically used mathematics to discipline the whole class for talking. Of course I told my parents I was not the one talking, but I am sure I was. I don't recall the exact numbers, but she gave an overnight assignment to subtract, say, 13 from 3,000 then subtract 13 again from the result and again and again until there was not enough left to subtract. I worked all night worried I had made many mistakes and wouldn't have the correct answer the next morning. Then it hit me, just divide 3,000 by 13 and the remainder would be the correct answer. As I expected, my answer by multiple subtractions was wrong. Okay, I admit it. I then cheated. I went back several pages and made an intentional mistake so the answer would be correct in the end. I handed in the paper and was surprised to see the astonishment on the teacher's face. I was hooked on math: the language of what would be my greater interest, science.

I started to read about science even though I didn't completely understand it. Science popular at the time fascinated me. In grade school, I read about Einstein and physics. In high school, I read about chemistry and the discovery of the DNA molecule of life. This may sound arrogant, but as early as grade school, I had already set my goal to get a Ph.D. in science.

Little did I know where my journey would lead me. One of my favorite books on math, which I read in grade school, was an early edition by Dr. George Gamow, a theoretical physicist and cosmologist. That book gave me a hint of how my future journey would move from math to faith, but I wasn't paying attention. At its beginning Gamow wrote:

> "There was a young fellow from Trinity
> Who took the square root of infinity
> But the number of digits
> Gave him the fidgets;
> He dropped Math and took up Divinity."[22]

I have always enjoyed the adventure of travel. I have been blessed by the confluence of my science and engineering employment and faith career to be able to travel extensively. This ultimately led me to over 100 countries, a majority of the world, on all seven continents. It became an important part of my discovery of God's revelation in nature.

Preparing for those trips was almost as exciting as the trips themselves. This time I was instinctively and unconsciously preparing for the biggest trip of all, to find God in nature and later the afterlife. Before launching my journey, I felt it necessary to prepare the launch pad. I wanted to be sure I had the right vessel, instruments, and necessary fuel to make the trip.

I knew I had to start with some basic principles if my journey was to be systematic and goal oriented. This chapter provides the background explanation of my assumptions and resulting principles for this, the greatest of my journeys.

GOD'S REVELATION – God manifested in everything

> *"There exist two realms of knowledge, one which has its source in Revelation [Faith] and one which reason [Science] can discover by its own power. To the latter belong especially the experimental sciences and philosophy... The two realms ... have points of contact. The methodologies proper to each make it possible to bring out different aspects of reality."*
> ST. POPE JOHN PAUL II

I wanted my trip to be based on accurate maps and expert advice. My maps consisted of principles, primarily reason, to discern how God reveals Himself to us. I sought advice from a diverse group of experts: theologians, philosophers, ethicists, anthropologists, paleontologists, neuroscientists, physicians, historians, linguists, mystics, and many more. Though I was prepared to make my own final informed conscious decision, I needed more than just my individual interpretation of nature. In hindsight I realized I was using a hermeneutic approach, which is a term most often applied to the interpretation of scripture, meaning using all available sources of true information. It is certainly also applicable to science.

I acknowledged faith believed God reveals Himself in three ways and, if necessary, I was bound and determined to reconcile them. I describe these ways in reverse chronological order.

Scripture — God's Word became flesh

> *"There are only two ways to live your life: as though nothing is a miracle, or as though everything is a miracle."*
> Albert Einstein

> *"Miracles are not contrary to nature, but only contrary to what we know about nature."*
> St. Augustine of Hippo

393 A.D. was the date of the Catholic Council of Hippo, which was the first to create the list, or canon, of Old and New Testament books that exist in today's Catholic Bibles. Martin Luther included all those books in his 16th century translation of the Bible into German. Subsequent non-Catholic Christian denominations have eliminated some of those books. For the sake of consistency when consulting scripture, I chose to use the modern Catholic translation, *The New American Bible*, which contains all the original books with their original languages interpreted and translated by interfaith experts.

I was prepared to accept what others believed: Scripture is the Divinely inspired word of God. I was not interested in fundamentalism, i.e., a belief in the literal interpretation of scripture, which to a certain extent occurs in all faiths. The reason is literal interpretation can lead to numerous contradictions and misunderstandings. Hermeneutics helped me avoid this pitfall.

Tradition — Holy Spirit's truth dwells within everyone

> *"It is a duty for theologians to keep themselves regularly informed of scientific advances in order to examine if such be necessary, whether or not there are reasons for taking them into account in their reflection or for introducing changes in their teaching."*
> St. Pope John Paul II

28 A.D. is the approximate date Jesus started His public ministry. I used that date as the start of the verbally transmitted Christian tradition, even though some theologians may not traditionally think this way.

Occasionally I considered the traditions of some non-Christian faiths, which often began much earlier. The reason is Jesus was a historical figure affected by history. Examples include: The first burial of humans with tools, suggesting a belief in an afterlife, as early as 25,000+ B.C. More recently, possible Sun worship at Stonehenge, England, about 3100 B.C. Perhaps more relevant for my purposes, the emergence of Zoroastrianism, the first monotheistic religion, in the early 2nd millennium B.C. Zoroastrianism influenced Judaism, Christianity's predecessor religion.

Scripture originated from the verbal tradition of the early Christians as documented by 2nd- to 4th-century historians. They had to be Divinely inspired to decide what writings were valid, that is, Divinely inspired by the Holy Spirit. Historically, without tradition scripture would not exist. Those traditional beliefs were codified into the canon[23] as described in the previous section.

Nature – God is manifested in all His creation

> *"The scientist's condition as a sentinel in the modern world . . . the first to glimpse the enormous complexity together with the marvelous harmony of reality, makes him a privileged witness of the plausibility of religion, a man capable of showing how the admission of transcendence, far from harming the autonomy and the ends of research, rather stimulates it to continually surpass itself in an experience of self-transcendence which reveals the human mystery."*
> ST. POPE JOHN PAUL II

13,700,000,000 B.C. is the estimated birth date of the Universe. It was at this point God started to reveal Himself. He has been manifesting Himself in nature ever since.

Theologians sometimes refer to "infused knowledge" as a separate way God reveals Himself. They say it is knowledge not acquired by personal effort nor by the instruction of others, but rather is produced directly in a created mind by Divine illumination. But it is not separate. It is also knowledge through nature since it affects the brain. Without nature, tradition and scripture would not exist. God was revealing Himself sequentially through nature, tradition, and scripture. I was mystified why God's revelation in nature wasn't given more consideration in my Catholic education or in the seminary when I studied for the priesthood.

Scientism is the belief we can learn all we need to know strictly through science. Scientism[24] is to science as fundamentalism is to religion. I must admit, early in my rebellion, I danced with this concept. But ultimately I realized legitimate science itself did not believe in scientism. So my approach was not scientism, but instead legitimate science with an awareness of all its possibilities and limitations.

As I proceeded on my journey to discover the Divine, I would normally think in logical, systematic steps, which were the scientists' discoveries in chronological order. But my journey was not always chronological because I needed some transitional thinking to better understand the road signs on my journey.

FAITH PRINCIPLES – Love others as God loves us

> *"Science and religion can renew culture . . . which embraces everything of which man is at once the center, the subject, and the object."*
> St. Pope John Paul II

I needed principles for my journey. I started with faith principles, which by definition are unchanging. The key faith principle described by theologians is Jesus' commandment to love one another as I have loved you, which leads to a sharing in the Divine; to live as unique individuals, uniquely loved.

It is necessary to address, and then adopt, belief in non-dualism, which means certain things are meant for each other and cannot co-exist unless they are mutually non-contradictory. It does not mean they are equivalent. This includes faith and reason, body and soul, God and man. The very concept of addressing the asymptotic convergence of faith and science, that is approaching but not touching, would have to rest in this principle. For example, this principle guides people not to commit suicide, if they have the necessary freedom, knowledge, and faith to not do so. Fortunately, most people do not have that desire.

This logic seemed obvious to the Western mind because the opposite gives discomfort. Some faiths, which often are called philosophies by their original practitioners, believe in reincarnation, which requires a belief in dualism. This could logically result in different outcomes, such as condoning suicide, if the cause is just, since a new body awaits us. They are not killing their soul, hence it is not suicide. During my travels to Burma, present-day Myanmar, I was reminded of this belief by Buddhist friends of the monks who immolated themselves in protest of the oppressive political regime. But I was not comfortable with that concept, hence why I adhered to the principle of non-dualism.

Though I didn't know at the time, the following principles became important in my spiritual journey. I discovered the disconcerting dissonance was due to my head and heart not being in synchronization. My body and soul, faith and reason had to match. My spirituality[25] and religion by themselves were not enough.

As a scientist, I know assumptions can preordain outcomes if not chosen carefully. A fair criticism could be made I preordained these principles; I loaded the deck to draw preconceived conclusions. As I proceeded, I found just the opposite. My science reinforced these principles in amazing ways as became apparent in my journey.

Faith & Reason – Use God's gift of reason to love

> *"Faith can never conflict with reason."*
> St. Pope John Paul II

Many strongly believed,[26,27] if the understanding of faith contradicted the understanding of reason, based on an informed conscience, then one or both of these understandings are incorrect. This was at the core of my journey, since to exclude reason from the equation is to exclude a gift God lovingly gave me.

Body & Soul – Jesus always heals physically and spiritually

> *"The human person is a unique composite – a unity of spirit and matter, soul and body, fashioned in the image of God and destined to live forever. Every human life is sacred, because every human person is sacred."*
> St. Pope John Paul II

Body and soul are meant for each other. Thomas Moore, among others, wrote effectively about this.[28] They affect each other and are meant to be in peaceful harmony. This is why in all eighteen of Jesus' healings in scripture, the one common thread is He heals both body and soul. It is also why I expect both to somehow be reunited in Heaven. My faith and science journey led me to better understand how it could happen. So non-dualism of the body and soul had to be one of my principles. Body and soul are meant to be with each other.

God & Man – God and man seek mutual union

> *"Let him kiss me with kisses of his mouth! More delightful is your love than wine."*
> Song of Solomon 1:2

God wishes to share His divinity with humans. That is not to say we become God, but to be at true peace, we are meant to share in His divinity, just as He shared in our humanity. Those words are said by the priest or deacon at every Mass. By sinning, we break that sharing; it is not God who breaks it. My mystical experience made my belief in this union visceral, not just intellectual. It propelled me in my spiritual journey.

SCIENCE PRINCIPLES – Always seek truth

> *"Change your opinions, keep to your principles; change your leaves, keep intact your roots."*
> Victor Hugo

The most basic principle of science is the belief patterns exist in nature and experiments are used to identify them and reason to understand them—even to the level they might allow future events to be predicted. If the term "faith" means believing in something that can't be proven, then scientists have faith in this unprovable scientific principle. Scientists start with a mental construct and then experiment to establish a theory or model, which can be tested. Consistent with that, I offer the following explanation to delineate additional information and principles I followed in pursuing God's awe in nature.

Definition of Terms – Know God's manifestations in nature

> "I . . . see also the science of faith on the horizon of rationality understood in this way. The Church wants independent theological research, which is not identified with the ecclesiastical Magisterium."
> St. Pope John Paul II

One of the most misunderstood terms, shared by many, is "theory." It does not mean opinion, but rather a construct used to help predict future events. Contrary to popular belief, scientists are primarily interested in disproving a theory, rather than affirming a theory. More can be learned if a theory is demonstrated to not be applicable. This can lead to tweaking the theory to make it more broadly applicable or even to initiate a major paradigm shift[29] to the theory.

It is necessary to understand theories have the following attributes: Science never proves, only attempts to disprove theories. The strength of an explanation lies in the rigor of attempts to disprove a theory. Theories are not opinions, but a collection of rigorously tested hypotheses. Theories can, and do, change; they are thrown out or modified. They may be changed to be more powerful and/or inclusive. It is especially important to acknowledge and accept not all phenomena are subject to scientific testing, for example, beauty and love.

Deduction & Induction – Reason is God's gift

> "Logic will get you from A to B. Imagination will take you everywhere."
> Albert Einstein

When in college I took a course in logic and statistics, which was fascinating and, for my journey, indispensable. Here is a summary of what I learned and what I applied in my spiritual journey. At first it may seem like a strange, overreaching concept, but I often used it without realizing it. When I took the course, I never dreamed I would later apply it to both faith and science, so please bear with me.

There are two forms of logic, deductive and inductive.

Deductive consists of formal logic going from the general to the specific, which results in conclusions that are certain. A deductive example is called a syllogism:

1. All men are mortal (major premise)
2. Socrates is a man (minor premise)
3. Therefore, Socrates is mortal (conclusion)

Inductive logic consists of informal logic going from the specific to the general, which results in conclusions that are probable, not certain. An inductive example:

1. Smokers have a higher probability of cancer
2. Bill is a smoker
3. Therefore, Bill is more likely to get cancer

I considered deductive logic in order to apply it to God's very existence. I had heard the phrase "God is dead." It was first used by Friedrich Nietzsche,[30] which initiated the so-called God Is Dead period extending into the early 1900s. During that time, scientists believed if you couldn't measure something, it didn't exist. They were using flawed deductive logic as scientism. Later scientists came to realize inductive logic was preferable in certain circumstances as described later in quantum mechanics.

The first question: Can logic be used to prove God exists? Proving the existence of God is impossible with deductive logic. But to deductively prove God didn't exist was even more difficult, indeed also impossible.

Playing scientist, let us conduct a mental experiment to reason this to conclusion. If the major premise is large enough, as God would certainly be, there is a problem. If a certain type of rabbit is capable of living anywhere and the premise is it does exist, stumbling on such a rabbit, say in Ohio, would immediately stop the search. If the premise is the rabbit does not exist, it would be necessary to explore every square foot of Earth and all other planets in the Universe to prove it does not exist. Truly an impossible task.

On the other hand, I knew I could inductively show God most probably existed, but others would have to draw their own conclusions. Little did I know I had entered an inductive journey of exciting and monumental proportions.

Concepts & Tools – Build a strong foundation for truth

> *"In . . . the last few decades we have witnessed more basic advances in our understanding of physical reality than had been made during the entire previous history of our planet . . . Scientific achievements proclaim the dignity of the human being and greatly clarify man's unique role in the Universe."*
> St. Pope John Paul II

Fr. Roger Bacon (1219–1292 A.D.) is credited with being one of the earliest European advocates of the scientific method, which scientists use to this day. He was an English philosopher and Franciscan friar, who placed considerable emphasis on studying nature through empiricism. Scientists continue to use his scientific method as I did in my journey to God's awe.

Summarizing its principles: The scientific method starts with an observation, leading to a question, which leads to a hypothesis; an experiment tests the hypothesis. The results of the experiment are compared to the results predicted by the hypothesis. If the conclusion of that comparison supports the hypothesis, it normally provokes a new question for further study. If the conclusion of that comparison does not support the hypothesis, an alternate hypothesis is usually proposed. Either way, supports and does not support, the cycle is started again. I often found myself in that veritable loop of science while on my faith and science journey.

Fortunately, my interest in math was helpful, since my journey was going to require I deal with very large and very small numbers. The following are a few useful scientific notations, which are also needed by non-scientists. Large and small numbers are expressed by moving the decimal point. For example, 1,000,000 becomes 10^6 by moving the decimal point to the left 6 places. And 0.000001 becomes 10^{-6} by moving the decimal point to the right 6 places.

Nature has self-consistency because it has fundamental physical constants. Some constants are a fundamental part of nature and an indication of God's awe. There is no need to recite the lengthy list of the 26 currently known fundamental constants in the Universe. They are everywhere: in the speed of light, gravitational force, celestial physics, molecular chemistry, etc.

With that general understanding, I arrogantly thought I was ready for my trip. But as it turns out, I had no idea where the road was going to lead me.

I ask you to join me as I share the backstory of my multilayered journey from science to faith, which shows where the road ultimately led me.

Bon voyage!

3
PHYSICS TO CREATION

Figure 5 Light Echo V838 – Photo[31]

"The Heavens declare the glory of God; the sky proclaims its builder's craft."
Psalm 19:2

My journey started after I left the seminary and discovered girls. I was a lifeguard at a public pool, which afforded me the wonderful opportunity to see them. I spotted my future wife there but didn't meet her until my family took me to a church function. How prophetic. She was just as beautiful in a dress as in her swimsuit. We dated for four years, falling deeper in love along the way.

Linda and I were virgins when we got married. That was rather unusual during the free-love days of the hippie era. Linda came from a family of three girls and I from a family of three boys. From that sheltered background, we discovered and explored each other. I found God's awe in Linda's natural beauty.

After graduate school, I enthusiastically accepted a job at Shell Development, Exploration and Production in Houston, Texas. Linda and I saw it as an opportunity to leave St. Louis. We both had a few negative memories there: I with Fr. Tom and she with the nuns who taught her in grade school. Even though we initially attended church and got married in the Catholic Church, once in Houston neither of us was attending church.

While at Shell, I took courses in geology and obtained a patent for determining in situ oil saturation. I didn't get much initial satisfaction from it partly because it was many years later I learned Shell had invested millions of dollars in it. But the real reason I missed out on that satisfaction? I was laid off after just over a year of employment. There was a massive layoff following the philosophy, last in, first out. I sent out over 800 letters looking for a job during that pre-internet market downturn.

I got a job with Alco Standard Corporation in Cleveland, Ohio. We had to move from palm trees to snow drifts. My boss and I were the only ones in the corporate research and development department. Alco was a conglomerate of over 80 acquisitioned, small, entrepreneurial, privately owned companies. It turned out to be a career opportunity I didn't recognize initially. I had to troubleshoot many different industries, which required me to quickly learn a lot about a broad range of science and engineering. I traveled widely to consult in chemical plants, long-wall mining operations, paper mills, industrial combustion equipment manufacturing, food-cooking equipment manufacturing, metal stampings plants, plastic extrusion plants, and many more industries. I was forced to become a jack of all trades and not humble enough to know I was a master of none.

UNIVERSE'S MAGNITUDE – God is Awe

> *"For in him were all things created, in the Heavens and upon the Earth, things visible and things invisible . . . All things have been created through him, and unto him."*
> COLOSSIANS 1:16

I was spiritual, not religious. I entered a parallel journey of secular science and spiritual faith. I still believed in God, but was seeing Him in the awe of His creation, not in church and not in His people. Only later in my journey did I realize what was ascribed to the early mystic Dionysius as the first stage of the spiritual journey, the Purgative Stage. To only sense God in what I could see with the eyes. I began to see God everywhere in nature. I entered into a mission of discovery in the physical secular world.

The quest for God's awe led to nature in: the powerful Angel and Iguacu Falls, the expansive Arctic and Antarctic Oceans, the unending Alps and Andes Ranges, the majestic Fuji and Matterhorn Mountains, the mighty Mississippi and Irrawaddy Rivers, the deep Grand and Waimea Canyons, the silent Mojave and Sahara Deserts, the clear Superior and Louise Lakes, and the mysterious Dead and Black Seas.

It was not a braggadocio travel log, although it came in handy at cocktail parties. It was really my drunken wanderlust for God's awe. I discovered Him everywhere. I was in awe of His natural creation, which made me in awe of Him. My name for God became "Awe of Nature."

Despite all those wonderful experiences, I was hungry for more. My appetite was insatiable. Where else was I to look? I found the answer in my childhood.

As a child I was a counter. It started when I would count the number of steps in each concrete square on the sidewalk. Soon I was counting my steps to the store. This may sound strange, but I had a propensity for math. I liked numbers and was a little obsessed with accuracy. I figured, given enough time, I could count everything.

Then I was blown away. I was about six years old when my dad took me to the Missouri Ozarks. It was my first trip to the country away from city lights. On that cloudless night I saw the Milky Way for the first time. It was mind boggling! I could not begin to count the stars. It was inconceivable each was like our Sun.

Though it was natural for me to constantly seek God's awe in the natural wonders on our Earth, I gradually realized I needed to expand my search. With the Universe filled with what seemed like an infinite number of other heavenly bodies, how could I discover His awe there? I pondered all the undiscovered mountains, rivers, oceans, everything I was missing.

At the time, scientists, including Einstein in his early career, thought the Universe was static and finite. If that is true, why couldn't I somehow count the stars? I certainly could have used some humility. With that trait missing, I had the audacity to launch my trip into the Universe. I wanted to know *how* it was formed. But the deeper, unconscious question was *why* it was formed. Unwittingly I was asking science to answer both questions, but it addresses only the how. As I would learn later, it led to a hint of the why.

How big is big? I knew the rough dimensions of my house, my city, and even the Antarctic, but I wanted to know the dimensions of the Universe.[32] After all, it embodies all of what God has created. So to better understand God through His creation, I had to at least know its size. I started my journey through the Universe, which continued over the years.

My adventure necessarily required the use of very large and very small numbers and symbols. Remember scientific notation allows 1,000,000 to be represented as 10^6 and 0.000001 as 10^{-6} just by moving the decimal point.

It was necessary to address large distances in the Universe, which are so vast, to use miles and kilometers became unwieldy. I used the astronomers' measurement based on the speed of light. Light travels at a constant 186,000 miles per second. The distance light travels in one year is 5.9 trillion miles, which is called a light-year. To understand my journey, I had to use the distance measurement of light-years.

Using imagery helped to understand the map of my journey. I pretended to use a camera and started taking pictures from outside the Universe looking in. The zoom lens focused on Earth, started moving backward in consecutive mental and real images hoping to end with a wide-angle lens of the entire Universe. I ask you to join me as I retrace my journey.

PHYSICS TO CREATION

Solar System – Warmed by God's love

"We believe in one Lord Jesus Christ, the only Son of God, eternally begotten of the Father; God from God, Light from Light."
  Nicene Creed

I went from the Earth, with its wonderful nature observed and described in my travels, to a wider view of our "solar system," which consists of our Sun and all the planets that orbit it. The next figure clearly shows the Earth is not very big. My awe of God in nature on Earth didn't accurately capture the bigger AWE of God in our solar system.

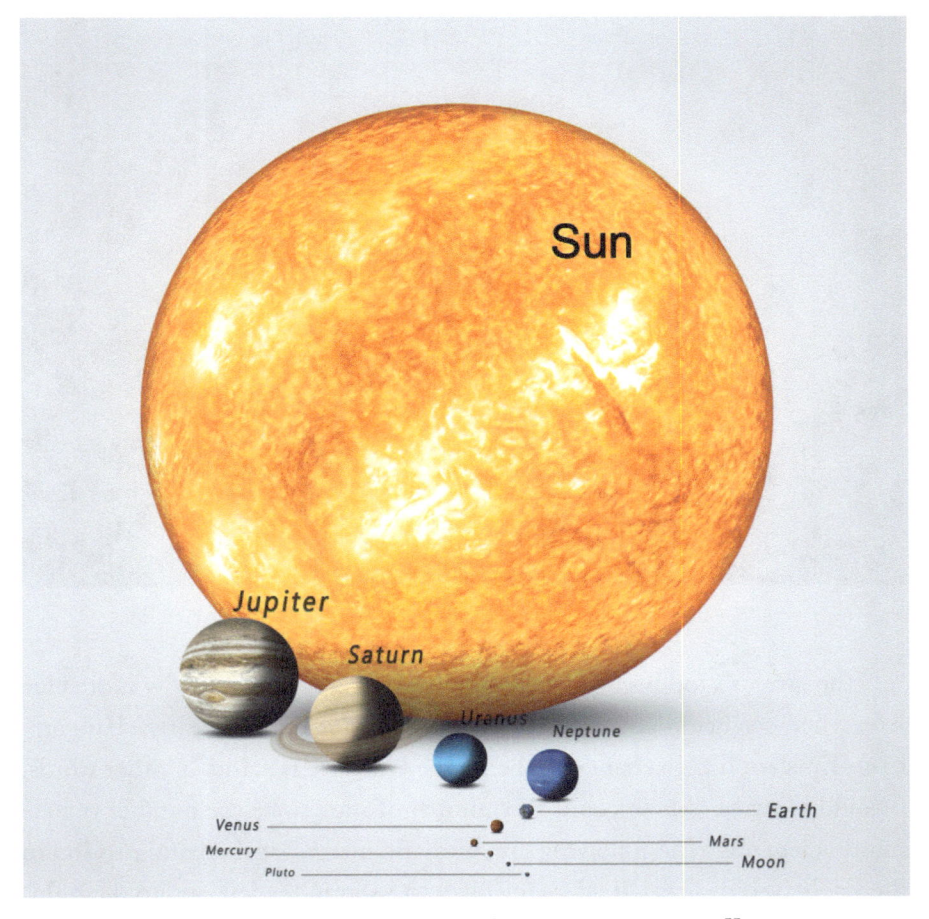

Figure 6 Solar System Relative Sizes – Image[33]

Stars & Galaxies – Light to true light

"I am the light of the world. Whoever follows me will not walk in darkness but will have the light of life."
John 8:12

The Sun's relative gigantic size compared to the Earth puts in perspective why early civilizations worshiped it. It is so large about 1,300,000 planet Earths can fit inside of it. But nearby stars like Antares are even bigger than our Sun. Only Antares' edge is visible in the following figure. I was starting to realize how small even our Sun is; our solar planets including Earth are not even large enough to be visible in this image.

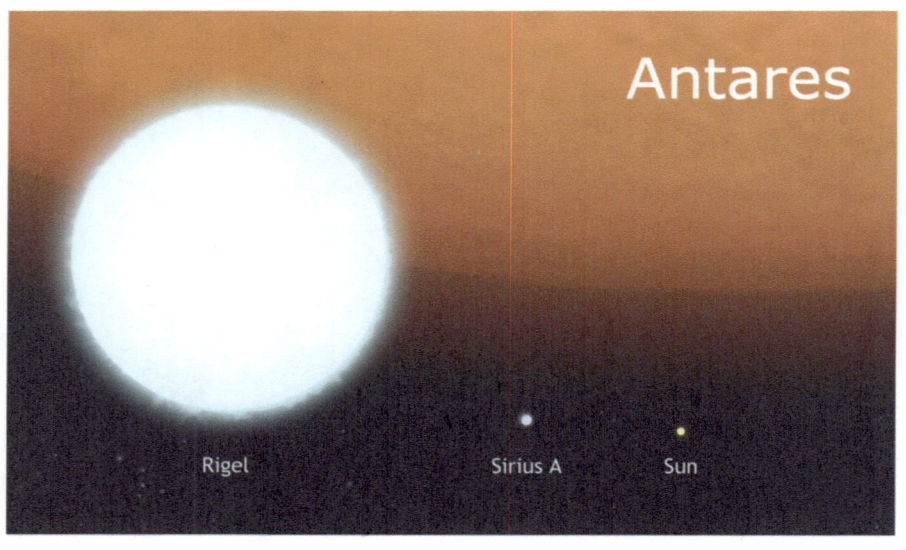

Figure 7 Nearby Stars' Relative Sizes – Image[34]

The awe of God became even more impressive, yet somehow more elusive, when science discovered the number of stars is constantly changing. Even Einstein had to change his belief the Universe is static. In other words, I would never be able to count the number of stars since the number is constantly changing. The following are dramatic images of the hand of God in the Eagle Nebula Gas Cloud giving birth to a star to the left, and to the right, a star similar to the size of our Sun dying.

PHYSICS TO CREATION

BIRTH **DEATH**

Figure 8 Birth & Death of Stars – Photos[35]

When I first saw the Milky Way as a child, I thought the millions of stars were perhaps too numerous to count. Was I in for a shock! What I was seeing is only a very small part of our Milky Way Galaxy, much of which is not visible. The following figure shows our Milky Way Galaxy as an image of a galaxy similar to ours since we cannot physically get far enough away from our Galaxy to photograph it. This shows our Sun is actually miniscule and located on the tail end of the swirling disc of our galaxy. It is only that tail I first viewed as a child.

Figure 9 Milky Way Galaxy – Image[36]

Our Milky Way Galaxy is estimated to contain about 200 billion stars. Invisible are the estimated 100 billion planets orbiting those stars. Our galaxy is a gigantic 100,000 light-years (lys) across. It is 5.9 trillion miles times 100,000 or 5.9 hundred thousand trillion miles.

As the television advertisements often say, "But wait, there's more." There are other galaxies. Our galaxy is considered only average in size. There are some very dense galaxies such as the Sombrero Galaxy, which is 28 million light-years away and contains an estimated 800 billion stars.

While I was continuing my search for God in His awe, I was fortunate to be living during the time of tremendous growth in knowledge of the Heavens. The Hubble telescope undertook the Hubble Ultra-Deep Field (HUDF) Project in 2003 to 2004. That project discovered 10,000 additional, previously unknown, galaxies. The HUDF Project took the following photo into what appeared to the naked eye to be empty blackness. To get an idea of the telescope's field of view, it is the equivalent of holding up a U.S. dime at arms-length and looking at the area behind the dime. The image below shows what Hubble discovered behind my dime.

Figure 10 Galaxies Ultra-Deep Field – Photo[37]

At first appearance, I thought the white spots were stars. Wrong again. They are galaxies! I remember reading about this discovery in the *Houston Chronicle* on a back page in a small paragraph. It was becoming clear the press didn't understand the magnitude of this discovery; indeed didn't understand the Universe itself. If a respected newspaper didn't understand that fact, how could it understand the Awe of God?

Once the wide-angle lens was moved out, I was satisfied I had seen all of what I could of God's awe. The assumptions for the estimated total number of galaxies and stars in the galaxies in the entire Universe were brazen. First, it was assumed all galaxies have about the same number of stars as the galaxies in our celestial neighborhood. Second, it was assumed the Universe has the same density of galaxies per dime in areas of the heaven not explored. These assumptions led to the conclusion of the approximate magnitude of the Universe. It was a stunning conclusion. The Universe contained 200 to 700 billion stars per galaxy. There were about 100 to 170 billion galaxies. Hence there were about 20 to 1,190 billion trillion stars in the Universe. The large ranges of the estimates showed the inaccuracies of the assumptions. I would never know the actual numbers. But for sure, my mind was numbed.

Visible & Invisible — God's love outnumbers the sands

> *"How precious to me are your designs, O God; how vast the sum of them! Were I to count them, they would outnumber the sands . . ."*
> PSALM 139:18

I had gone from finding God's awe in rivers, mountains, lakes, oceans, and much more on Earth to His awe in the Universe itself. Yet I had not reached the final conclusion of the Universe's magnitude. I was about to be served the *pièce de résistance* on my journey.

All the numbers of visible objects in the Universe actually make up only 4% of the Universe. The other 96% is invisible, made up of 23% dark matter, which contains black holes, and 73% dark energy. This is incredible! The Universe is huge, beyond-the-imagination in magnitude. Only 4% is visible. God is truly Omnipotent.

But the number of stars is changing, thus adding further confusion to a scientific approach. The Universe is not static. God's complete awe was again elusive. The scripture quote at the beginning of this section, "things visible and things invisible," is certainly apropos.

I was forced to go deeper to find God; to explore the matter and energy seen and the vast majority not seen. How did science know invisible matter and energy existed if it could not be seen? The answer: Dark matter and energy exert force on neighboring visible objects in the Universe, so dark mass and energy could be calculated. I needed details.

I had to rethink my image of God, just as Einstein had to rethink his images of the Universe. God's awe must also be in the invisible.

MATTER & ENERGY – Jesus the Man energized us

> *"At present we see indistinctly, as in a mirror . . . At present I know partially."*
> 1 CORINTHIANS 13:12

As a youngster, I often thought of God as the energy that created the material world. The Creator! Now I was challenged to put the image to the test. As an added blessing, this challenge led to the field of my graduate education, physical chemistry. Dark energy and dark matter intrigued me.

Many scientists believed in the concept of conservation of matter and energy. In other words, the total matter and the total energy in the Universe each remained constant, which meant the percentages in the previous section, 73% dark energy and 23% dark matter, would never change. In my pursuit of God, I might have analogously said, there was no ongoing creating taking place. That, not coincidentally, was the error both scientists and theologians made in the past.

During this same period, one of the most brilliant scientists was alive. Einstein said conservation of matter and energy was wrong; they were changing in accordance with his famous equation $E=mc^2$, where E=energy, m=mass of matter, and c=speed of light. Have no fear, this is the only equation you will see in this book. Imagine if c is squared, 186,000 miles per second, the result is a huge number. It is so huge that even if it is multiplied times a small number for m, the result is still a very big number for E.

This is why it took such a small atom bomb in Hiroshima, about 25 pounds of fissionable U235, to create such a huge explosion. Uranium 235 is used because it is unstable, making it easier to fission. But what is intriguing about God's creation is 25 pounds of rose petals contains the same amount of nuclear energy. This is not like burning logs in a fireplace, which is an exothermic, chemical reaction that merely changes molecules from one form to another, solid to gas. No, Einstein was talking about a nuclear reaction, which changes the subatomic.

As the word implies, fission is breaking atoms apart as was done in the atom bomb on Hiroshima. But a hydrogen bomb is so much bigger in energy, it takes an atom bomb to detonate a hydrogen bomb. A hydrogen bomb consists of fusion, or combining subatomic material.

As discussed earlier, there are many stars. They are driven by nuclear fusion reactions, hence why they seem to never run out of material fuel or m. Though our Sun does have a life span, don't worry: it won't run out of fuel for a long, long time.

Newton's Gravity — God and man mutually attracted

> *"Draw me after you and let us run together!"*
> Song of Solomon 1:4

Matter and energy are interchangeable. Even so, all the matter of God's beautiful creation observed all over our Earth is still interesting, which leads to Newton.

As legend has it, Newton discovered gravity when focusing on matter, namely an apple. Intuitively, it probably didn't fall on his head. Nonetheless, he probably saw one fall and it had a mental impact on his brain, figuratively falling on his head. This subtle interpretation became meaningful when I later learned about consciousness.

Newton asked: Why would it fall? Only a scientist would ask that question. Everyone else would just eat the apple. He postulated there was an invisible force drawing it to the Earth, which became the term "gravity." That led him to ask the obvious corollary question: Why did the Moon not also fall to the Earth like the apple? His intuition led him to postulate: There must be an opposite and equal force keeping it away. He knew the Moon was orbiting the Earth. He called it centrifugal force.

Visualize centrifugal force by thinking about a kid swinging a rock on a rope around his head and it stays extended. Centrifugal force was throwing the rock out and gravity was the invisible rope counterbalancing the centrifugal force holding it in. Our Moon is centrifugally held out in orbit in perfect balance with the gravitational force of it being drawn to Earth. This is the same principle that holds man-made satellites in orbit.

To summarize Newton's equation: First, it shows the magnitude of gravity is greater for the heavier of the two objects. Second, it shows the greater the distance between the objects, the gravity becomes far less than would otherwise be expected by just a proportional change in the distance.

Suddenly Newton's theory provides more insight. The apple also exerted a force of attraction on the Earth, but due to the apple's relatively small mass, the force was too small to measure. Thinking bigger, I applied the concept to galaxies and a question that had been dogging me. Why don't the massive galaxies fly apart in their spiral spinning? Applying Newton's theory, the answer must be due to a large mass at the center of the galaxies, which exerts a gravitational pull on the spiraling heavenly bodies to keep them from flying off. But no one could see anything there. Ah! This is where the dark matter resides, which, together with dark energy, came to be known as a black hole. It is the invisible mass, which holds our Milky Way galaxy together by gravity. This is where dark energy also resides. The gravitational force is so great in a black hole, nothing that gets too close can escape it, not even light energy. Hence, dark energy and dark matter are both there.

Scientists were saying attractive force is universally part of nature. All bodies in the Universe from celestial to human attract each other.

I started to question my childish image of God as energy and think of Him more as incarnate matter. I put my science hat on and tried to draw analogies to see where it might lead. Was my attraction to God's awe part of the grand design of the Universe? If so, was my attraction to God's awe actually small compared to His huge attraction to me? I pondered where this would lead. This concept of gravity was too intriguing to not go deeper.

General Relativity – Eternity free of space and time

> *"When forced to summarize the general theory of relativity in one sentence: Time and space and gravitation have no separate existence from matter."*
> ALBERT EINSTEIN

The bigger question of Divine attraction led me intuitively to suspect there must be more than Newton's concept of gravity. Einstein had a different way of thinking about gravity, which he postulated in his general theory of relativity, which he called General Relativity. It is a paradigm shift from Newton's theory of gravity without contradicting it. It provided fresh insight into the Universe and God.

Einstein believed space and time are curved, not linear. What this meant was not immediately clear. But it became very important in my spiritual journey into God's awe, so please stay with me. The following figure helps visualize what Einstein's theory is saying. It shows the mass of the Sun curves space around it. That curvature forms a dimple in space, which causes Earth and the Moon to be dragged into the dimple. It is called a dimple since it looks like the dimple on a person's face. When a marble spins around the top of a funnel, as the marble slows, it gets sucked down into the funnel. Another image is the roulette table and the ball spinning around it. When it slows, I hope to hit a jackpot as it falls. Similarly, the Sun's mass creates a dimple in space for the Earth to rotate around. The Earth also creates a dimple for the Moon to rotate around.

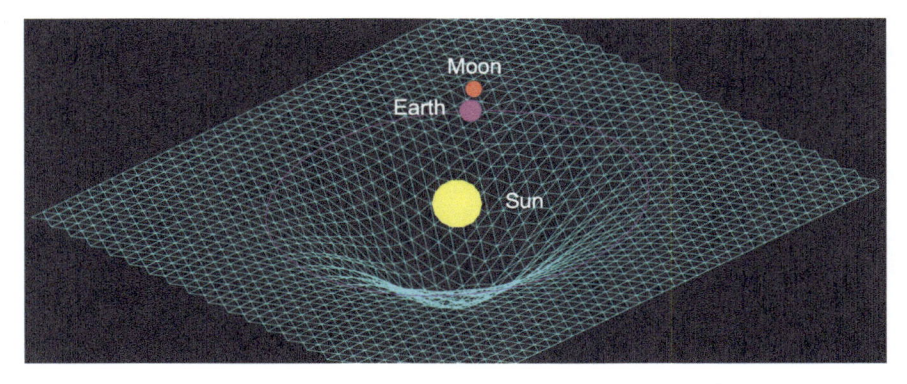

Figure 11 Gravity in General Relativity – Image[38]

But that was not all. I was challenged to let go of my images of God as energy or matter, but somehow incorporate both energy and matter. The reason is Einstein's General Relativity also applies to the energy of light, which also bends by the dimple of space. The following figure helps imagine how the concept works.

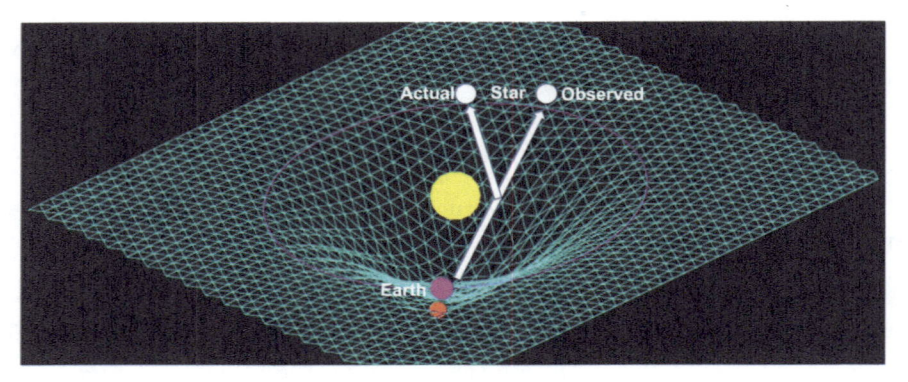

Figure 12 Light Bent in General Relativity – Image[39]

The observer on Earth in the bottom is looking at a distant star and viewing it as the observed location at the top. But it is an illusion! As the star passes behind a large heavenly body like our Sun the light is bent, so the real position of the star is behind the heavenly body. Light is not linear, but curved, due to the pull of the dimple in space caused by the large heavenly body.

Initially hard to believe, but Einstein's theory is confirmed by actual measurements depicted by the previous figure. The light from a distant star was measured behind our Sun during a solar eclipse to avoid the glare of the Sun. Since the dimensions of the Sun and the distance from the star are both known, one can calculate what the predicted time of the reappearance of the star's light would be. The experiment showed it appeared sooner, confirming Einstein's General Relativity theory.

There is another consequence of Einstein's theory called the Equivalence Principle. It states that regardless of the mass of objects, all bodies attract each other at the same rate. During the first lunar landing in 1969, the astronauts demonstrated the principle on the atmosphere-free Moon. They simultaneously dropped a hammer and a feather, both hit the ground at the same time. The reason it doesn't happen on earth is our atmosphere causes unseen resistance to the feather. In 2018 it was also demonstrated on large-body, astronomical objects.

I had to refine my thinking as to why God and I had mutual attraction. As I said at the beginning of this chapter, I had been avoiding people. But is God attracted to them too and equally? Was I, by the laws of nature, also attracted to others and they to me? These were scary thoughts. I was not ready to deal with them in my spiritual journey.

Somehow, I needed to look at the awe of God in a different way. I knew frequently in science new discoveries caused tweaks in theories. But rarely was there a paradigm shift like Einstein's General Relativity Theory was to Newton's Gravitational Theory. My journey to God needed a paradigm shift.

I turned to my personal scientific experience for an analogous example of the paradigm shift I needed in my spiritual journey. It was the Moebius Curve. It is a three-dimensional object with only one side and one edge. Mathematicians worked on the problem for some time. They knew it existed. Engineers used it to create continuously-playing tape cassettes, which looped back on themselves. This was accomplished very simply by the manufacturer twisting the tape 180 degrees and reattaching it. A piece of paper cut into a narrow strip, twisted once with the ends taped together creates a Moebius curve. The resulting strip only has one side and one edge even though it is three dimensional. I needed to twist my brain's thinking-tape and look at my images of God's awe in a different way. Using three-dimensional, curved space, I approached God's awe with a new perspective. I tried to visualize how a curved Universe would affect my journey toward God.

During my search, I was stunned to learn there is actually a Flat Earth Society that still believes the Earth is flat. The concept of the Earth being a sphere is not that new; it dates back to the early Greeks. If I traveled East, I would eventually return from the West. I once flew in a corporate jet cruising at about 55,000 feet elevation, which was high enough to clearly see the curvature of the Earth. Most commercial flights fly at only about 35,000 feet elevation, which pretty much eliminates that perspective. Early mariners did not need that high elevation perspective. They saw the bottom of the ship disappear while the top of the mast was still visible, thus suggesting a curvature.

I visualized the Earth as a basketball. Walking around the basketball, I wouldn't fall off, as some predicted Christopher Columbus would, when he went on his voyage to the New World. I also would not perceive an edge. Einstein showed the Universe is also curved; it would be like walking around the inside of a basketball. If traveling in one direction fast enough, which is impossible, I would return from the other direction without perceiving any edge to the Universe. I would not fall off.

Hence it is nonsensical to ask what is outside the Universe, what is beyond its edge. It would be like asking a fish what it is like to swim without water. If the fish could talk, it wouldn't even understand the question. It would be nonsensical. Everyone is a prisoner trapped in the Universe's dimensions of space and time.

The paradigm shift in my spiritual journey happened when I realized, if there is eternal life, as I believed, it also could not be trapped by the dimensions of space and time. Language is incapable of describing it. If such language existed, I would be like the fish who couldn't understand the question. Questions like what is outside space are nonsensical since the word "outside" implies space. Questions like what is eternal life are also nonsensical because the word "eternal" implies time forever. I was entering the ineffable awe of God. I was strangely undaunted in my journey by such ineffable awe. I had to push on and better understand space and time.

Special Relativity – God visible and invisible

> *"Time performs the miracles. Time is in fact the hero of the plot."*
> GEORGE WALD, Nobel Laureate

I went back to Einstein for inspiration on space and time. I had read about Einstein's Special Relativity Theory. My initial reaction was a cringing feeling I wouldn't be able to understand it. That passed quickly when I read how he conceived of the idea. It turns out to be rather simple, but requires another paradigm shift in thinking, like the Moebius Curve. Please stay with me since this led me to more incredible insight into God's awe and love.

Einstein had a special fascination with light. When he worked in a patent office in Switzerland, he looked out the window. If he had been caught, he probably would have been accused of daydreaming. But like all good scientists, he was conducting a thought experiment, summarized in the following Figure and explanation.

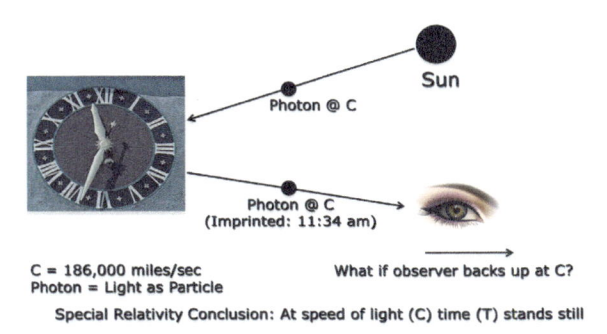

Figure 13 Einstein's Space-Time Thought Experiment – Image

In 1905 he looked at the town clock, which in this image is registering 11:34 am. He asked: How am I able to observe the time? He mused it was because the Sun's light was reflecting off the clock face and bouncing back to his eye. The image was carried by a series of photon energy particles imprinted with the image of 11:34 am. He asked: What if I travel at the same speed, the speed of light, away from the clock? Einstein of course gave the simple answer to his own question. When he traveled at the speed of light away from the clock, he would constantly be seeing the same photon imprinted with the same 11:34 am image. For him, as the traveler, time would stand still. His astonishingly simple reasoning and logic led him to the concepts space and time are relative to each other. It is called Special Relativity and indeed it is special.

Humans have worshipped the Sun for millennia. Light has always been a big part of religious ritual and liturgy. It is a reliable and necessary part of life. Einstein's theory identified its reliability by determining its speed is constant and the fastest thing in nature. How could he say it is constant? According to his theory, the faster matter moves, the more mass it gains, until it reaches the point where it can't be moved any faster. Hence, why it reaches a maximum and why it is an essential part of his $E=mc^2$ equation.

Time is inextricably linked to light. Time always moves forward, not backward. Yet science still struggles with why time only moves forward even though the reason seems obvious or at least intuitive.

The past is no longer just remembering, but directly observing. God provides an opportunity to travel back in time. You may say that sounds crazy, but suddenly my awe took on an unexpected dimensional time-warp. Because of the known speed of light, distant galaxies are visible as they existed billions of years ago, since it takes their light billions of light-years to get to Earth. In fact, they can't be seen as they exist now. They may have died light-years ago; we on earth wouldn't know it.

Even the art world reflects the new concept time does not pass at a constant rate. Salvador Dali's famous painting, *The Persistence of Memory*, depicts a melting clock.

And if that wasn't bizarre enough, scientists suggested something that seemed even more bizarre, the Wormhole Theory. It involves combining Einstein's General and Special Relativity. Special Relativity shows space and time are inextricably linked so scientists referred to the space-time continuum. General Relativity proves the space-time continuum is curved. Visualizing that continuum as a very simple two-dimensional piece of paper, it can fold back on itself as shown in the following figure.

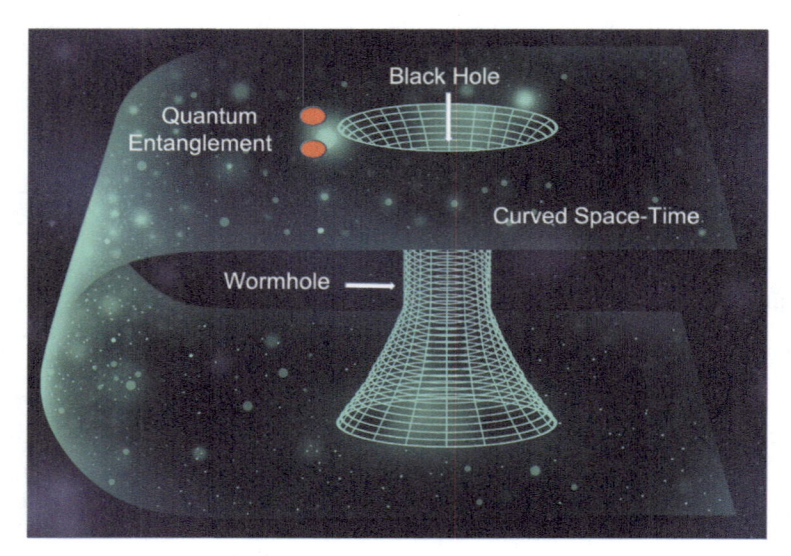

Figure 14 Wormhole Theory in Space-Time – Image[40]

The theory says there are so-called wormholes, which theoretically connect two points in spacetime. They would, in principle, allow space and time travel. They are related to black holes since they consume everything around them, including space and time.

I almost started to freak out. One of my favorite 1985 movies, *Back to the Future*, could save a bunch of time in my journey to God's awe. In 1935 Einstein first postulated the basis of this concept as part of his General Relativity Theory. In 1988 researchers at the California Institute of Technology worked out how to convert a wormhole traversing space into one traversing time.[41] Though accepted by science, it applies only to the very small quantum, subatomic level, so it is impossible to apply to human time travel. Little did I know this would play a significant role in my future journey.

In spite of all this wonder and knowledge, science still didn't completely understand light; in fact, it still doesn't. Fortunately, we scientists are a practical bunch willing to live with some tension and ambiguity. People of faith also live with and accept ambiguity. Because of the simultaneous belief in one God and three Persons, even my faith has to feel comfortable with ambiguity. Similarly, scientists sometimes visualize light as a particle as Einstein did in his photon thought experiment. Sometimes they visualize light as a wave when that model made better predictions.

When light is viewed as a wave, it looks like the image in the following figure. Be careful not to confuse this with a physical wave such as water in the ocean or sound in the air. Though analogous, light is different; it is actually energy, not matter like water or air.

Wavelength (Peak-to-Peak Distance)
Wave Frequency (Speed)   FM = Frequency Modulation
Wave Amplitude (Height)   AM = Amplitude Modulation

Figure 15 Visible Spectrum – Image[42]

Visible light or white light is composed of all colors. Water droplets in the air act as a prism refracting white light into the colors of the rainbow as shown in the visible spectrum figure. When talking about the spectrum, the terms used to describe it are revealing. The height of the wave is called wave amplitude, peak-to-peak distance called wavelength, and speed of the wave called the frequency. The terminology "frequency modulation" (FM) and "amplitude modulation" (AM) are used for radios. But radios are clearly not capturing light. As the wavelength increases the color turns from purple to red.

There is more to the story than just visible light. Stay with me. This explains something wonderful about the Universe. The light visibly seen is only a very small part of the overall electromagnetic energy spectrum. In fact, it is only one ten-trillionth of the total spectrum, which is represented in the following, not-to-scale, image.

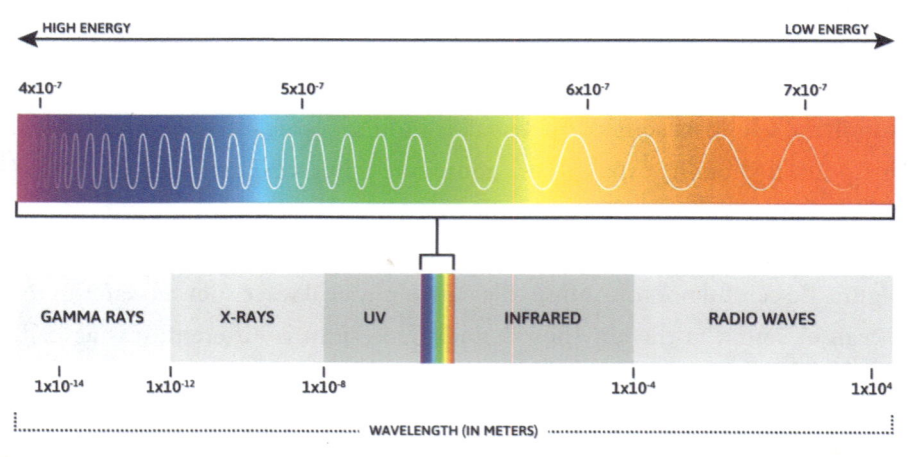

Figure 16 Electromagnetic Spectrum – Image[43]

I began to realize why the scripture quote at the beginning is so accurate: "At present we see indistinctly." Engineers created technology in order to view the invisible parts of the spectrum by converting their signals to a visible image or audible sound as in FM and AM radios. Engineers built scopes for this purpose, which range from microscopes to telescopes. They are all based on the general principle: If the spectrum wavelength is similar in dimension to the object observed, then an appropriate instrument can be designed.

In the 20th-century, multiple applications were developed. For example, radar, which is in the radio range, has large wavelengths, so is used to view large objects like airplanes. Microwaves, used in our ovens, as the name implies, uses microwave energy to vibrate the water and food, thus causing friction and heat. By accident, a microwave telescope contributed to a major discovery that the Universe is expanding, which is discussed in a later chapter. Small wavelengths off to the left are used to study the human body and large molecules using X-rays are in electron microscopes.

Though I was fascinated by all this, for a time I thought I was going off on a tangent. Or perhaps getting further into the weeds away from God's awe. But was I? This all led to a major discovery.

BIG BANG – God's creative love is explosive

> "The Big Bang theory does not conflict with the Catholic concept of creation."
> Pope Pius XII

Georges Lemaitre was both the father of the Big Bang Theory and a father in the Jesuit order. How did Fr. Lemaitre earn this Big Bang title? To answer that question, I needed to go deeper.

Expanding Universe – Growing with God

> "The account of the beginning [Genesis 1] is natural science but so profound that it is cloaked in parables." "Study astronomy and physics if you desire to comprehend the relation between the world and God's management of it."
> Maimonides, Rabbi and Mystic

This is what I discovered about the theological importance of seeing outside the visible light range—what led me to a better understanding of electromagnetic energy and waves and their importance in understanding the awe of God's creation. Electromagnetic energy, when considered as a wave, actually shows the Universe is expanding at an accelerating rate. It is not static as Einstein once thought. Here is how.

I always had a sinking feeling when I saw a policeman pointing a radar gun at me. He is able to clock my speed due to the so-called doppler effect. He is using the radar end of the electromagnetic energy spectrum. When the radar waves from his gun hit my oncoming car, they are bounced back to his gun's detector. But they are compressed waves, like an accordion, thus making the wavelengths, peak-to-peak distance, shorter than when they were sent. This is a direct and calculatable result of the speed of my oncoming vehicle, squeezing the waves flatter like an accordion.

Another image helps explain this phenomenon. Though a train's whistle is not based on electromagnetic energy, but on physical sound waves, it provides a better understanding of the same effect. When approaching, the whistle is high pitched because waves are being compressed to shorter wavelengths. When receding, the whistle is low pitched because the waves are being stretched longer.

I was delighted to learn I didn't always have to relate this to a speeding ticket. Scientists used this wonderful effect when they discovered distant stars and galaxies are lengthening, that is, stretching the wavelengths. Since it was first noticed in the red end of the spectrum, it is called the "red shift." Scientists discovered the Universe is expanding, and not only expanding, but accelerating in speed. It is not like having the car on cruise control, but like "putting the pedal to the metal" before I got my ticket. I was young and really amazed because I had bought into the idea God had created a Universe and, once created, it was static, unchanging, but science discovered it is not static. But was the red shift just a one-off, an anomaly?

Because of the red shift discovery, separately and independently, Arno Penzias and Robert Wilson were searching for communications from extraterrestrials using a microwave telescope by trying to see outside the visible range. But Penzias and Wilson had a problem. They were getting static in all directions. As with many scientific discoveries, they first thought something was wrong with their equipment. After much mechanical inspection and retesting, they realized there wasn't anything wrong. They had discovered the same source of static old televisions would get; the echo from an explosion in the distant past. In 1978 Penzias and Wilson were awarded the Nobel Prize for Physics.

The mutually affirming red shift and microwave echo experiments had profound implications. They enabled the calculation of when the explosion took place at the beginning of the Universe, about 13.7 billion years ago. The Universe is expanding at a high, accelerating rate. So high, the diameter of the Universe, as of today, is about 156 billion lightyears. But since the expansion is accelerating, that number is also constantly increasing. The diameter will be different tomorrow. It is difficult to even imagine that great of a distance. I was blown away that two separate experiments confirmed the same truth, which reaffirmed my theological faith. There was a beginning to the Universe. At the time, I thought this was the holy grail of my Awe.

Then I met Gerald Schroeder[44] and listened to his amazing presentation. He is a Ph.D. physics graduate from MIT who conducted a mental experiment, just like Einstein conducted a mental experiment. He asked: What if he was riding on the wave front, the shock wave, of the original explosion? Because the shock wave was traveling so fast, though not at the speed of light, for him as traveler, time would dramatically be slowed down in accordance with relativity theory. Schroeder calculated what the elapsed time, since the original explosion, would be for him, the traveler, on the wave front, compared to me traveling on Earth. Remember for me on Earth, the age of the Universe is 13.7 billion years. But Schroeder calculated, for the traveler riding the wave-front, the age of the Universe was 6.5 to 7.0 days. This is an astounding result consistent with Genesis. My only concern was a rush to literalism in scriptural interpretation.

But where was Einstein in all of this? I normally thought of him first. I was in for another surprise.

Unified Theory — United in God's love

> "... to comprehend with all the holy ones what is the breadth and length and height and depth, and to know the love of Christ that surpasses knowledge, so that you may be filled with all the fullness of God."
> EPHESIANS 3:17–19

I found myself back with Einstein. He had been trying to develop one equation for combining the only known forces at the time, namely gravity and electromagnetic energy. Called the Unified Theory, he thought he had come up with an answer, but there was a problem. His resulting equation predicted a beginning to the Universe. Einstein was uncomfortable with that major paradigm shift in thinking. He, like most scientists and theologians of faith, believed there was no beginning, the Universe was static. So he introduced a fudge factor into his equation.

A fudge factor is sometimes inserted into an equation to adjust, or fudge, the result to better match our perception of the real world, or to adjust the margin of error. It is most often added retrospectively. Fr. Lemaitre and Einstein were friends and fellow cosmologists. After meetings with Einstein, Fr. Lemaitre was successful in convincing Einstein his fudge factor was not necessary. He convinced him his original equation was correct. There was a beginning to the Universe. That is the reason why Lemaitre is considered the father of the Big Bang Theory. Einstein's Unified Theory predicted the age of the Universe, which was experimentally confirmed by both the red shift and microwave echo experiments. This was the Big Awe I was looking for in my search for God's creation.

Figure 17 Meeting of Fr. Lemaitre & Einstein - Photo[45]

After Einstein two additional forces were discovered, the strong and the weak nuclear forces. The strong holds atoms together and the weak allows decay for nuclear stability. But like the Universe itself, I was confused as to how big the four forces are relative to each other. I arbitrarily set the magnitude of the weak nuclear force at "1". The calculation showed the strong nuclear force became 1,000 and electromagnetic force became 100. Shockingly, the gravitational force became 10^{-39}, the dot followed by 39 zeros before the one. Astounding! Gravity was the first force to be discovered, yet it is incredibly weaker than the other three forces. The dismaying possibility is there are probably additional forces yet to be discovered.

As usual, the story doesn't end there. Scientists needed to expand Einstein's Unified Theory equation to include all four forces. Here is their thinking. Perhaps an existing equation, describing some other system, could be modified to fit their need. The equation they chose described a system consisting of multiple, one-dimensional strings. This came to be called String Theory. A string is really three-dimensions, but in the equation, they described something more like the one-dimensional line used in geometry.

Scientists are never satisfied with a theory. They always want to disprove it, which often leads to further tweaks. Different systems were considered for a more accurate equation to reflect the four forces. Subsequent theories used systems consisting of more dimensions. This led to Membrane Theory, based on two dimensions, then ultimately P-Brane Theory, based on multiple dimensions, "P" dimensions. I have to admit scientists do have a sense of humor to call it P-Brane Theory.

There is a progression to greater accuracy each time more dimensions are considered in the formulation of the equation. That means the Universe itself is more likely made up of those additional dimensions. As it turns out, some scientists think it could be made up of as many as eleven-plus dimensions.[46] The only reason it is impossible to directly experience beyond the four—length, width, depth, and time—is because the other dimensions are subatomic. This is breathtaking. Like the view of light being very limited, the view of the other dimensions of the Universe is also limited. Everyone is trapped in the multiple dimensions of our Universe like the fish trapped in its water. God's awe kept expanding in my brain.

Something very interesting happened on my journey to the Big Bang beginning. It turns out the unified equation has time as one of its variables, which enables a better understanding of the expansion of the Universe depicted in the following famous image.

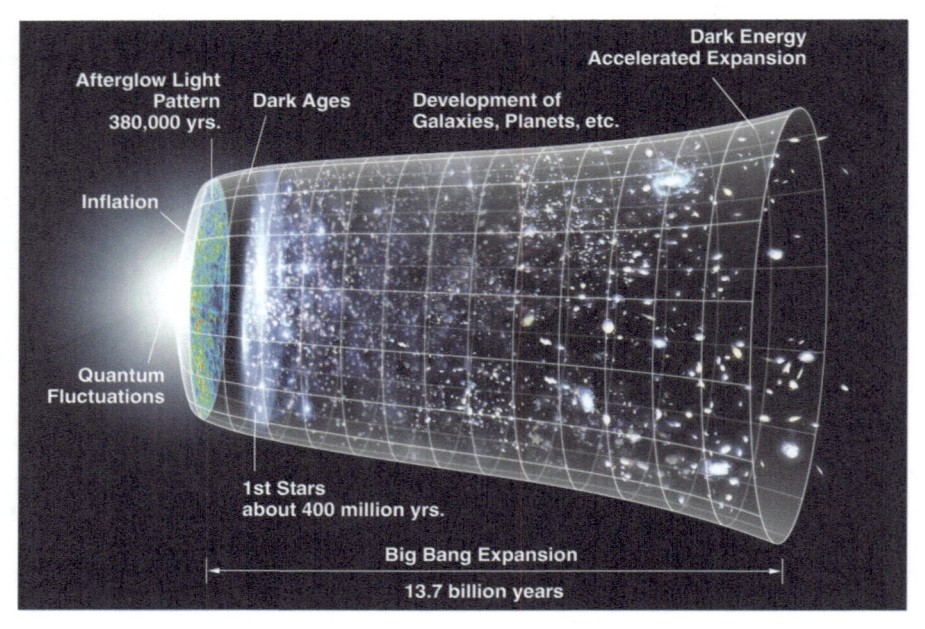

Figure 18 Expanding Universe Creation Process – Image[47]

Note the ongoing expansion is not linear, but greater at the beginning. The equation shows such good accuracy, it could predict the makeup of the Universe within fractions of a second after the Big Bang. The Unified Theory equation enables us to look back in time to the very beginnings of the Universe with finer detail than can be imagined. The results are stunning in their detail. It provided context or a map for my journey.

It showed at zero-time, what scientists called the Singularity, the four forces were unified. Then between 10^{-43} to 10^{-10} seconds after the Big Bang, the four forces started to separate into their individual characteristics. During that same time, the temperatures were cooling from 10^{32} to 10^{15} °F. Remember the number of zeros involved in making these numbers is incredibly small for time and large for temperature. Absolutely amazing.

The plot thickened! Between 10^{-4} to 180 seconds after the Big Bang, elementary chemistry started to evolve from subatomic to hydrogen. At the same time, the temperatures were continuing to cool from 10^{12} to 10^9 °F. This is attention-grabbing because life is primarily made up of hydrocarbons, meaning hydrogen and carbon. What is the next step?

Then it happened! Between 400 million to 500,000 years ago, with continued cooling, light atoms formed, then the stars. Chemically every atom in our bodies was once part of the stars. I immediately recognized that, separate from this scientific discovery, the wisdom literature of almost all faiths refers to light as a symbol of life. The rest is history: galaxies at 500 million years to our solar system at 9 billion years after the Big Bang.

It is almost inconceivable an equation could yield so much information in the infinitely small time frames immediately after the Big Bang. The chemistry of life led to refining my search for God's awe. But first, I focused on the characteristics of the "Singularity," the word scientists use to describe what existed at the beginning of the Big Bang.

Singularity & Anthropic – Universe to Heaven transcendence

> *"The more I examine the Universe . . . the more evidence I find that the Universe in some sense must have known we were coming."*
> FREEMAN DYSON, Physicist

> *". . . He chose us in Him, before the foundation of the world."*
> EPHESIANS 1:4

The attributes of the Singularity at the beginning of the Big Bang are intriguing. Einstein's theories, including his Unified Theory equation, suggest there are primarily four attributes of the Singularity.

1. *DIMENSIONLESS* – As the Unified Theory equations are continually improved, scientists changed their predictions of the dimensions of the Singularity. They started from the size of a baseball, to a golf ball, to the dot at end of this sentence. Then ultimately to the size of a photon of energy. Wow! The Singularity was outside space, or more accurately, not constrained by space.

2. *TIMELESSNESS* – Gravity takes on a much more dominant role because the distance between the matter is so small. In fact, gravity is so strong, even light cannot escape its gravitational pull. This is also a characteristic of the Black Holes at the center of galaxies. Without light there is no time. The Singularity is outside time, or more accurately, not constrained by time.
3. *ORDERED* – From chemistry, scientists knew the 2nd Law of Thermodynamics states the Universe is continually getting more disordered. Entropy is a measure of that disorder, which is always increasing. At the Singularity, entropy was zero. The Singularity was perfectly ordered.
4. *UNIFIED* – The four known forces converged into a true unified force in accordance with Einstein's Unified Theory. The Singularity is unified. The force was with us from the beginning, not just in the *Star Wars* movies.

This was mind blowing. It finally addressed the issue of why scientists struggled with time only moving forward. Science postulated three possible explanations. One is cosmological because the Universe is expanding not contracting; it is always creating not uncreating, which is addressed later in my journey to the Big Bang. The second reason is thermodynamic because the 2nd Law of Thermodynamics says entropy, a measure of disorder in the Universe, is always increasing not decreasing. The third reason is psychological because only the past can be remembered, not the future.

I conjectured a fourth theological reason in my search for God's awe. I can only learn from my sins and mistakes of the past, not the future. My attraction to God's awe could only be satisfied if time moved forward.

I must admit I had real problems wrapping my head around the four attributes of the singularity, especially the last one. At first, I was somewhat a doubting Thomas. I asked: How was it possible to fit the immense magnitude of the Universe into such a small space?

When the Singularity was predicted to be the size of a baseball, each atom has a huge amount of void space. Theoretically this would allow a huge collapsibility in volume. But this obviously did not come near to solving the volume problem. The second explanation is the concept of potential energy. Small towns have water towers, which use small pumps to slowly lift water to the top of their tower at night when the demand is low. This is called kinetic energy. It is being stored as potential energy. In the morning, by simply opening a valve, gravity allows the water to flow at high rate and with proper pressure due to the height of the tower. There is no need for a big pump to meet the high demand in the morning when everyone is showering. Perhaps the Singularity is potential energy ready to explode into kinetic energy. But both atomic collapse and potential energy didn't satisfy scientists' bewilderment.

When equations predicted the Singularity to be the size of a photon of energy, applying Einstein's famous equation, the only one in this book, the Singularity is primarily energy, not matter.

Suddenly the Singularity took on real significance for my faith because the Singularity was at the transcendence between Heaven and Earth. I needed to focus on it; it became very important to my journey. The attributes of the Singularity are consistent with my faith belief: Heaven is not constrained by space and time, it is perfectly ordered and it is unified in God's existence. I recalled this aha moment later when my journey of awe entered into mysticism.

If that weren't enough, on my way to the origin of the Universe, there was an additional shock. Physicists tried tweaking the values of the four forces in the equation at the Singularity to see what kind of Universe would have resulted if those forces were different. What they discovered came to be known as the Anthropic Principle.[48]

Hold onto your chairs for this one. In a nutshell, the Anthropic Principle states the four forces at the Singularity were so incredibly fine-tuned as to predictably enable the later emergence of life. For example, if either the gravitational force or the weak force varied by only one part in 10^{50}, the Universe would have collapsed or exploded. Fr. Spitzer, a Jesuit scientist, has compared the pure chance likelihood of the emergence of a single cell in the Universe to "a tornado sweeping through a junk-yard assembling a Boeing 747 from the materials therein."[49] Or the pure chance formation of a single protein in the Universe to a solar system full of blind men solving Rubik's Cubes simultaneously. I could only drop to my knees when I understood this.

At this point, my hero Roger Penrose weighed in. He said there is also an exceedingly small probability of a pure chance occurrence of a low-entropy beginning to our Universe. He calculated the probability to be one in $(10^{10})^{123}$. It was impossible for me to get my brain around that number. I had left humans only to be dragged back to life itself during my journey to the stars.

Not surprisingly, some scientists had trouble with that kind of major paradigm shift, just like Einstein had trouble with his paradigm shift to a non-static Universe. They postulated a multi-universe theory as a solution. They said humans were just lucky to be living in the one Universe that allowed for the existence of life. That meant there had to be $(10^{10})^{123}$ more universes. Curiously, I thought with some sarcasm, this could not be experimentally challenged, since scientists generally agree our physics and science collapse before the Big Bang.

Surprisingly, a brilliant and sophisticated proof was proposed by leading cosmologists Arvin Borde, Alexander Vilenkin, and Alan Guth, known as the BVG Proof. They scientifically showed even multiple universes had to have a beginning. The attempt to discount the Anthropic Principle failed.

Clearly, I had met the Omnipotent Creator, the ultimate Awe of the Universe. We are not here by chance. The Universe was created by God for life. When I started this chapter, I was no longer in need of organized religion and, more particularly, didn't need people. All I needed in my spiritual journey was seeing God in the material awe of His creation. Now I had to confront my error. My pursuit of the stars had led me back to life itself, including people.

Both the Anthropic Principle and the Universe timeline summarized at the beginning of this chapter drew me inexorably into fundamental subatomic and atomic chemistry at the early beginnings of the Universe. To truly understand creation, I needed to look at chemistry. The simplest atoms throughout the Universe existed relatively immediately after the Big Bang, exist in the stars, and, literally from the stars, exist today in life itself in my own body. After all, life is part of creation and is made up of atoms and molecules. From my discovery of the very large in the Universe, I now needed to explore the very small.

4
CHEMISTRY TO LIFE

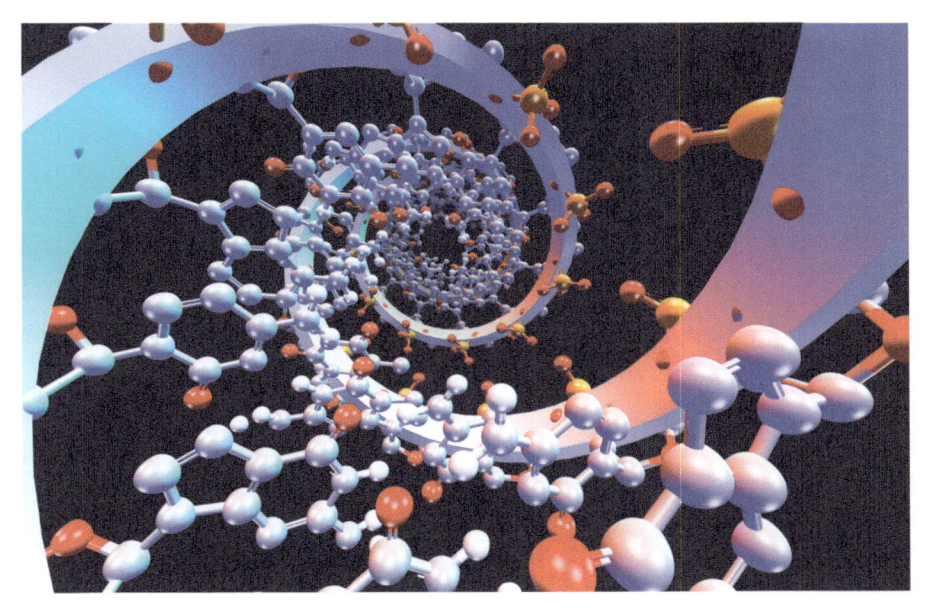

Figure 19 DNA Helical Molecule Viewed Axially – Image[50]

"Before I formed you in the womb I knew you, before you were born I dedicated you, a prophet to the nations I appointed you."

JEREMIAH 1:5

It was prophetic when the Universe led me to life. My wife gave birth to our son David. Our beautiful child turned our lives as parents into a new dimension, but this was different. My wife suffered from severe post-partum depression and was hospitalized. Visiting her every day and taking care of a newborn would have been impossible without the help of our families. Suddenly, I was no longer in control. I was clearly in need of a faith community, which I had shunned. But I wasn't ready yet. Instead, I unconsciously converted my quest for God from the stars to life itself.

The quest for God's awe led to searching for life in: the mysterious Muir Woods and the Black Forest; the beautiful tropical fish in Hanauma and Phang Nga Bays; the majestic Big Five animals in the Serengeti Park and Ngorongoro Crater; the powerful humpback whales and elephant seals in the Antarctic Ocean.

I logically concluded life must exist on other planets and moons. That belief is legitimately based on the gigantic size of the Universe, hence the high probability of intelligent life elsewhere. But the focus had to be on known science and the emergence of life on Earth.[51] This chapter follows a chronological timeline of life on Earth.

Starting with the Big Bang 13.7 billion years ago, Earth was formed about 4.5 billion years ago. Fossil records show the earliest single cell formation about 3 billion years ago. Later in this chapter, the discovery of the Cambrian Explosion and Pangea breakup 543 and 175 million years ago respectively is discussed. Dinosaur extinction was about 65 million years ago. The primitive apes and hominid-humans appeared about 27 and 6 million years ago respectively.

Here is a striking fact: If the age of the Universe is on a 24-hour clock, humans would not appear until the last 38 seconds. We are latecomers to the Earth. My lack of humility at the beginning of the previous chapter was starting to become even more obvious to me.

Chemists know science's chronological process of discovery went from atoms to larger molecules to subatomic particles. Instead of following that historical chronology, I needed to approach my journey more simply and sequentially. I used the same visualization method I used for studying the gigantic Universe. Only now I was looking at the infinitesimally small, subatomic world.

Again pretending to use a camera, I started taking pictures from outside of life beginning with a zoom lens focused on subatomic particles. Moving the camera backward expanded the view to atoms, molecules, DNA, cells and microbes. I hoped to end with a wide-angle lens of life. I ask you to join me on my journey toward a deeper understanding and experience of God's awe in life itself.

CHEMISTRY TO LIFE

SUBATOMIC TO ATOMS – The smallest among us loves

"Both religion and science require a belief in God. For believers, God is in the beginning, and for physicists He is at the end of all considerations ... To the former He is the foundation, to the latter, the crown of the edifice of every generalized world view."
   MAX PLANCK, Physicist & Nobel Prize winner for Quantum Theory

God Particle – God is the core of all things

"Am I a God near at hand only, says the Lord, and not a God far off?"
   JEREMIAH 23:23

My mental journey started in Switzerland, home of the Large Hadron Collider (LHC) shown in the following figure.

Figure 20 Hadron Collider Map[52] and Tunnel,[53] Switzerland – Photos

Cyclotron accelerators accelerate subatomic charged particles. The LHC is a synchrotron accelerator, a descendent of the cyclotron. The cyclotron uses the same principle as a linear accelerator at the amusement park to launch a roller coaster with its huge initial acceleration. The polarity of the magnets below the amusement car constantly and rapidly move the car down the track. The magnets alternate polarity between pushing and pulling, pushing and pulling, on and on. A set of simple bar magnets can help visualize the process.

Michael Faraday discovered the relationship between magnetism and electricity. Unlike a car battery, which maintains polarity with direct current

(DC), the cyclotron operates on alternating current (AC) as in a US home's wall socket. Every time the polarity switches, the magnetic field flips from push to pull. House current switches polarity 60 times per second, known as 60 cycle current, which is why it is used to accurately run clocks at 60 seconds per minute. The cyclotron also switches polarity, but at a much faster, constant rate.

The synchrotron changes the rate at which polarity is switched to account for, or synchronize with, the continually increasing mass of the subatomic particle, which it is accelerating. Hence, its name, the synchrotron. It works in accordance with Einstein's $E=mc^2$ equation, mass increases with speed. The synchrotron LHC in Switzerland accelerates subatomic particles in a tunnel over a very large circumference distance. By alternating polarity fast enough, a charged particle can be accelerated to very high speeds.

When applied to charged subatomic particles, collisions with other particles are produced, which means the masses can be calculated based on their altered trajectories. This is similar to the calculations on the effects of dark energy on visible celestial objects. So even though they cannot be seen directly, they can be measured indirectly. But how?

They can be measured using a cloud chamber filled with smoke. It is analogous to seeing the condensation trail on an overhead jet plane. Sometimes the aircraft is not visible, but the jet is at the head of the condensation trail or contrail. A contrail is produced by the water byproduct of burning hydrocarbon fuel being condensed in the extremely cold temperatures at high altitudes.

Like the number of celestial bodies in the Universe being finite, although immense, so the number of subatomic particles is also finite. There had to be a finite fundamental particle. Scientists were in search of the smallest subatomic particle they called a Boson, colloquially referred to as the "God Particle."[54] I found it humorous physicists used the term euphemistically, but the secular press treated it literally. For them, the particle became God. To my delight, on July 4, 2012, the Boson or "God Particle" Peter Higgs predicted was discovered using the Hadron Collider.

Scientists were still not sure they had discovered the ultimate, smallest particle. The subatomic world is a magical world of God's awe populated by

CHEMISTRY TO LIFE 57

many strangely named particles like Quarks, which came into existence at 10^{-4} seconds after the Big Bang.

As my imaginary camera lens moved back, it reached the atom. I had studied the history of atomic discoveries. I was starting to feel a bit more comfortable since my degree is in this field. But have no fear, this concept is not complicated; it will lead to life itself.

The discoveries related to atoms were made by clever, indirect means, since what was being studied was so small. In 1808 Dalton discovered the atom. In 1897 Thomson discovered electrons using a cathode ray tube like old televisions. In 1911 by bombarding gold foil with helium, Rutherford discovered the nucleus around which the electrons flew. And in 1913 Bohr proposed an atomic structure that, to a certain extent, is still used today. The figure below shows Bohr's model of the simplest atom on the left, hydrogen, and a more complex atom, with multiple electron orbits, on the right. The hydrogen atom first came into existence 180 seconds after the Big Bang. Please, be patient! This chapter reveals some explosive discoveries about my faith and God.

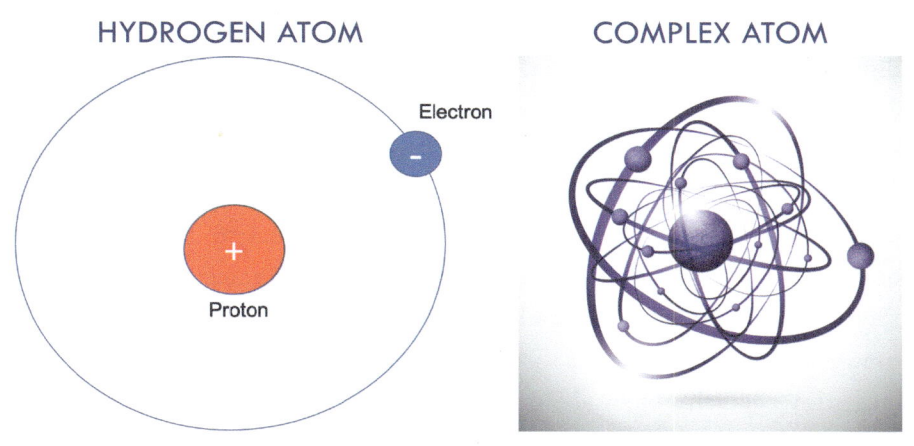

Figure 21 Hydrogen and Complex[55] Atomic Models – Images

It turns out there is a greater void in atoms than thought. Taking the simplest atom, hydrogen, and comparing the distance between its one proton (+) nucleus and one electron (-) by using proportional dimensions, it is easier to relate to. If the proton in the center was 1 inch in diameter, the practically dimensionless electron would be in a 0.8-mile-diameter orbit around the proton.

Uncertainty & Chaos – Knowing God by unknowing God

> *"Where can I hide from your spirit? From your presence, where can I flee? If I ascend to the heavens, you are there."*
> PSALM 139:7–8

My wife healed from her depression and came home from the hospital. Our experience caused me to pray a lot more often. During the process I pondered, would God help Linda and me? My parallel journey into science would lead me to an unexpected answer to my prayer.

On my journey I discovered uncertainty and chaos in nature. This was, for me, a weird twist in God's plan, yet led to a wonderful surprise. I will address these subjects separately. But I had to draw conclusions on how they related, which led to the unwrapping of a wonderful surprise.

HEISENBERG UNCERTAINTY PRINCIPLE[56] – Heisenberg made a discovery in 1927, that would have a profound impact on initiating a paradigm shift in scientists' views of, not only the atom, but the Universe.

Researchers could not simultaneously locate both the electron and its momentum, which is its mass times its speed. They realized this when they used electromagnetic energy in an electron microscope to view molecules. The electromagnetic energy itself, with a wavelength similar to the dimensions of the molecule they were studying, actually excites the electrons and causes them to change momentum and location. They were on to something more fundamental than just some sort of confusion they thought they may have created. Called the Heisenberg Uncertainty Principle, it states that a very fundamental characteristic of nature itself is our inability to know nature completely. Here's why.

During the "God is dead" period in the early 20th century, scientists believed if they couldn't measure something, it didn't exist. Therefore, God didn't exist because He couldn't be measured. Now they had to eat crow and accept the electron exists even though we cannot measure it completely. You

CHEMISTRY TO LIFE 59

may say: So what? It turns out this had profound philosophical implications; scientists now believed in the Uncertainty Principle. Their conclusion was science can only give a probability of where the electron is in its orbit around the nucleus of an atom. Science was undergoing a paradigm shift from deductive to inductive logic, from Newtonian mechanics to quantum mechanics, or the Quantum Theory. So, God may exist, even though we cannot measure Him. As ridiculous as that statement may sound, it is the logical consequence of the Uncertainty Principle.

The following figure shows the new quantum depiction of the hydrogen atom with color-coded electron probability density.

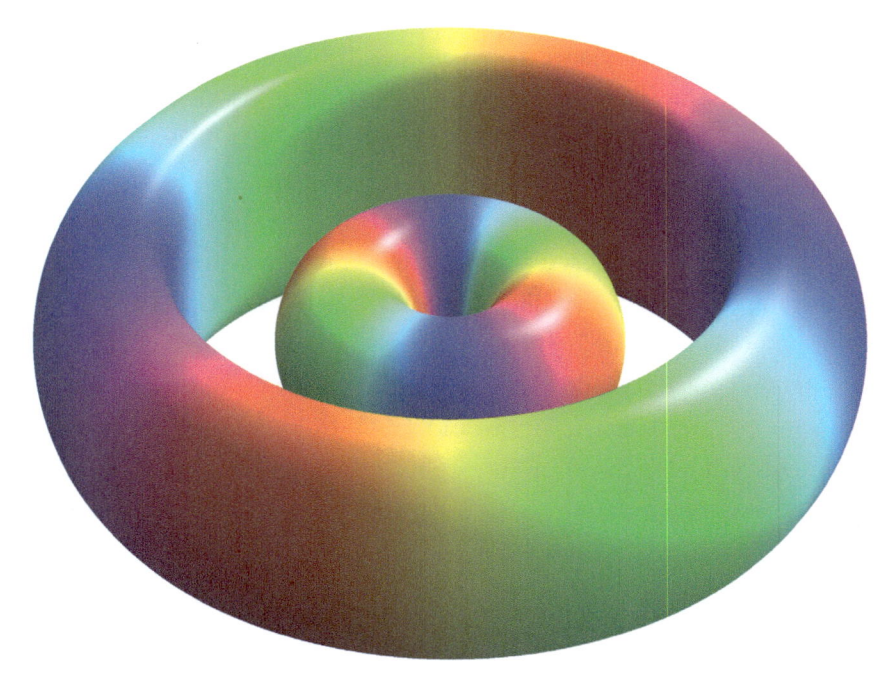

Figure 22 Hydrogen Electron Probability Density – Image[57]

Bohr's image of more complex atoms in Figure 21 shows more electrons in progressively higher and higher orbits. If such an atom is excited by external energy, the electrons will jump to higher orbits. The classic Newtonian explanation is you can see the electrons transition between orbits. Quantum theory says they are actually taking so-called quantum leaps with no time spent between orbits. Weird!

It would be like walking to the market and suddenly, instantly, being one block further with no observable transition to get there or time elapsed. It is difficult to relate to this experience or imagine it in daily life, yet it exists at the atomic level, predicted by Quantum Theory. This discovery required adjusting to another major paradigm shift.

I wondered is this what it's like to go to Heaven? No discernible transition to the next life just a quantum leap. If it is possible to make such a transition in the atomic physical world in accordance with Quantum Theory, why not in the spiritual world?

During the mid to late 19th Century, there were discoveries of many new atoms, with many more electrons, all exhibiting the same uncertainty. Mendeleev helped scientists catalogue those discoveries when he organized his famous Periodic Table of Elements.

CHAOS THEORY[58] – Chaos is not chaotic! The following true story demonstrates what seems to be a very strange statement.

When powerful computers became available, scientists decided to apply them first to one of the most difficult, complex problems: predicting weather. This was important because billions of dollars are lost in crops when weather cannot be predicted. One night the researchers inputted their data into the computer and got the results the next morning, but they didn't make sense.

I could relate. I was using an old IBM 1600 computer to calculate data for my graduate dissertation research. Every evening I submitted my punched cards, which contained the program and data, and the next morning I received the results. Like any good scientist, if the results didn't make sense, I rechecked my data and programming for errors and resubmitted.

The weather researchers did the same thing. The results didn't make sense; they discovered a very minor error in their input data. They didn't think it would have much effect on the results because it was so small. But they corrected the minor error and reentered the data. The next morning the results were dramatically different. They thought they had made another error. Frequently scientific discoveries are made accidentally, or more aptly, serendipitously.

After extensive rechecking, the weather researchers realized they had discovered something fundamental in nature: When there are multiple variables in nature, the slightest change in even just one variable can have a dramatic, unpredictable effect. This is called the Chaos Theory, which is accepted by scientists. They euphemistically, yet accurately, used an example called the Butterfly Effect, which states that if a butterfly in Beijing flaps its wings, it will change the weather in New York.

Not only was I stunned by this theory, but also by the beauty of the images when the data processing was plotted. The images were called Mandelbrot Fractals. Examples are shown in the following figure.

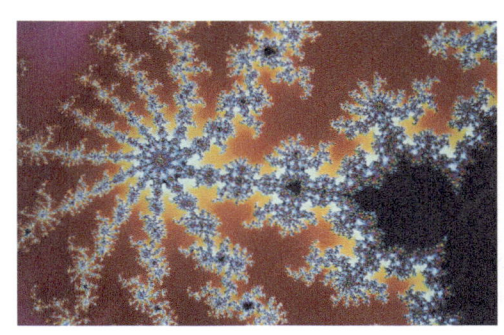

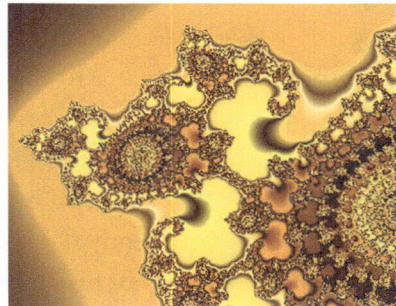

Figure 23 Mandelbrot Fractals from Chaos – Images[59]

But these are strange images of chaos. Even more incredibly, using a microscope, repetition of the same macro pattern at the micro level can be seen, no matter how deep the microscope zooms. For me, nature was becoming increasingly more incredible and beautiful with each passing moment. However, these images were still a plot of chaos that was not certain, hence not completely knowable or predictable!

This meant one human could have an incredible impact on the environment and other human beings by the simplest of actions. It also meant models would have an equally incredible inability to measure or know the impact, since usually there are too many variables involved. Chaos Theory told me I am not in as much predictable control over reality as I might think. This was a very humbling revelation on my spiritual faith journey.

Remember the quote by St. Augustine of Hippo in an earlier chapter that says miracles are not an exception to the laws of nature, but an indication we don't know the laws of nature completely. Science is saying we can never even deductively know all the laws of nature.

Some scientists, and even theologians, proposed the Clockmaker Theory for describing God's involvement, or lack thereof, in creating the Universe. It essentially states: He created the Universe and then left town, leaving it ticking without any further involvement.

The Uncertainty Principle and Chaos Theory put an end to the Clockmaker Theory and supported my faith belief that God can intercede in a way we may not be aware of. St. Augustine was right.

Heisenberg's Uncertainty Principle said God can, by making microadjustments to the atomic electrons, intercede and not violate His laws in a way impossible to recognize or measure. Chaos Theory[60] said these microadjustments can affect macro changes and again would be unable to measure or recognize it. These are successive indeterminacies built into nature. This later led to a better understanding of my faith journey into mysticism.[61]

This conclusion answered my question about God helping my wife and me. I knew more fervently God had answered my prayer for Linda's healing from depression after our first child. Science said He could intercede; my faith convinced me He did intercede.

Linda and I sought to leave the snow and move to San Francisco, one of our favorite places. I was offered a job at Bechtel, the premiere engineering firm in the world at the time. My expertise in liquefied natural gas (LNG) at Alco Standard Corporation on small LNG peak shaving plants in the Northeast U.S. qualified me for the job. Bechtel hired only two of us with cryogenic experience to work on one of their first grassroots LNG projects, at the time a $600 million investment. My colleague had worked with liquefied hydrogen on the Saturn V rocket for the space program and I had LNG experience. For a person in his late twenties, I was thrust into having incredible responsibility at this plant in Indonesia. My world had opened up more internationally and scientifically.

Our family was growing. In San Francisco we had our second child, our beautiful daughter Kristin. It was with much trepidation we planned for her birth, concerned Linda might again have postpartum depression. God was with us and that didn't happen. We lived in and enjoyed the golden era of San Francisco. Unfortunately, we were only there a couple of years before Bechtel transferred me to their office in Houston. Linda would jokingly say

CHEMISTRY TO LIFE

she suffered from hill withdrawal. Her real suffering was destined to get much worse.

Non-Local Universe – God is everywhere

> "... an Earth-shattering result. This is the kind of result that should take your breath away."
> BRIAN GREENE,[62] Physicist

> "... spooky action at a distance."
> ALBERT EINSTEIN

When I realized God could intercede in His creation without violating His laws, it was exhilarating and liberating. But that begged another question: In His creation, how encompassing can that intercession be? The answer to the "how" question is found in science.

Based on the new Quantum Theory, there is another astounding discovery. Scientists bombarded a calcium (Ca) atom, one of the atoms in the periodic table, with electromagnetic energy. The Ca atom emits a pair of photons with opposite spins, up and down. When the spin on one is changed, the other photon also instantly changes spin. At first, researchers thought they might be communicating with each other at the speed of light, the fastest speed in the Universe. They devised an experiment to test for that. They deflected the electrons out 7 miles in opposite directions. The same phenomenon happened again. Not at the speed of light, but instantly. Astonishing!

The scientists had discovered a fundamental characteristic of nature called quantum entanglement. Because of the relative dimensions of the very tiny photon, compared to the huge distance of 7 miles, this phenomenon can just as easily occur across the entire Universe. The phenomenon is named the Non-Local Universe; it could have been just as descriptively called the All-Local Universe.

At first glance this appears to be an interesting theory, but not necessarily practical. However, there is a practical side. Arbitrarily our arithmetic uses a base-10 numbering system, 10 symbols from 0 to 9. Computers use a base-2 system, only 2 symbols, 1 for electricity on, and 0 for electricity off. The same numerical value can be expressed in either system. For example 13,546 in the base-10 system can also be represented in the base-2 system. The problem is page after page of 0s and 1s is needed to express the same number. Despite this, engineers and scientists immediately recognized the inherent usefulness of quantum entanglement as a base-2 system with spins up or down. The quantum-entanglement phenomenon can be used to communicate information across vast distances, instantaneously.

In July 2017 the Chinese announced the first successful satellite-to-ground quantum network, sometimes referred to as quantum teleportation.[63] At more than 300 miles, it is the longest distance over which entanglement has been measured. This was a significant, practical step in making communication of data at least 10,000 times faster than the speed of light. It would have been instantaneous, except the equipment sending and interpreting the signal slowed down the process. How can this be? Since nothing is faster than the speed of light, another paradigm shift was needed. This is a subatomic quantum effect transmitting information, not an energy effect transmitting mass, thus limited by Einstein's famous equation. Even Einstein was shocked by this phenomenon; per his quote at the beginning of this section, he called it "spooky."

Stranger still, this led some scientists to suggest there may be a 5th force, the Unparticle Force, to explain this long-range spin-spin interaction in quantum entanglement, though many scientists didn't necessarily agree. It was necessary to deal with the realization there may be, indeed probably are, more undiscovered forces in nature beyond the four already known.

I almost discounted the usefulness of quantum entanglement. There is more usefulness beyond the imagination. Quantum entanglement and wormholes, discussed in the previous chapter, are inexorably linked. Logically called Wormhole Entanglement,[64] some say Wormholes can only exist if the entanglement is intact. Break the entanglement and the wormhole breaks. This was subtly implied in Figure 14 in the previous chapter by the two red spheres representing the quantum entanglement of two photons from a calcium atom mentioned earlier.

Originally concerned about time travel with the body, now in theory, it may be possible to receive information from the past and the future. This raised the question: Is information the same as knowledge? That question is answered later in my journey, but it haunted me. For the time being I assumed it could somehow be done.

Wormhole Entanglement shows information may simultaneously exist throughout the Universe, bridging space and time. I realized immediately the implications on my faith journey. It enhanced my faith belief since I knew even more clearly, if information can exist everywhere, then God could certainly exist everywhere simultaneously. God is truly Omnipresent. He can exert His loving influence everywhere, even though I may not perceive it or understand how. I can only have knowledge that His love is universal in the Universe.

Without life this subatomic transmission of information was not adequate in my journey; I needed to know more about knowledge. All I could do for the moment was to refocus on exploring molecules.

DNA TO CELLS – God imprints His love in us

"The meaning of the message conveyed by the DNA is not given by the laws of chemistry . . ."
   Ian Barbour,[65] Physicist

Amino Acids – God is the cornerstone of our being

"What came to be through him was life, and this life was the light of the human race."
   John 1:3–4

My next move was to molecules, combinations of atoms, which can be simple or very complex.[66] Nature has a way of trying to make things more chemically complex, recalling that entropy always increases. The challenge was to try to understand how this would lead to life itself.

Stanley Urey and Harold Miller pursued a search for life. They recognized the importance of some of the building-block molecules of life such as complex amino acids. Chemists would call them complex molecules, but biochemists call them simple molecules. One of the strange attributes of these molecules is, in life, they only come in the left-handed versions, even though chemically right-handed versions, called enantiomers, also exist. Left-handed versions are simply mirror images of right-handed versions, yet have different properties. To help understand the concept, visualize the difference by looking at human hands, which are mirror images, called in the chemistry of life the chirality of amino acids. It is impossible to put a left hand into a righthanded glove. Similarly chemicals could not react in the same way with other chemicals if they are not of the right chirality.

Urey and Miller were very clever to try to understand how nature, on its own, could produce these complex amino acid molecules. They devised a rather simple experiment that would attempt to duplicate the environment when the Earth was young and soupy.

The experimental equipment Urey and Miller built consisted of blown glass vessels. At the time, I was blowing glass in the lab for my doctoral dissertation experiment. My so-called glass rack was similar to theirs. It consisted of tubing, valves, and spheres.

In one vessel, they included primitive simple molecular gases such as water, carbon dioxide, ammonia, and methane. They added an electric spark simulating lightning. It was amazing what they discovered. Complex amino acids start forming naturally. They are one step closer to life from molecules.

It is mind-boggling what eventually happened in their equipment. After Miller died in 2007, the sealed vials of his original experiment were examined. It turned out over 20 complex amino acids were present, many more than originally reported. Nature was still building a course to life on its own! Or was this God's ongoing creation?

Eventually the probability of life on other planets was confirmed. The Murchison Meteor landed on Earth. It contained contain amino acids and other complex hydrocarbon molecules, the building blocks of life, similar to those found by the Urey-Miller experiment. Nature is much more adept at complexity than originally thought.

CHEMISTRY TO LIFE

Primordial Soup — God's loving embrace

> *"God said, 'Let the water teem with an abundance of living creatures.'... And so it happened: God created the great sea monsters and all kinds of swimming creatures with which the water teems... God saw how good it was, and God blessed them, saying, "Be fertile, multiply, and fill the water of the seas."*
> GENESIS 1:20–22

I wanted to go beyond Urey and Miller's experiment, which was a simple system. I knew catalysts participate in accelerating a reaction, but remain unchanged by the reaction. I was surprised to learn Earth itself was able to act as a catalyst. The geological catalysts were clay templates, which brought together the necessary chemicals for life's reaction.

I learned this is apparent in deep sea chemistry such as volcanic sea vents. Aleksandr Oparin and John Haldane independently hypothesized what would happen in a primitive reducing atmosphere. Such an atmosphere would lack enough oxygen but have enough energy, as in the previous experiment, to spontaneously synthesize a wider range of organic compounds. This could lead to the more and more complex molecules necessary for life. Oparin referred to this as primordial soup, which became a powerful symbol of the Oparin-Haldane view of the origin of life.

I still had no idea how complex the molecules of life could get until what happened next.

DNA in Cells — Total Body of Christ interstitially in each cell

> *"If you accept the belief that baptism incorporates us in the mystical body of Christ, into the Divine DNA, then you might say that the Holy Spirit is present in each of us."*
> FR. THOMAS KEATING, Monk & Former Abbot

I was nine years old when I first read about chemistry. I loved the subject and learned about simple molecules. So you can imagine how shocked I was to learn of the discovery of such an incredibly complex molecule of life as DNA.

68   **FAITH and SCIENCE**

In 1953 James Watson and Francis Crick discovered the main building blocks to life. They are deoxyribonucleic acid (DNA) and ribonucleic acid (RNA).[67] This discovery meant chemists had jumped from large molecules in nature to a molecule whose complexity defied the imagination: a double-helical structure. Its complexity was further verified by Rosalind Franklin using X-ray crystallography. X-ray is a wavelength in the electromagnetic spectrum, outside the visual range, but convertible to the visual by instrumentation. The following figure shows that complexity.

Figure 24 DNA Molecule, Watson & Crick – Photo[68]

This discovery should not have been surprising. Among the 26 constants in nature, one is the Constant Logarithmic Spiral equation, which mathematically defines the spiral in nature, most obviously demonstrated in seashells. Even an early proposed periodic table of the elements was a helix but didn't get wide acceptance due to the difficulty of representing its three dimensions on a two-dimensional piece of paper.

For my spiritual journey, the most important aspect of the DNA discovery is its properties. My question: How big is it? Here are some of its staggering characteristics. There are 4,600 trillion DNA molecules per human body. Each DNA molecule is 6.6 feet long. The next logical question: How in the world could that fit into a cell whose average diameter was only 0.0012 inches? The crazy answer? It is twisted very compactly like a super-thin rubber band so its length fits within a cell. It represents a DNA-to-cell compression ratio of 100,000 to 1. But the absolutely most amazing finding? One DNA molecule contained a complete code for the whole body.

I thought of how this affirms my faith. Together all my cells make up my body and separately each of my cells contains the full map of my entire body all dwelling within it. Does this sound familiar in my faith?

Together we are all the Body of Christ; separately each of us contains the full Body of Christ dwelling within us. Why shouldn't the physical world be indicative of the spiritual world? Especially if there is non-dualism between my body and my soul?

This is not the complete picture of the chemical progression from the subatomic to life; there are gaps in science's understanding. Though RNA is a messenger for passing information for DNA to produce proteins, it was unknown how it got from DNA to energy to adenosine triphosphate (ATP), which is a complex organic chemical that provides energy to drive processes in living cells. How does ATP go to enzymes and back again to DNA? How does DNA move from cells to microbes? Science appeared to lack the necessary understanding. Or at least at the level of my capability of understanding. I continued to follow the ongoing speculation, hypotheses, testing, and experimentation in the biochemical field.

To review what is known: Stars send atoms to Earth. Of those, hydrogen and carbon atoms go to amino acids as a result of atmospheric and geologic activity. Amino acids go to proteins with the catalytic help of clay templates on Earth. I had learned something very profound about DNA, but had to move on to better understand the implications of my DNA aha moment.

The synchronicity of the Body of Christ and science's understanding of DNA was having an impact on my spiritual journey. That knowledge and my wife's progressively worsening illness were drawing me back to my faith. I started to surreptitiously attend Mass. I sought the sacrament of confession although only much later would I learn about the science of forgiveness. I started to realize it was both possible and necessary for me to be both spiritual and religious in my faithful communion with others.

MICROBES TO HUMANS – God's ongoing creation

> *"The world of molecules evidently has an inherent tendency to move toward emergent complexity, life, and consciousness."*
> IAN BARBOUR, Physicist

Cambrian & Pangea – God's love is timelessly non-linear

> *"I will make your descendants as numerous as the stars in the sky, and I will give them all these lands, and in your descendants all the nations of the Earth will find blessing..."*
> GENESIS 26:4

Cell fossils first appeared on Earth about 3 billion years ago. Some very important macro events also took place.

The first is the so-called Cambrian Explosion about 541 million years ago. Before this event most organisms were simple, mostly composed of individual cells. This is startling because in geologic time the Cambrian Explosion happened almost overnight. The formation, at an accelerated rate, of advanced organisms closely resembled today's organisms. They all, almost simultaneously, started to have two eyes, two ears, etc. This change was testimony to the fact that evolution is non-linear. It is prone to short-term bursts of ongoing creative change.

The second was the Pangea Breakup. As a youngster, I was always intrigued by the map of the Earth. It looked like a jigsaw puzzle fitted together by the contours of the existing continents; the East, or right shoulder of South America, seemed to fit into the West, or left indentation of Africa. Geologists proposed the existence of a supercontinent on Earth called Pangea, which broke up about 175 million years ago. This enabled migration of primitive life to the future seven continents, thus giving all life common ancestry. I could relate because of my travels to those continents.

Alan Turing's proposed Morphogenesis Theory gives an explanation of the process by which identical cells differentiate—for example, into an organism with arms and legs, a head and tail. In 2014, 60 years after Turing's death, researchers provided experimental evidence to validate his theory.[69] Sheldrake[70] also wrote extensively on the subject.

I was a bit overwhelmed by the seemingly crazy effects and implications of the Cambrian Explosion, Pangea Breakup, and Morphogenesis Theory. I tried to maintain focus on my map and on the further science of the emergence of life on Earth.[71] It was becoming increasingly clear I needed to understand Evolutionary Theory.

Evolutionary Theory — God and man continuously co-create

"I am in my Father and you are in Me and I in you."
JOHN 14:20

The famous, or unfairly infamous, Charles Darwin[72] came from a religious family and believed in God. He was a brilliant observer of nature. He left England and circumnavigated the globe in his ship, the *Beagle*, with his most productive stop on the Galapagos Islands off the northwest coast of South America.

One of Darwin's first critical observations was how different finches evolved with different beaks. He observed that the cactus finch adapted to its environment by developing longer, more pointed beaks than the ground finch, thus protecting itself from the barbed prickles on the cactus, their main food source.

Darwin founded Evolutionary Theory,[73] which is based on three rather simple principles: *variability, adaption and fitness,* and *natural selection. Variability* means some forms are better adapted than others. *Adaption and fitness* means forms that are better adapted will leave more offspring and thus increase in population frequency. Finally, *natural selection* means, as environments change, some new form may become better adapted and increase in frequency so new species may arise.

The following figure is a visual overview, part of which depicts what happened when applying Darwin's principles to life on Earth. It shows a timeline of life on Earth from the Earth's formation to man's appearance.

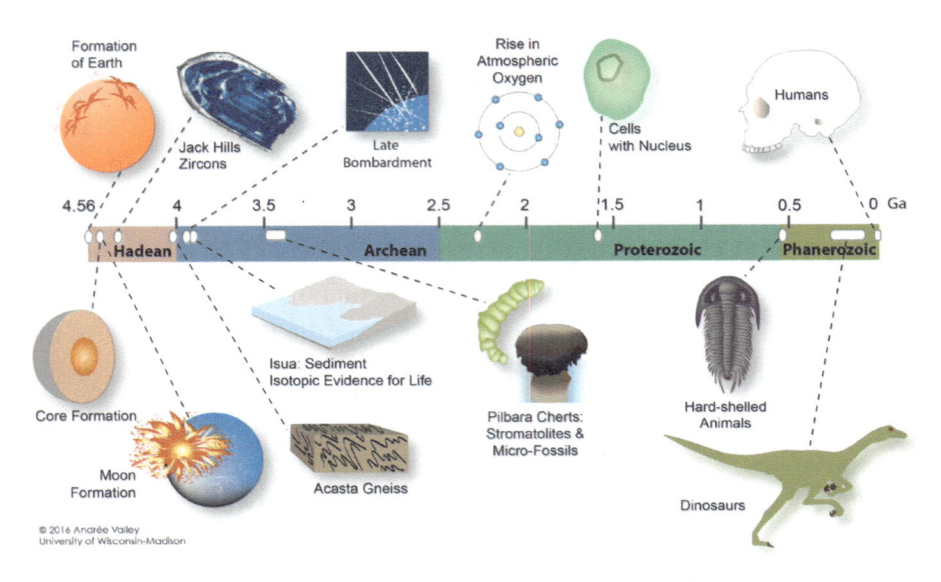

Figure 25 Evolution Overview – Image[74]

Darwin's theory is frequently misinterpreted. The most misunderstood concept is humans evolved from apes, which is not part of the theory. Humans and apes have common ancestors, some of which led to dead-end extinction. The following figure helps demonstrate that fact.

Studying this figure, it is easy to imagine why some may mistakenly interpret Darwin's theory. In the next chapter, I will address this misconception when I explore consciousness.

Darwin was not the only one who had an interest in faith and science. Gregor Mendel did as well. Darwin and Mendel were contemporaries, though they didn't know each other. Yet separately and independently they contributed immensely to the cornerstones of biological evolution. It is interesting to note both were initially discounted by fellow scientists.

Mendel was a scientist and a Catholic Augustinian friar and Abbot of St. Thomas' Abbey. His Gene Theory in the 1860s made him the father of genetics. He initially studied seven traits in peas that seemed to be inherited independently of other traits: seed shape, flower color, seed coat tint, pod shape, unripe pod color, flower location, and plant height. Mendel cultivated and tested some 28,000 plants, the majority of which were pea plants. Later he moved on to mice.

CHEMISTRY TO LIFE

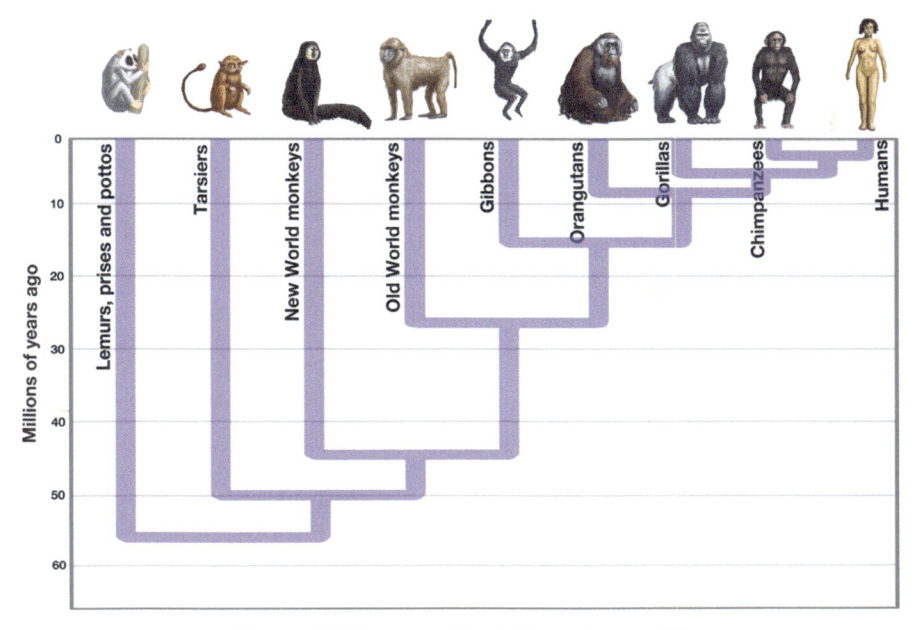

Figure 26 Primate Evolution - Image[206]

Mendel showed when purebreds of different varieties were crossed to each other, two out of four were hybrids, one out of four were purebred. His experiments led him to discover the differences between recessive and dominant genes. Mendelian Heredity is an inherently biological process, which later became known as Mendel's Laws of Inheritance.

Evolution had finally led to humans, powerfully confirming my faith God was continually creating and we were part of that creation. However, it didn't give me much satisfaction on the different kind of humans I would see while traveling the world.

Migration & Races - Love is relational with all humans

"If you accept the belief that baptism incorporates us in the mystical body of Christ, into the Divine DNA, then you might say that the Holy Spirit is present in each of us."
Fr. Thomas Keating, Monk & Former Abbot

In 2015 a 2.8-million-year-old specimen was discovered in Ethiopia. Scientists believed it was 400,000 years older than what was previously thought to be one of the first humans. From Ethiopia migration began to populate the world. Humans and Neanderthals migrated together until reaching the New World.

The evidence for this migration route came from multiple sources including the study of common ancestry, recent or micro-evolution, experimental evolution, discovery of transitions, missing links, and perhaps most importantly, from DNA. Knowledge was starting to build on the previous understanding of DNA. Partially using my worldwide travel experience, let's reconstruct the migration route discovered by science.

In central Africa, near Ethiopia, there are black descendants of the first human. This is the first migration split that started in Northeast Africa going East and West.

EASTERN BRANCH: The Eastern branch headed from Ethiopia into the Middle East. Visiting nine of the Middle Eastern countries, I observed generally brown-skinned people, which I ascribed to the sunny climate. Not eating pork is a cultural habit. Local religions early on had banned its consumption, since people were dying from its bacteria count. The warm climate led to poor preservation of meat. Bacteria was not discovered until the late 1800s. Religion became the source of good advice, since science was not yet advanced enough.

Somewhere in Eastern India, a split took place going North and South. The Northern split went to Mongolia with its uniquely featured people. The Southern split populated China and Southeast Asia. The indigenous Indian descendants of the migration are in seven countries in Southeast Asia. The Aborigines in Australia developed a uniquely different physical appearance.

WESTERN BRANCH: The Western branch went from Ethiopia to North Africa. In Tunisia there are lighter-complexioned people; they moved to Spain and the rest of Europe and Scandinavia.

I am familiar with the peoples of Europe from visits there. My ancestors are from Germany and Poland. The migration descendants in all the Scandinavian countries plus twenty-three visited European countries have lighter complexions. The Western branch migration tour veered to the East, including six visited Eastern European countries, then into Russia.

Throughout this leg of the journey, there are generally lighter-complexioned people. I ascribed this to the overcast weather, which meant they needed more thermal radiative heat from the Sun to keep warm. Eating pork is culturally accepted. It is easier to preserve meat in colder climates, so it is easier to avoid food poisoning.

This Western branch continued to be traceable via DNA, leading to the Bering Strait, which was a walkable land bridge at the time of the migration and led to establishing the indigenous Indian cultures in the New World. There was a split in central North America leading East and West. The West split continued South through Central America. The indigenous people in these countries have unique Mayan features.

It split again in Northern South America going East and West. The South American West split continued through seven countries, all the way to the Southern tip of South America, the final terminus of human migration.

In Punta Arenas, Chile, in the southern tip of South America, there is a museum devoted to the Fuegian Indians. They belonged to one of the three tribes of indigenous inhabitants of Tierra del Fuego. What is striking was the primitive light clothing in such a cold climate. The Fuegian Indians clearly had ancestral toughness to have made that long migration journey to its terminus.

Taking an overview of our journey: Of the 115 billion people who ever lived, 7 billion are alive today. And stunningly, each human is composed of approximately 7×10^{27} atoms. Try to visualize the magnitude by comparing it to the estimated number of sand grains on Earth at about 7×10^{20}. It is mind blowing.

Comparative genomics uses tools, including computer-based analysis, to compare the complete genome sequence of the DNA of different species. Though only a few animals have had their full genome sequenced, those that have demonstrate the DNA from different species is astonishingly similar to humans. For example, human DNA is 60% the same as a fruit fly's DNA, which was humbling; 80% the same as a cow's DNA; 90% the same as a cat's DNA; 82% the same as a dog's DNA. I apologize to my fellow dog lovers, but cats are closer to humans.

The discoveries got even scarier, yet more informative and relevant. Human DNA is 97% the same as a chimpanzee's DNA. And, are you ready? I wasn't. Between humans of all races the match is about 99%.

I had to accept I was truly one with nature and other human beings.[75] It gave me a better understanding of how, as I observed in my travels, the first human developed and migrated into our current races.

In the middle of my euphoria over these discoveries I got a cold feeling when, in my journey from physics to creation, I recalled entropy. It was wonderful to discover entropy was zero at the Singularity before the Big Bang, which by definition means the Singularity was perfectly ordered. But with that joy it was necessary to grapple with the concept that the 2nd Law of Thermodynamics said entropy is always increasing. If so, how could organized life, including humans, develop without violating that law?

Ilya Prigogine provided a solution called dissipative structures, for which he won a Nobel Prize. Sparing me and you the intricacies of thermodynamics, think of this fancy theory describing humans as parasites living off the disorder in the Universe. Humans consume organized food, corn, and steak and eliminate disorganized waste. Hence, humans contributed to the overall increase of the Universe's entropy, while staying organized. My bout of doubt was rectified.

Was it necessary to consider adding dissipative structures to the previous list of indeterminacies? Was God able to intervene in nature successively from subatomic quantum uncertainty to macro-dissipative structures to living non-chaotic chaos? And would I ever know it? Pondering these questions, I tried to maintain my focus forward.

My propensity to constantly ask questions led me to ask: Where is all this evolutionary creation leading? There is an intrinsic commonality to all races and genders down to each cell in our body, just as God dwells in each of us as the Body of Christ. How can I not love others, since I am part of everyone, sharing the same source of love?

Fr. Teilhard de Chardin, a paleontologist and Catholic priest, insightfully addressed this question. He was way ahead of his time when he postulated evolution applied to the physical brain and yet "there is something through which material and spiritual energy hold together and are complementary."[76] We are being drawn toward the God, Whom he called the "Omega" point. Since he was initially rejected by the Catholic hierarchy, I thought I was being rebellious in high school by reading his book *The Phenomenon of Man*.

I actually learned something in the process. Later Pope Benedict[77] gave credit to Fr. Teilhard.

Relying upon an example of his thinking helped me understand the bigger picture he was proposing. Survival of the fittest would indicate, in primitive times, if someone had bad eyesight and couldn't see the lion coming, he would be eaten and not further pass on the genes of his bad eyesight. This would cause the species to evolve with better eyesight. I wear glasses to compensate for my bad eyesight. When I see a lion coming, I can avoid being eaten. Obviously I don't see lions very often, but stay with me. I pass on my bad-eyesight genes, which causes my offspring to evolve with worse eyesight. To compensate, my offspring's brain evolves and continues to improve technology, which leads to passing on genes of better and stronger brains, thus, better survival. Similarly, my brain and soul were marching together toward God.

Ilia Delio[78,79] a scientist and nun, contributed to the rediscovery of Teilhard and to the expansion of the application of his concepts. Beatrice Bruteau[80] also described, as did Chardin, the Universe as God's ecstasy.

Let's look back on what I learned: My journey led me to the stars, then to the very atoms that come from the stars, which become part of life's molecular structure. Think of the words of the Nicene Creed: "light from light, true God from true God." Through sharing common DNA, I learned of the oneness of God's creation and awe in all of life on Earth. My name for this Omnipresent God began to shift to Awe of Life.

I was relentlessly being drawn back to humans, the source of both love and anger in my spiritual journey. I kept asking why? If humans share so much DNA with other life, why didn't the chimpanzees build skyscrapers and land on the Moon? What was so special about humans? I knew enough not to be anthropomorphic in attributing human traits to all of life. Yet I kept asking what made humans more conscious than other forms of life? I was inextricably drawn to the research on consciousness, which is the current frontier of science.

While Linda and I were living in Houston, it was becoming increasingly obvious her mental illness was getting worse. It wasn't just depression, but wild mood swings, which were ultimately diagnosed as bipolar condition. It is very difficult to treat. My interest in the science of the brain, particularly its synapses, intensified with her illness. Doctors were trying numerous medications to improve her synapses. She suffered through it all, beyond what I could possibly imagine.

My interest in science was being driven by a convergence in my personal journey between the brain science of my wife's suffering and my faith interest in consciousness.

5
BIOLOGY TO CONSCIOUSNESS

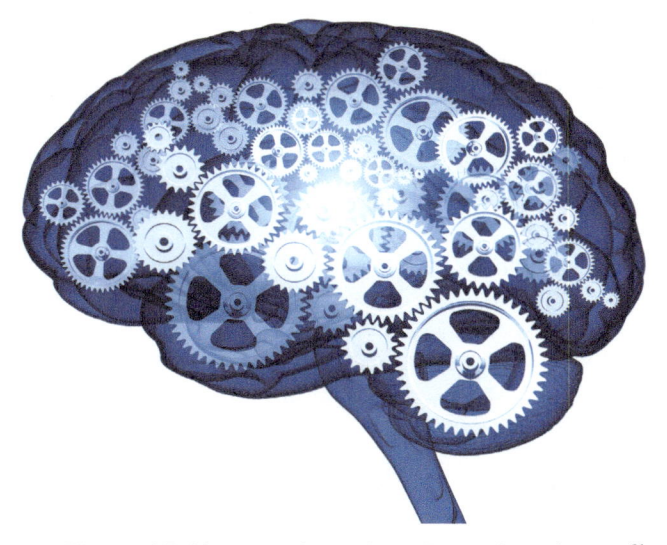

Figure 27 Abstract Conscious Brain Art – Image[81]

"I regard consciousness as fundamental. I regard matter as derivative from consciousness. We cannot get behind consciousness. Everything that we talk about, everything that we regard as existing, postulates consciousness."
MAX PLANCK, PHYSICIST & NOBEL PRIZE WINNER FOR QUANTUM THEORY

I had reached a dilemma using the same metaphorical technique I used in Chapters 3 and 4: the use of a camera to focus on the small and then back up with a wide-angle lens to see the big picture. That made me, the photographer, an objective observer to nature.

But Teilhard's challenge was my brain and my consciousness are part of the evolutionary process. The logical result was I could not be an objective observer, like a photographer, but had to be part of the picture. In modern mobile phone lingo, I had to take a selfie. It is with that thought I launched my search into God's awe in life to human consciousness.

The search for God's awe was inspired by seeing Him in human creations, including: His grandeur on Jungfrau and Machu Pichu mountains; His beauty in Louvre and Hermitage museums; His majesty at Versailles and Peterhof palaces; His power in Hoover Dam and the Great Wall; His heavenly abodes in Windsor and Neuschwanstein castles.

BRAIN & FUNCTIONS – Seeing God dwelling within

> *"When I look at the human brain I'm still in awe of it."*
> BEN CARSON, M.D., Neurosurgeon

Biology & Scans – We see God in our true self

> *"Consciousness seems to me to be such an important phenomenon that I simply cannot believe that it is something just 'accidentally' conjured up by a complicated computation. It is the phenomenon whereby the Universe's very existence is made known. One can argue that a Universe governed by laws that do not allow consciousness is no Universe at all."*
> ROGER PENROSE, Cambridge Physicist

Some scientists hesitate to use the term "mind" because it cannot be easily defined. Some think of it by analogy to computers: the brain and its stem are the hardware and the mind is the software or operating system. Most scientists do not use the term "subconscious," which is a layperson's term for the unconscious.

Scientists know very little about the brain, partly because only recently have tools been developed to study it. And even those tools don't show as much detail as they would like. One of the tools is magnetic resonance imaging (MRI), which is best for measuring general geographic locations in the brain.

In chemistry graduate school, I used nuclear magnetic resonance (NMR) to study hydrocarbon molecules, which by definition contain hydrogen and carbon. At the time, I would never have dreamed of sticking my head into

BIOLOGY TO CONSCIOUSNESS 81

that small instrument; it wouldn't have fit anyway partly due to my huge ego. Later NMRs were made larger for humans, but the term "nuclear" in NMR would have caused many to decline to participate even though the word was referring to the nucleus of a hydrogen atom, not radioactive nuclear energy. I had to laugh when the term was changed to magnetic resonance imaging to lesson people's fears.

What does science know about the brain's anatomy and functions? The stem is the oldest part of the brain, which contains the animal instincts retained through early evolution. The prefrontal cortex and frontal lobes are the newest parts of the brain, which include moral decision making. The figure below shows an overall map of the brain labeled by function.

BRAIN FUNCTIONS

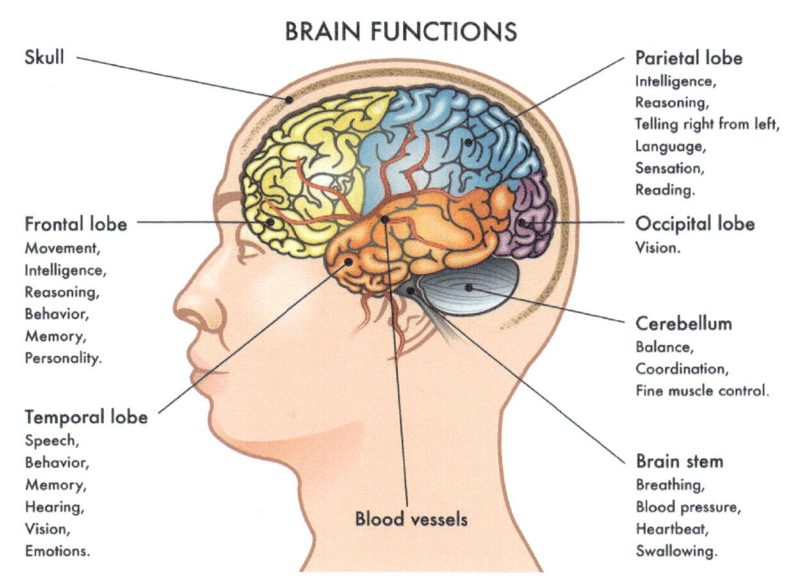

Skull

Frontal lobe
Movement,
Intelligence,
Reasoning,
Behavior,
Memory,
Personality.

Temporal lobe
Speech,
Behavior,
Memory,
Hearing,
Vision,
Emotions.

Blood vessels

Parietal lobe
Intelligence,
Reasoning,
Telling right from left,
Language,
Sensation,
Reading.

Occipital lobe
Vision.

Cerebellum
Balance,
Coordination,
Fine muscle control.

Brain stem
Breathing,
Blood pressure,
Heartbeat,
Swallowing.

Figure 28 Brain Map of Functions – Image[82]

Be careful reading too much into that image. The margins of each function are not like the fixed border crossings of countries. The brain is much more complex. Study of the brain leads to its cells' micro-level workings and the all-important synapses. This is where the action is. My wife's bipolar treatments mostly revolved around medications meant to improve synapses in her brain.

This leads back to electromagnetic energy, which the brain uses to process information through the synapses. This is the same energy contained in the physics of the Universe. Here it is again. The brain's electromagnetic waves, brain waves, are in four distinct wave lengths generally related to different states of consciousness, which are recorded by electroencephalography (EEG). They are: *delta* (Δ), while in a coma; *theta* (θ), while asleep, hypnotized, or in contemplation; *alpha* (*A*), while daydreaming or in meditation; and *beta* (β), while actively at work. When my journey led to mysticism, I would later bump into the theta and alpha wave lengths.

Suddenly the oneness of God's creation was starting to hit me hard because electromagnetic energy permeates both the Universe and the brain. The following[83] is an amazing comparison between the brain's circuity and its stunning similarity to the Universe's networking.

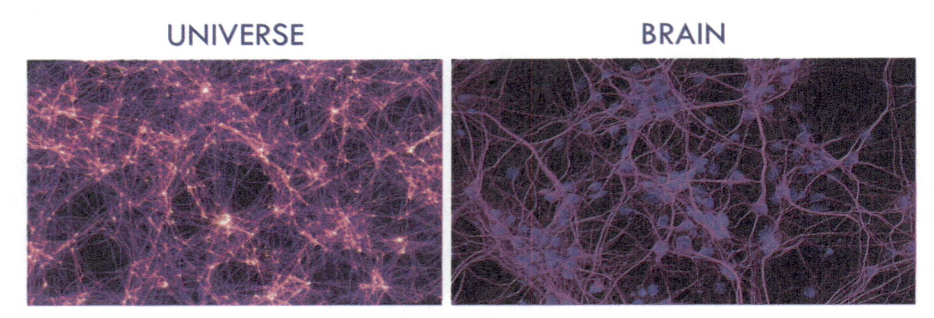

Figure 29 Universe Network[84] & Brain Circuitry[85] – Images

The left image shows the web-like network of the aggregated matter of the known Universe, formed over billions of years, as the Universe evolved from the Big Bang to the present. The right image shows the web-like network of connections among the nerve cells in the brain of a mouse.

This is reminiscent of the journey through the magnitude of the Universe. The relative magnitude of the brain compared to the Universe is fascinating. The Universe has 100 to 170+ billion galaxies and the brain has 100 billion cells. The Universe has 200 to 700+ billion stars per galaxy; the brain has 1 billion neurons or nerves. The Universe is 4% visible and 96% invisible. The brain is about 5% conscious and 95% unconscious. Something was going on here. Even though these are all just estimates, it seems to be a creepy coincidence.

The stages of sleep were going to be relevant to my search for God's awe. The sleep sequence can be described in terms of the brain's waves. The beginning stage is the sensations in *alpha* wave lengths. The drowsiness sleep stage is in *theta* wave lengths for about 5 to 10 minutes. The next stage is rhythmic waves for about 20 minutes. The transitional stage is in *delta* wave lengths, which leads into deep sleep for about 30 minutes. Finally, sleep ends with rapid eye movement (REM) in which dreams occur for about 90 minutes. Obviously this doesn't add up to a full night's sleep, which is explained by recycling between rhythmic and transitional stages.

Scripture is replete with references to God speaking to prophets and saints in their sleep. It continues to happen to people today, including in my prayer experiences. Science seemed once more to be reaffirming my faith.

The brain is incredibly complex, the last frontier of science, but it did not discourage me from continuing to read about the relevant science and technologies. Think about the relative arrogance of science and engineering trying to replicate the brain's function. The goal was to program a computer to perform at least as well as, and preferably better than, the human brain. In my business career, as computers became more powerful, there was almost hysterical euphoria at those attempts.

Expert Systems (ES) or Fuzzy Logic is one that was moderately successful. Programming is based on interviewing an expert or experts in a field and developing a logic diagram reflecting their thinking process. A computer is programmed to execute the diagram. Artificial Intelligence (AI), on the other hand, is a much bolder attempt. Its overall program includes subprograms that attempt to teach the computer to learn from its mistakes. It often uses parallel processing to calculate more efficiently. I am uncomfortable with this approach. I question how a computer could be programmed to calculate emotions.

Thankfully along came my hero, Roger Penrose,[86] a Cambridge physicist and colleague of the famous Stephen Hawking. Penrose actually advised Hawking on the mathematics he needed for his work. Penrose published his mathematical evaluation of the attempts to replicate the brain's function with a computer. His postulated proof contains page after page of mind-numbing zeroes and ones in computer base-two logic. After reading Penrose's evaluation *ad nauseam*, I finally reached his mathematical conclusion: A computer could never replace humans.

One issue, which I find rather humorous, is the concern of some that computers will take over from humans. I laughingly muse that computers need power and maintenance. Pull the power plug. Problem solved! An interesting reflection: Does our death come when God pulls our plug before we go AWOL (Absent Without Leave)?

Since I was already skeptical, I agreed with Penrose. My faith journey was questioning the arrogance of thinking a computer could calculate the love and anger I had experienced. I surreptitiously disposed of these AI attempts from my pursuit of God's love. But I did continue my journey to see God's awe in the brain.

Competing Dualities – Spiritual growth through choice

"Do I contradict myself? Very well then, I contradict myself. I am large, I contain multitudes."
    WALT WHITMAN, "Song of Myself"

My whole premise was non-duality between faith and reason, body and soul, God and man. Then I was confronted with the fact science is saying the brain is full of dualities. I realized my terminology was getting in the way. My non-duality principles still applied. This was something different. It was offering options to the brain. In hindsight I can say this ultimately led me to a deeper understanding of my awe of the God dwelling within. These options confirmed the necessity of free will to make decisions—part of what made me human. But I digress; I am getting ahead of myself.

The brain is made up of multiple dualities that compete with each other for the brain to make decisions. The dualities do not violate my principle of non-dualism, but did require the discovery of the non-dualistic answers to the apparent dualism challenges. These dualities are not necessarily located in one area of the brain. What follows is an overview of the five known brain dualities.

1. RIGHT-LEFT HEMISPHERES – The two brain hemispheres have different functions. The right hemisphere's functions are primarily visual-spatial perception, fact checking, and scientific observation.

The left hemisphere's functions are primarily language, organization, problem solving, storytelling, and theological constructs.

Learning about epilepsy helped clarify understanding of this particular duality. One of the early, last-option treatments for epilepsy, no longer practiced, was to sever the Corpus Callosum, which is the bridge connecting the two hemispheres of the brain. This treatment terminated brain communication between the hemispheres. Though it was often successful, it had some bad side effects. For example, if a person is handed a pencil and asked to describe it, he might say it is a plate. His right brain sees it as a pencil, but can't communicate the information to the left brain, which is responsible for language and speech.

2. PRESENT & FUTURE – Humans are constantly faced with evaluating and making choices between the present and future. It can be thought of as delayed gratification or suffering, "pay now or pay later." There are numerous examples in life of such dual choices: adjustable-rate mortgages, marital infidelity, alcohol-free house, advanced directives, and sugar versus diet. For example: If a person is an alcoholic, removing all alcohol from the house means if the person was later tempted to imbibe, the alcohol would not be available.

3. MULTIPLE-STABLE STIMULI – Visual illusions called multiple-stable stimuli are fascinating. One famous example comes to mind, no pun intended. It is shown in the following figure. It is almost impossible to see the image of two people facing each other and the cup simultaneously.

Figure 30 Multi-Stable Stimuli: Cup or People? – Image[87]

4. **EMOTION & REASON**[88] – The prefrontal cortex plays a major role in reason and emotion; both are inseparable and necessary. The left side processes positive emotions for relationships, and the right side processes negative emotions for avoidance. This is at the heart of the decision between fight or flight. Emotion may say fight, but reason says flight. Surprisingly, there are many subtleties of emotions the brain has to process. Resilience is needed to recover from adversity and sustain a positive outlook. Intuition is needed to pick up on social signals and self-awareness of bodily feelings. Sensitivity is needed to recognize and regulate reaction to the context of a situation, and attentiveness is needed for clarity and focus.
5. **CONSCIOUS & UNCONSCIOUS** – The final duality hit me like a brick: understanding the difference between the conscious and unconscious brain. This is the most important duality of the brain. I had to explore it in more detail.

Conscious & Unconscious – God protects us from false self

"Consciousness will never fully understand itself [unconsciousness], no matter how much we peek inside the brain."
KEVIN NELSON, Physician

I should not have been surprised there are two brains. After all, biologically, there is a lot of redundancy in twos: eyes, ears, arms, legs, lungs, kidneys. God was surely trying to tell me something when He gave me only one month; I always seem to overuse it. I started looking for a definition of two brains, conscious and unconscious, both of which are part of the evolutionary process.[89]

To be conscious is to have the quality or state of being aware of an external object or something within oneself. To be unconscious is to operate well outside the attention of the conscious: an altered state of consciousness with limited conscious awareness.

These definitions seemed to be lacking. Perhaps a description of their respective attributes or characteristics would help. The conscious brain is slow and systematic, the unconscious brain is fast and automatic. The conscious brain is explicit and analytic, the unconscious brain is implicit and heuristic. The conscious brain is rule-based and proactive, the unconscious brain is intuitive and reactive. The conscious brain is reflective and neocortex-based, the unconscious brain is impulsive and limbic system–based. Finally, most intriguing, the conscious brain is younger and smaller at about 5%, the unconscious brain is older and larger at about 95%. This was mentioned earlier in the chapter when the brain was compared to the Universe.

Since I started this quest to determine what made humans different from animals, I had to ask, is there a test for consciousness? David Eagleman's[90] description of a famous test is a simple experiment. Cheese is given to a rat; it eats the treat with apparent glee. Then an electrode is connected to the cheese and the rat is shocked whenever it tries to eat it. The rat goes into a catatonic state because it is unable to make a risk decision. It can't decide which risk to its life is greater, not eating or getting shocked. The conscious, healthy, human brain would know how to deal with that dilemma. It would reconcile the dualities of the brain by disconnecting the power or finding cheese elsewhere or whatever. But the rat cannot. The rat does not have a conscious brain like humans. This wonderfully captured in the following poem, by Katherine Craster and shared by Eagleman.

"A centipede was happy quite,
Until a frog in fun
Said, 'pray tell which leg comes after which?'
This raised her mind to such a pitch,
She lay distracted in the ditch
Not knowing how to run."[91]

Eagleman also gave a human example. The workers on an assembly line follow a daily pattern of assembly without having to think much because the pattern is imbedded in their unconscious. They can be thought of as the unconscious part of the company's brain. If they had to think about each move, they would be very slow and inaccurate and probably go crazy. When the assembly line manufacturing machine breaks down, they report it to the President. He can be thought of as the explicit conscious part of the company's brain. He can solve the problem through reason. But he would be terrible at the unconscious actions of the assembly workers. Both are needed for efficient production.

I thought it sounded insulting to the assembly line worker, as if he couldn't learn anything. I was wrong again. The unconscious brain can indeed learn unconsciously or heuristically. Eagleman told a delightful true story to demonstrate that truth.

In the poultry industry, it is important to determine the sex of the chicks as soon as possible in order not to waste a lot of money feeding non-egg-producing roosters. Sorry guys, the males are not as valuable. As it turns out, baby chick sexing is a very difficult task. The U.S. poultry industry heard the Japanese had perfected the ability to do just that, so they sent a team to Japan to learn their trick. They observed the Japanese chicken sexers, as they were called, fast at work examining each chick and quickly throwing them into separate bins, one for hens, one for roosters.

The Americans asked them how they were doing it. They answered they didn't know how they were doing it. Puzzled, and a bit annoyed, the Americans sat with them and tried to do it themselves. With much observation and practice, they too became skilled in the sexing process.

Here is the interesting and rather funny part. When the Americans returned to their bosses in the U.S., they were asked how the Japanese did it. They answered they didn't know. Obviously, the bosses were a bit frustrated until their researchers showed them they could do it. They had learned unconsciously.[92] There are many examples demonstrating this learning process is actually possible and real.

This fact hit my psyche hard. This is a description of faith. I know something is true by my faith, but I can't explain it. Faith is a form of unconscious learning. Please note: The previous stories are not meant to be demeaning to the grandeur of faith itself.

Non-Christians often think the term "faith" is used only by Christians since we use the term so often. I once had a discussion with a prominent Buddhist at a conference and said she also had faith. She claimed she didn't. I pointed out she had faith reincarnation was real but couldn't prove it. Scientists also have faith there is order in nature for them to study. So on my journey I started to think of my faith as unconscious learning. I later modified that thought, which will become apparent.

Given the brain's many dualities, this thinking led back to the obvious necessity of free will. After all humans, don't go catatonic like the mouse. Science was saying there must be free will. That was consistent with my faith. But where is it? How does it work? After all, didn't I freely choose to pursue this venture into non-dualistic faith and science? Furthermore, how does the brain decide right from wrong, that is, whether I should be doing this in the first place? I was getting a little annoyed with science.

CONSCIENCE & FREE WILL – Free choice to love

> *"He went about doing good and healing all who were oppressed by the devil, for God was with Him."*
> ACTS 10:38

I knew I was not the first to ask questions about conscience and free will. The early Greeks used only one word, *Syneidesis*, to mean both conscience and consciousness. Surprisingly, like Greek, most Romance languages have only one word for both these concepts. I learned this the hard way. I was giving a presentation with simultaneous translation at the Pontifical University in Rome. The translator didn't know how to translate the two words "conscience" and "consciousness" into Italian, since Italian has only one word for both. I only speak English, and frankly, not that well. But at least English has two words, which allows important distinctions between them. The translator consulted with me in advance; I gave her the following definitions and somehow she finessed it.

Conscience is the internal moral guide to determine right from wrong; it can be sincere or insincere. Consciousness is true external self-awareness; it can be true or erroneous. Intuitively, the ideal is both a sincere conscience and true consciousness. Sincere conscience is based on internal evaluation without rationalization. True consciousness enables us to honestly say we see a tree outside when there really is a tree outside.

I recently took my grandchildren on their first fishing trip. They were so excited. Until I placed the hook through the worm. My seven-year-old grandson tearfully asked, "Doesn't that hurt the worm?" I was uncharacteristically speechless, thanking God for only one mouth. I tried to explain what we must do to eat. My explanation was really feeble and lame. It was clear, deep down, his conscience was expressing itself and I intuited his free will was ready to act by asking the question.

This true story, and many other anecdotal examples, indicate conscience and free will exist, but science has not definitively located either in the brain.[93] So where to look? This was important because I needed to know how to make morally correct decisions as part of my study of faith and science in nature. Sometimes faith and science have to look for truth in odd places, including in brokenness. In the case of faith, a wonderful spiritual book titled *The Spirituality of Imperfection*[94] addressees this when dealing with the disease of alcoholism from which my wife suffered while unsuccessfully trying to self-medicate her bipolar disorder. In the case of science, I got some hints from case studies of brain disorders.

Brain Disorders – God teaches us not to condemn others

> *"I cannot grasp all that I am."*
> ST. AUGUSTINE OF HIPPO

The fascinating story of Phineas Gage is studied even today in psychology classes. He was a God-fearing, churchgoing, sober teetotaler, a non-womanizing, upstanding, loyal member of the community. He worked for the railroad in Vermont in the late 1800s. His job was to pack dynamite charges into vertically drilled holes in rock spaced about 10 feet apart. The charges would later be detonated simultaneously, causing a large slab of rock to break away to make room for railroad construction. There are remnants along Vermont highways of multiple vertical, semicircular cylinders where the rock broke away from the charges.

In the 1800s a crowbar was designed differently than the ones used today. It was about six feet long and straight with a point on one end and flat on the other. One day Phineas put the flat end of his crowbar into a hole not realizing it already contained a charge. He inadvertently detonated the charge. The full force of the explosion launched the crowbar's pointed end through his skull. The figure on the left is a recently discovered photo of Phineas holding his crowbar. Notice his left eye is closed. The figure on the right shows the path of the crowbar, which went directly behind his left eye.

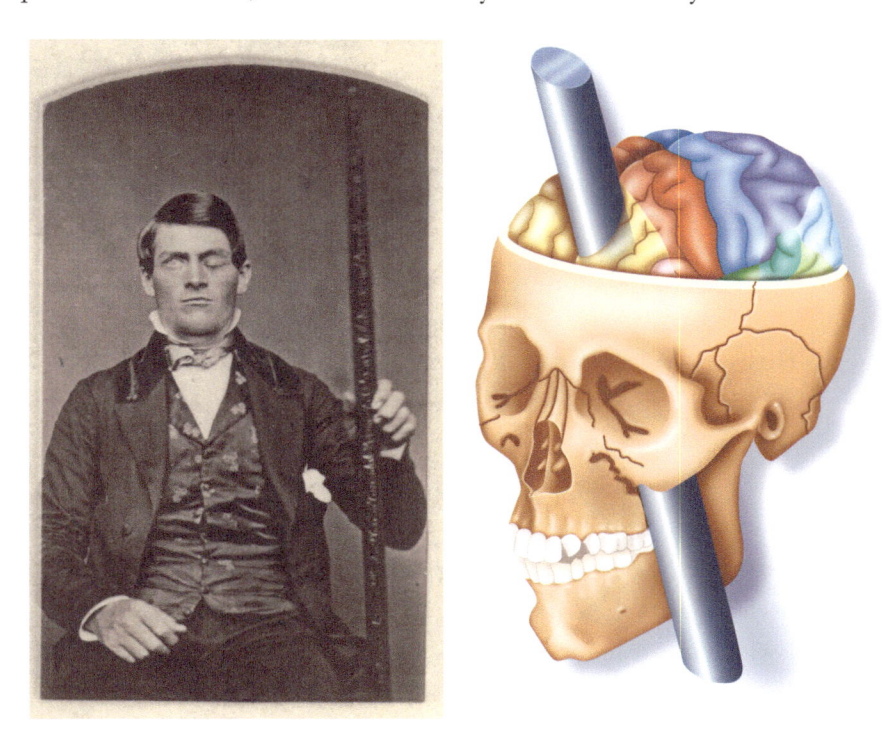

Figure 31 Phineas Gage Injury – Photo[95] & Image[96]

He miraculously survived because it was a clean, straight wound and the heat from the explosion cauterized the wound. This was a very rare combination of events. He was blinded in his left eye, but otherwise looked normal on the outside. But he was not normal on the inside. His personality changed dramatically. He avoided church, drank, cursed, womanized, and was condemned by the community. In the late 1900s, his body was exhumed and his skull was scanned. The macro problem was identified. His frontal lobes had been completely eliminated.

This reconfirmed what neuroscientists later understood. Though the entire brain is involved in making moral decisions, the frontal lobes are especially important. They are the youngest part of the brain and essential to discern right from wrong.

There is a more recent case study. Michael May lost his eyesight in an accidental explosion when he was just a few months old. He grew up, got married, had children. When someone loses their eyesight, it is very rare for surgeons to be able to restore it. Michael was exceptionally fortunate. When he was in his 40s, medicine had advanced to the point it was possible to surgically restore his eyesight. When it came time to remove the bandages, his wife and children were right in front of him. They were the first people he would see.

Everyone was happy at his joyous reaction when he saw his family. But it quickly became apparent there was a major problem. He couldn't remember his wife's face from one day to the next. He couldn't distinguish depth of field, couldn't distinguish the trees from the forest. Objects moving toward him had indistinguishable shapes.

Since such surgeries were rare, there wasn't much precedent to go by. The medical community finally determined his brain had not developed the necessary skills to efficiently utilize his conscious and unconscious brain. This normally occurs during the critical brain development growth period of early childhood, which he missed. His micro-synapse problem couldn't be detected by macro brain scan technology.

His conscious brain, including his parietal lobes, were trying to process a huge amount of data. Remember, the conscious brain is slower and more analytic; it couldn't handle all the data. Fortunately, with time, he improved and the side effects subsided.

His brain was starting to rewire itself as it normally would have done during childhood. His unconscious brain had to learn to build paradigms, so his conscious brain didn't have to process so much information. It had to develop a mental caricature or picture, for example, a beauty mark on his wife's face, to unconsciously trigger his unconscious brain to recognize the mark was part of his wife's face. That way he didn't have to consciously process every aspect of her face.

This is how I learned. As a student, I memorized large amounts of data. I used acronyms and mnemonic devices to form a word from the initial letters of many words, which meant more data stored in my unconscious for quicker recall during final exams.

What is stored in the unconscious? The answer went down an unexpected path. It yielded wondrous insight into the awe of God.

A lot of things are stored in the unconscious. A big one is involuntary breathing. If the conscious brain had to think about every breath, humans would certainly die. Worldviews and images of God are stored in the unconscious brain. If I had grown up with Muslim parents, I would probably be Muslim and not think of a triune image of God. The unconscious stores past traumas to protect itself. If injured in an explosion and later hear fireworks, say on the Fourth of July, the brain would unconsciously move into fight-or-flight mode. It is the basis of post-traumatic stress disorder (PTSD).

But what is most intriguing is the unconscious stores habits, both virtues and vices, which is why it is such a struggle to overcome habitual sins and to forgive. Prejudicial "isms" are stored in the unconscious brain: racism, sexism, nationalism, politicism, classism, economism, religionism, naturalism, culturalism, fundamentalism, scientism, and others. They all share the common definition of prejudice, taking the actions of one or a few in a group and condemning the whole group. This relegates humans to be judgmental of those who don't belong to the same groups. This was why the first unconscious reaction can be to distrust or dislike someone or some group. This is a profound systemic problem in humans and our society.

St. Paul had the same problem, but of course didn't have today's science. "For I do not do the good I want, but I do the evil I do not want ... but I see in my members another principle at war with the law of my mind, taking me captive to the law of sin that dwells in my members"[97] (Rom 7:19, 23).

This was hitting very close to home vis-à-vis my past traumas and prejudices. This information was starting to have a profound effect on my spiritual journey. How could I condemn the individuals who hurt me in my life, since I could not climb inside their brain and know their culpability? They included Fr. Tom and my wife during the manic phases of her bipolar suffering.

I needed to know more in order to make moral decisions and determine culpability. I got more involved in the study of my faith, since science was not giving me all the answers. What I found actually reinforced the science.

The interplay between my understanding of faith and my understanding of science was, by necessity, becoming a two-way street.

This led me to the seminary to take classes on my faith. This was the start of my discernment process to become a Catholic permanent deacon. Little did I appreciate how this would continue into a four-year program in preparation for ordination. Only later did I realize I was entering what was ascribed to the early mystic Dionysius as the second stage of the spiritual journey, the Illuminative Stage. I was starting to recognize there was something more, the Spirit's presence in my life.

Informed Conscience – Faith and reason are God's gifts

> *"You shall not eat it or even touch it, lest you die . . . The moment you eat . . . you will . . . know what is good and what is bad . . . The eyes of both were opened and they realized that they were naked . . . I was afraid because I was naked."*
> GENESIS 3:3–10

What did I learn from Phineas Gage and Michael May? I learned I need three things for what my faith aptly calls an "informed conscience." The first was biological, a properly functioning brain. The second was informational, truth in my knowledge. The third was spiritual, an internal guide, the indwelling Holy Spirit. Science didn't and couldn't give me the last one. My upbringing, my grandson fishing, my intuition, my faith gave it to me.

I need a working brain before I can even hope to get to true information and spiritual guidance for the conscience. I need true information, which Michael May was getting, but his conscious brain couldn't process it efficiently. I need spiritual guidance for my conscience, which Phineas was not getting because his brain was damaged. In other words, for me to be fully culpable for my actions in the eyes of God, I need to meet these three criteria. In the end only God knows my culpability and relationship with Him, my spirituality.

This is consistent with my faith belief of full moral culpability in the eyes of God, as described by Aquinas.[98] The act or omission has to be morally wrong. Fortunately, that can be determined using the informed conscience.

Full knowledge and full freedom are required. Only God determines those last two because only He can climb inside our brain. The clincher: Only He can climb inside the brains of others, hence the reason we can't judge others' culpability in the eyes of God.

We are not only obligated to make moral decisions, but we are also capable of making moral decisions; hence the first item is up to us. The operative word is "informed." But because of possible brain disorders, which by definition, we may not be able to introspectively know, the brain may not have cognitive understanding of full knowledge and full freedom. By the same token, we certainly cannot judge others since we cannot climb inside their brains. Please note: I am talking about culpability in the eyes of God. God is able to climb into everyone's brains as He did with my grandson while fishing.

I needed a hypothetical example to evaluate and apply this concept. I needed to understand how and why I reacted negatively to people, especially those who angered me. I assumed I could climb into the brains of other people and predict what God would do; I needed to know why my lack of humility led me to believe I was good at playing God.

A man is on a vacation. He is in a tall hotel looking at the beach below. He sees two people. One is obviously drowning. The other is onshore looking toward the ocean.

The man in the hotel wants to help but can't get there in time or call someone to get there in time. He is getting angry at the man on the beach who clearly could do something to help. He judges the man on the beach is committing a sin of omission by not helping.

The man on the beach doesn't have time to seek help; he is the only one on the beach. He also has no rope or life-saving equipment. He can't help because he can't swim. In fact, he didn't immediately and clearly see the man drowning. His perspective view was not from a tall building.

The man in the water may be angry at the man on the beach for not saving him. But more than likely, he is in such panic, he has no time to be judgmental of others.

I was starting to realize how often I was quick to judge others, as if I could climb inside their brain. I rationalized part of my judgmentalism was due to the limitations of language. Though this was a weak attempt at blaming others for my actions, it did have some validity. The following may help explain my concern and proposed remedy.

I sent a letter[99] to Cardinal Müller, at the time the Prefect of the Congregation for the Doctrine of the Faith in the Vatican. It was shortly after my presentation on the subject at the Pontifical University *Regina Apostolorum*. I had briefly met the cardinal in the Vatican when he was made a cardinal. A quote from my letter:

> Science is validating the teachings of the Church, particularly as they relate to informed conscience and moral culpability. However, it is becoming apparent that our linguistics is not adequately keeping up with either science or faith. More specifically the term "sin" is being used to convey both a subjective and objective meaning, which can lead inadvertently to implied personal condemnation, when in fact there is no such intent. Perhaps using "sin" for subjective individual culpability and "morally wrong" for objective moral decisions would be helpful. Pope Francis has alluded to this quite often, when he says he cannot judge someone, only God can judge them. Furthermore, Catholics are more and more painted with the same broad brush of judgmentalism that is provoked by the wrongful teachings of fundamentalists. Dealing with this issue would be a natural follow-up to the change in the Church's position in allowing funeral Masses for suicide victims.

I sent the letter because my spiritual journey had taken me from condemning my Church to actively trying to reform it from within. To clarify, I was not proposing moral relativism. And the reference to funeral Masses refers to a time when a funeral Mass for a suicide victim was not allowed.

When discussing and presenting this subject, there was often a need to clearly address some potential confusion. Moral culpability is not the same as civil culpability. Society still has the right, and indeed obligation, to protect itself through incarceration based on true justice. However, I became concerned when neuroscientific brain-scan studies showed a much higher rate of brain damage among the incarcerated.

Applying these ethical issues to myself was more difficult, especially since I was having to reevaluate my anger at those who hurt me. That led me deeper into my spiritual recovery. Because of my interest in consciousness, it logically led to bioethical issues.

One of the most challenging situations is at the confluence of making moral decisions and evaluating brain damage. This can occur in unconscious patients near death. This actually often gives rise to conflicting interests and tensions between recovering a patient from an unconscious state and acquiring their organs for transplant based on their previous donation agreement.[100] Help in understanding the more severe states of disorders of consciousness came from experts in the field. One such expert, whom I had the privilege of meeting, was Calixto Machado, M.D., Ph.D.[101] He is one of the world's experts at bringing people back from unconscious states. At the time I didn't realize the importance of our meeting.

Sometime later I made arrangements for Calixto to give a presentation at The Institute for Rehabilitation and Research (TIRR) in Houston. This is the world-famous hospital where Congresswoman Gabby Giffords recovered from her severe brain injury due to an attempted assassination. At the presentation, Calixto reported his discovery in Jahi McMath of a new state of disorder of consciousness, a permanent, minimally conscious state, which he termed "responsive unawake syndrome" (RUS).[102] Unfortunately, as the name implies, it is near death and not treatable for recovery. However, this made me realize how little science and I knew about the different states of consciousness.

It dawned on me to ask him if he had many patients say they had a near-death experience (NDE). He answered, "Oh yes, many, many times." I excitedly asked, "You must have brain scans of those patients." He said yes but couldn't say if they were done when the patients were having their NDE. It turns out, an NDE is quite common and the vast majority of those who have them report pleasant experiences. There has been a lot written on NDEs and their common attributes. For a moment I thought maybe I was unnecessarily going down a rabbit hole in my spiritual journey. That turned out not to be the case.

There are four distinguishable NDE attributes: *Cognitive*, a sense of timelessness; *affective*, a sense of peace; *transcendent*, a sense of the Divine such as angels or God; and *paranormal*, a sense of being out-of-body as reported by the famous Dr. Raymond Moody.[103]

Suddenly it hit me like a ton of bricks. Those NDE attributes were similar to the attributes of the Singularity at the beginning of the Big Bang discussed in the "Physics to Creation" chapter. I asked: Why were they similar? My question should have been: Why shouldn't they be similar since both are at the transcendent point between Earth and Heaven? God is truly Omniscient. This is consistent with my faith belief.

This whole subject of making moral decisions and different states of consciousness was logically leading me to bioethics. I realized I had to go deeper to appreciate God's awe.

Ethics & Bioethics – God gives us principles to live by

> *"For everything created by God is good, and nothing is to be rejected if it is received with gratitude."*
> 1 Timothy 4:4

In my spiritual journey, it became increasingly apparent, in a sense, all ethics is bioethics[104] since the brain is involved. I needed to come to terms with my own unforgiving attitude. Having reviewed cases of brain damage and altered states of consciousness, I had to ask: How do I put this information to practical use?

The operative word is the "informed" conscience. Informing the conscience is often quite a challenge, especially in medical bioethics.[105] I started by applying the prime principle Jesus taught, to love God and love others as "I have loved you." I put the phrase in quotes because of a question about the golden rule.

Most religions, including Catholicism, have a version of the golden rule, "Do unto others as you would have them do unto you." In this day and age, where interreligious distinctions are shunned, it's especially important to note Jesus' commandment is not the golden rule. The golden rule does not yield objective, principled results. For example, if I were dealing with someone who believed in euthanasia and I did not, then I didn't want the person "doing unto me" what the person would want "done unto them." This line of reasoning only served to reinforce my commitment to Jesus' primary principle: To love other human beings as Jesus loved me. It avoids moral relativism because Jesus' love was the objective gold standard.

As a scientist, I was delighted to learn "informed" in my faith means to consult with all the expertise available. That includes, but is not limited to: scientific studies, sacred scripture, religious tradition, natural laws, civil laws, medical experts, spiritual advisors, family members, respected friends, and other sources of truth. It is the very non-dualism premise of my journey and this book. Interestingly the principle of "informing" is being applied by chaplains in most hospitals in spite of the fact many do not realize its origin is from Catholic teaching, primarily Aquinas.[106]

To apply Jesus's principle of love of other human beings, the first decision is very basic. Who is human and when do they become human? It was necessary to understand what faith and science have to offer, first about when life begins and ends, and second what makes us unique with human consciousness. I started with the first question, saving the second one for later. Research indicated both faith and science had struggled with this question.

A deacon friend pointed out faith's historic struggles. In medieval Christianity, the humanity of a fetus depended on its gender. A male became human much earlier than a female, or at least that's when the soul was implanted.

Having spent years exclusively in the secular world, I knew the beginning of life is currently deemed by some cultures, not necessarily religions, to be when a fetus is viable outside the womb. In that case, being human doesn't start until after a fetus reaches that point. When later it was discovered the fetus feels pain, even before being viable outside the womb, the secular culture moved back the date of becoming human. It became clear science currently knew very little about the brain and cannot say the experience of pain was the only measurement for life. Hence, as more knowledge became available, the secular culture might have to move the date back again.

I was bothered by this relativistic definition. It certainly was not principled, since by definition, principles don't change. Based on science's ignorance, the safest definition is human life begins at conception and ends with natural death. That is consistent with my faith's and Church's current teaching. We become human at the moment of conception.

Some time ago, I worked for several years as an engineering consultant in the same building that housed an abortion clinic. Every day I saw young people use the facilities. I felt immense compassion for them. Even though I had made my own informed conscious decision, I had to accept the fact I could not judge their culpability in the eyes of God, since I couldn't climb inside their brain. My faith's compassion and neuroscience's knowledge reinforced each other.

Scientific statistics had something else to offer. Conservative estimates are 40+ million humans are killed every year by abortion. For example, there were approximately 46 million legal and illegal abortions performed worldwide in 1995.[107] Of course the numbers were higher if assisted suicide and capital punishment were included. Most of those killed are females due to sex-selection killing particularly in China. I had a one-on-one conversation about that subject with a woman tour guide in Beijing who had many men suitors. She was handicapped with a crippled hand and said she was one of the first to be born under the one-child policy. She said the males in China were really struggling to find a wife.

What happens to a culture under such circumstances? The total fertility rate (TFR) is the number of live births per woman in a society. Sociological studies have shown, to maintain a culture, there has to be at least a TFR of 2.1. It's not 2.0 because some women die before child-bearing age. No culture has survived at less than 1.9. The U.S. native TFR is 1.9. The TFRs are published by country,[108] although they do not tell the whole story since immigration plays a role. For example, in the U.S. immigrant TFR is 2.2. Deeper analysis of the data is very revealing.

The cultures of many countries are sustainable, most of which are in Muslim countries. The cultures of many other countries are not sustainable, most of which are Christian countries in Europe, Russia, and South America. My faith teaching is correct but is not what fellow believers are practicing. The focus away from life by having fewer children leads to a diminishing number of descendants. A sort of genocidal suicide, the proverbial "live by the sword, die by the sword." My respect for life is not only a matter of human dignity, but also a matter of cultural survival.

Aquinas postulated there must be a prioritization of principles with human dignity being first. In bioethics, the following ranked priorities of principles each trump the ones after them.

The first is respecting life, which requires providing the basic necessities of life such as clothing, shelter, food, and water. The second is to not intentionally kill, which is fundamentally different than allowing natural death, provided it doesn't violate the first principle. The third is honoring patients' wishes, which means, for example, not giving antibiotics if they don't want them as long as it doesn't violate the first and second principles. The fourth is minimizing a patient's pain, which requires trying to make the patient comfortable without violating the first through third principles.

This became important for me since I had to implement the ranking of these principles for my parents. My mother did not want to precipitate death but didn't want antibiotics, so she could be allowed to die. My father did not want pain killers, so he could be conscious when he passed to the next life. Later my wife became ill with multiple problems resulting in loss of oxygen for a long time, which meant severe brain damage. I had her breathing tube removed. My science helped, but it was my principled faith belief that sustained me, informed me, in making those incredibly difficult decisions.

I knew my mother's wishes because I had a discussion with her when she had a stroke partially paralyzing her. I said quite often older people then fall and break their hip and need a catheter, which leads to an infection. I asked her if something like that happened, would she want antibiotics? We discussed whether it would be morally okay to withhold antibiotics, since we would not be killing her, but allowing her to die. When I thought about it, the death certificate never says the cause of death is withholding antibiotics but rather infection. We even discussed the case of Jacqueline Kennedy who refused antibiotics. My 89-year-old mother's answer was an emphatic no, she would not want antibiotics. I knew God inspired the discussion because that scenario is exactly what happened. I reported the conversation to my brothers, which helped in our decision to withhold antibiotics.

Unfortunately, an equally prophetic discussion was not held with my children. Jumping ahead for a moment in my spiritual journey, when Linda and I got older, our children knew of their mother's suffering and that neither Linda nor I wanted to have our lives prolonged if we were suffering. Selfless love had to be the driving principle in making the very difficult decision to stop intubation. The intubation tube was blocked due to aspiration of blood and she went without oxygen for over 10 minutes. Linda was not responding; brain damage was inevitable.

This decision was not only very difficult to make and carry out, but even more difficult to explain to my children. They didn't understand the bioethics; I didn't understand when I was their age either. Letting die is not the same as killing. Love meant letting go rather than using extraordinary means to keep my wife alive in a vegetative state, just so I could continue to have her with me. I knew my children loved their mother. Though it was difficult for them, I knew my prayers would one day lead them to understand my decision.

I quickly and intuitively realized medicine and science are not always simple and predictable. There are normally multiple effects from each action. Scholarly bioethicists have addressed this using St. Augustine's "just war" theory. Since he never anticipated a first attack annihilation by nuclear force, his just war theory does not apply in that case. But it does apply to bioethics.

His theory led to what is called the Double Effect Principle[109] for making decisions that have multiple effects. This helped me immensely. There are four criteria, all of which have to be met in making an informed, morally right decision. First, the act or omission can't be evil, in and of itself. Second, the intent has to be good. Third, the good can't result from the bad. Fourth, the good has to be greater than, or equal to, the bad. The degree of difficulty in implementing these principles certainly increases with each level.

On my personal journey I focused on bioethics, but recognized those same principles apply to other ethical decisions. For example, informed conscious decisions are required regarding political voting, environmental protection, jury duty, social justice, and much more.[110,111]

I intuitively knew free will exists. I found it rather humorous, when speaking to some secular scientists at one particular conference, they would argue its existence. When I rather sarcastically asked them if someone was

BIOLOGY TO CONSCIOUSNESS

holding a gun to their head, making them perform their research, or were they freely choosing to do so, the look on their faces was wonderful to see.

I kept asking where is the soul in all of this? Where are conscience and free well? Science had provided some insight into the brain, but then hit a dead end. I turned to my faith and tried to supplement it with what science did teach me. The *Catechism of the Catholic Church* describes the soul as follows. I inserted clarifications from science and faith in brackets.

> The soul is the subject of human consciousness and freedom [conscience and free will]; soul and body together form one unique human nature [including unconscious]. Each human soul is individual and immortal, immediately created by God [indwelling]. The soul does not die with the body, which is separated by death, and with which it will be reunited in the final resurrection [Divine Consciousness?].[112]

This was getting too complicated and unsustainable by just science or faith. I needed the following diagram to help visually summarize what I had learned, from faith and science, without compromising the truth of either. Before you freak out, please be patient. Read the explanation following it.

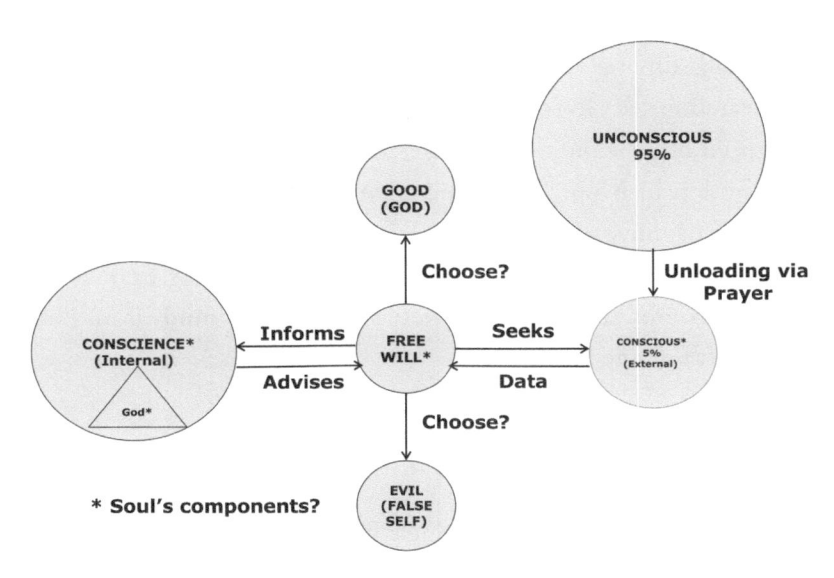

Figure 32 Free-Will Model – Diagram

My faith describes the soul as somehow an amalgam of consciousness, conscience, free will, and the indwelling God.

Following the diagram, free will seeks true, not erroneous knowledge, from the conscious brain, which returns the data. Free will informs the conscience with the data. The conscience, using that information, listens to the indwelling Holy Spirit's advice. The conscience then advises sincerely back to the free will what is morally right and what is morally wrong. The free will should accept it sincerely not insincerely. The free will then chooses good, God, or chooses evil, the false self. The free will is the gatekeeper at every phase.

Clarifications are needed. God is shown as a choice of the free will, but it is the same God dwelling within to advise the conscience. Our indwelling God, the Holy Spirit, is sometimes referred to as the True Self.

There is a major problem with this diagram. The conscious brain needs information from the unconscious brain, which is the issue I had to deal with. How does the unconscious brain unload into the conscious brain?

I continued to seek the answer in scientific studies. I had discerned who was human, so the next logical step was to look to additional valid scientific studies on the conscious and unconscious brain and what science has to say about religion. Science has a lot to say, as described in the next section. This became apparent when I was invited to join the interfaith Institute for Spirituality and Health.

The search to see God's awe shifted more to religious sites showing: His welcoming embrace statues overlooking Rio de Janeiro, Lisbon, and Havana; His redemption in Mont Saint-Michel and Our Savior on Spilled Blood Cathedrals; His universal love in the Temple Mount and Angkor Wat; and His blessings in the Holy Sepulchre and St. Peter's Basilicas. St. Peter is buried in its catacombs and his grave was discovered with funds from Houston philanthropist George Strake.[113]

HEALING RESEARCH – Divine Healer within

"He went about doing good and healing all who were oppressed by the devil, for God was with Him."
    Acts 10:38

I have had 29 medical procedures, 18 of which were surgeries. I was quite familiar with hospitals and doctors. I can't say I was interested in continuing my intimate relationship with that profession, but my journey took on a new twist.

I became vice chairman and a faculty member of the interfaith Institute for Spirituality and Health (ISH). This honor led me to discover research I had no idea existed. Founded in 1955, ISH is the oldest such organization in the U.S. and is located in the Texas Medical Center in Houston, the largest medical center in the world by multiple times. ISH was the first in the nation to train hospital chaplains.

There has been an explosion of studies on the healing effects of religiosity and spirituality on both the body and soul.[114] The internationally recognized authority on this subject is the *Handbook of Religion and Health*, edited by Harold Koenig, M.D.[115] He is a dedicated, faithful, Catholic psychiatrist. The book summarizes multiple research studies in the field of faith and science. Much of what I learned is from his book, which is discussed in this section.

The research applies regardless of the religion of the subjects, but since most of the research was done in the West, most subjects were Christian. It also contains more research on religiosity than spirituality, since the former is easier to quantify for research, such as frequency of church attendance.

An overview, based on J. W. Ehman's[116] survey, showed 66% of patients agreed a physician's inquiry about spiritual beliefs would strengthen their trust in their physician. Ninety-four percent of patients, for whom spirituality was important, wanted their physicians to address their spiritual beliefs and be sensitive to their values framework

Over 3,000 medical articles showed a significant correlation between religion and healing based on randomized controlled tests. The research is in three general categories: *faith*, belief in God; *liturgy*, religious involvement in regular church attendance; *prayer* on a frequent, regular basis. I jumped into the research with both feet. What I found led me again to change God's name to Awe of Love.

Faith & Liturgy – Knowing and visiting God

> "... so we, who are many, are one body in Christ, and individually members, one of another."
> ROMANS 12:5

Since my wife suffered from severe depression, I was intrigued that having a faith belief helped. Those who have a faith belief have less depression and faster recovery from depression, as confirmed in 272 of 444 studies. Of those, 67% showed significant improvement and only 6% moderate improvement. Lisa Miller, M.D.,[117] did studies showing less depression and faster recovery from depression was consistent with changes in brain structure.

The frequency of church attendance correlates dramatically with an increase in life expectancy: up to 7 years in the overall population and 14 years among African Americans. Those who attend a religious service once a week or more statistically have lower stress, blood pressure, and cholesterol. Studies show a significant correlation between a sense of wellbeing and church attendance, which is better than those who only reported intrinsic religiosity.

There are effects on the all-important immune system. Those attending church regularly are half as likely to have elevated levels of Interlukin-6 (IL-6).[118] High levels hurt the immune system. Decreased levels of IL-6 reduce the likelihood of many diseases, such as diabetes, atherosclerosis, depression, lupus, cancer, and rheumatoid arthritis. It was postulated such religious commitment may lessen stress because of richer social support and strengthened personal values and religious worldviews. However the effects are lessened if the faith has a vengeful rather than loving image of God.

Numerous studies showed regular religious involvement improves cardiovascular health. Of 63 studies, 57% showed lower blood pressure. Of 16 studies, 63% showed better cardiovascular functions. Of 19 studies, 63% showed less coronary artery disease.

Numerous studies showed religious involvement correlates with less addiction. Of 278 studies, 86% showed significantly lower use and abuse of and dependence on alcohol. Of 185 studies, 84% showed significantly lower use and abuse of and dependence on drugs. Of 135 studies, 90% showed less smoking, especially among youth.

Some early research related to marital wellbeing was further consistent with my faith belief. The divorce rate had been over 60% and rising. Early sociological statistical studies on cohabitation before marriage showed those who cohabitated had a 50% increased likelihood of divorce if they got married; in Europe it was 80%. As with any statistical study, there are no guarantees, only probabilities.

Two of the world's scientific experts on forgiveness research, Everett Worthington, Ph.D.,[119] and Ken Pargament, Ph.D.,[120] published extensively on the healing effects of forgiveness on the forgiver. This is consistent with my faith belief described by those with theological faith insight.[121,122] The research attested to the healing benefits of two important strategies for forgiveness: Ask God for help and support. Pray for the perpetrator.

I became friends with psychologist Dr. Pargament, who is Jewish and was a resident scholar at the Institute for Spirituality and Health. He said he looked forward to counseling Catholics because he could often recommend they go to confession as part of his psychotherapy and their healing. He wished more faiths had such a tool.

This scientifically reaffirmed why being spiritual and not religious had not been enough. It explained why earlier in my journey I knew God could forgive me without confession, but why I needed to have my confession heard. Confession is more accurately known as reconciliation. Science was affirming why reconciliation back into the community was both spiritually and psychologically necessary. It explains why the words of the Our Father, "forgive us our trespasses as we forgive those who trespass against us," were grinding on my psyche.

In 1969 Elisabeth Kubler-Ross, M.D., published her observations on the stages of dying. These stages were later successfully applied to the processes of grief and forgiveness. It seems everyone must go through all stages, without skipping any. Often there is recycling. When applied to forgiveness the stages are: First, *denial*, not ready to forgive. Second, *anger*, blaming others. Third, *bargaining* to protect oneself from future hurt. Fourth, *guilt*, it is my fault. Fifth, *acceptance*, which is needed for healthy moving on.

This research was hitting very close to home. I had to forgive Fr. Tom and did so. I had to forgive the priest who assigned Fr. Tom and did so. I had to forgive my wife when she was not herself during her manic states of bipolar condition and did so. I loved her!

Frequent Prayer – God's thoughts not my thoughts

"For my thoughts are not your thoughts, nor are your ways my ways, says the Lord."
Isaiah 55:8

At ISH my discovery of research on prayer[123] proved to be very timely. I learned Centering Prayer with Fr. Keating at a Trappist monastery. Due to my own profound mystical experience and possible benefits for my wife, I was particularly interested in its effects on the brain.

There are two types of prayer[124] common to all theistic faith traditions.[125] Even non-theistic traditions use variations of their methodologies, though obviously with very important differences in worldviews.

Meditation is the first, which comes from the Latin *meditatio*, meaning to think. The Greek word for this prayer form is *Kataphatic*. It is the engagement of the imagination and becomes discursive in thoughts, which may or may not be accompanied with spoken words. An example would be guided meditation.

Contemplation is the second form of prayer, which comes from the Latin *contemplatio*, meaning to focus on God alone. The Greek word for this prayer form is *Apophatic*. It is practiced by surrendering thoughts and resting in God.

Modern non-theistic, secular society has incorrectly modified the term *meditation* to also include the second form of prayer. For the purpose of this discussion the original definitions will be used, since they remain true to their etymology and my Christian tradition.

There have been many studies and testimonials[126] on the effects of prayer on the brain, but I decided to focus on only a few.

Some scientific studies investigated the effects of intercessory prayers, asking God for specific outcomes such as healing or safety. This is a form of meditation. Some of these studies were double-blind. But the results have been scientifically mixed and inconclusive. I believe that happened because the scientists were unable to judge if the outcomes were due to God or due to the researcher's or prayer practitioner's false or immeasurable expectations. This is consistent with my faith; God knows what's best for us better than we do.

A study on pain management and meditative prayer was conducted based on an American Pain Society questionnaire of hospitalized patients. It surveyed patients on what methods they used to manage their pain. Personal prayer was the most commonly used non-drug method for pain management. The results of the study[127] showed 82% used pain pills and astoundingly 76% used prayer. Other less-used methods: 66% IV pain medications, 33% relaxation, 19% touch, and 9% massage. Most were using several methods, hence why the total is greater than 100%.

While at ISH Peter Boelens, M.D., asked for my assistance negotiating a research agreement with Baylor College of Medicine. The research required the use of Baylor's functional magnetic resonance imaging (fMRI) equipment, the second largest number of fMRIs in the world. Baldwin and Boelens's[128] research showed meditation or discursive prayer, which focused on forgiveness, lessened the chance of depression.[129] Here are some of the details of the study.

Subjects were chosen who had post-traumatic stress disorder (PTSD) and were suffering from depression, but not on medication. It included a weekly one-hour prayer session for six weeks to recall hurtful memories, forgive the perpetrator, focus on inner healing, and end with deliverance from evil.

Self-administered tests, accepted by the professional psychiatric community, were used to measure the results. The tests were applied pre-prayer as a baseline, post-prayer, and in a one year follow-up. Called the HamD, HamA, and HOPE LOT, they measured, respectively, depression, anxiety, and hope. The results were dramatic between pre- and post-prayer. Depression was lessened four times from a factor of 20 to 5. Anxiety was lessened six times from a factor of 18 to 3. Hope was increased 33% from a factor of 15 to 20. But amazingly, one year later, without any further clinical prayer practice in the interim, the results still held firm. Separately pre-prayer and post-prayer fMRI scans validated the written evaluations of fewer ruminations and emotions and improved cognition, empathy, and reward.

Studies at the seminary were leading to my ordination as a permanent deacon. I had learned a lot about the complementary consistency between faith and science even though the professors were not necessarily aware of the science.

The research was fascinating. Because of my mystical and teaching experiences, my real interest was in research on contemplation. To that end, I spoke with Dr. Benson, a well-known Harvard expert in the field. He had shown daily contemplation was beneficial for the treatment of many things, including chronic pain, insomnia, anxiety, hostility, depression, premenstrual syndrome, and infertility. I was driven to explore contemplation or mysticism.

Confirmation Bias — Holy fault of Original Sin

> *"Then the Lord God said: See! The man has become like one of us, knowing good and evil!"*
> GENESIS 3:22

My spiritual journey led me to this point, then I got stuck. Some of the research didn't seem to be too healing. How was I to deal with my unconscious tendency to think my conscience was informed when I was actually rationalizing I had informed my conscience? My search for God's help continued. I inadvertently bumped into research on something very disconcerting: Confirmation Bias.

Scientists have conducted studies on subjects first asking their political, religious, economic, racial, gender, and other preferences. These were some of the prejudices I had difficulty with. They administrated a multiple-choice test, which gave scientific data, some of which supported the subjects' preconceived preferences and some of which refuted the subjects' preconceived preferences. Their research discovered a fundamental part of human nature called Confirmation Bias. The human brain is prewired to search for, interpret, favor, and recall information from the unconscious in a way that confirms its pre-conceived preferences. At the same time, the brain disproportionately gives less attention to information which contradicts its preconceived preferences.

I suddenly realized my brain was doing just that in order to protect me from hurtful memories and not waste my brain's conscious time inefficiently reassessing my preferences.

Even though Confirmation Bias may be protecting me, it doesn't easily allow me to change deep-seated prejudices and biases. This is a serious problem. If the brain stores virtues, true-self, vices, and false-self[130] in the unconscious, how am I to unload unconscious vices and prejudices? How am I to coax my conscious brain into transforming prejudices and biases into virtues and love?

This was becoming critical for me. I was preparing for my ordination to the permanent Catholic diaconate. My discursive prayer life sucked. I was constantly playing God by telling Him what I needed, when I needed it, and even how I needed it. He already knew what I needed, since He knew me better than I knew myself. What was I doing?

I realized my search for an answer to Confirmation Bias was more urgent. I needed to prepare myself spiritually for the challenges ahead with my ordination, but even more importantly for my journey to a deeper awe of God and union with Him. This naturally led me to psychology and how holy people through the centuries successfully and prayerfully dealt with this issue, even though they were not scientifically aware of the mechanism of Confirmation Bias. I had to launch more deeply into understanding contemplation, which is called mysticism in Christianity.

6
PSYCHOLOGY TO MYSTICISM

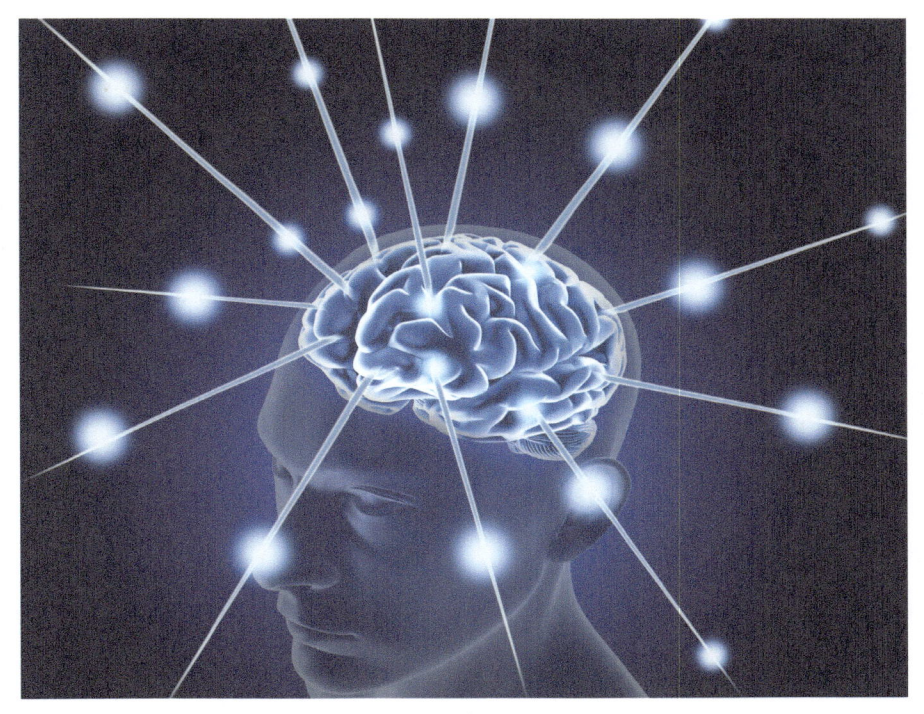

Figure 33 Abstract Mystical Brain Art – Image[131]

"The most beautiful emotion we can experience is the mystical."
ALBERT EINSTEIN

Research on prayer unexpectedly inspired a new search for God's awe in prayerful sites, which showed: His mystical love in Snowmass and Gethsemani Trappist Monasteries; His silent love in Christ in the Desert and Engelberg Benedictine Monasteries; His universal love in the Blue and Rumi Mosques; His love for His chosen people in Beth Israel and Western Wall Synagogues.

MEDITATION & CONTEMPLATION – Indwelling God

> *"Don't let the words get in the way."*
> ZALMAN SCHACHTER-SHALOMI, Rabbi

My focus was on contemplation because of my mystical experience. But because Confirmation Bias is a universal human condition,[132] my scientific search for help had to include all humans. This was why initially my interest was in interfaith prayer, which required me to explore the world's religions.

Though the numbers are shifting constantly,[133] in early 2000 about 87% of the U.S. population believed in God. Worldwide the largest faith by far is Christianity at about 2.1 billion; Catholics make up the largest denomination at about 1.5 billion, which is about the same number as Muslims, about 1.5 billion. The next is Hinduism at about 0.9 billion. Buddhism, primal faiths, and Chinese religions each make up about 0.4 billion, Sikhism 24 million, and Judaism 15 million. Other faiths make up the balance except for non-religious, which make up about 1.1 billion. It is noted every faith has denominations, most often multiple denominations.

Of the above faiths, most Buddhists preclude the existence of God or are agnostics, and about half of the non-religious are self-declared atheists. However, Zen,[134] a denomination of Buddhism, does allow for belief in a God.[135,136] Trappist monk Fr. Thomas Merton wrote about this.[137]

Studies show atheists often define their idea of God, then say they don't believe in that God. In the famous physicist Stephen Hawking's last work published posthumously, he explains why he was an atheist as follows:

"There was not time before the Big Bang ... that doesn't have a cause because there was no time for a cause to exist in. For me this means that there is no possibility of a creator, because there is no time for a creator to have existed in."[138]

Though I honored his right to his own informed conscience, I retained my right to challenge his logic.

Actually, I don't believe in that God either. The God I believe in is not constrained by space and time. I reasoned it would be like saying the builder of the first Volkswagen had to relegate himself to be within that Volkswagen when he was building it.

Why was all this important in an investigation of meditation? The science had spoken on Confirmation Bias. I needed to explore if that is consistent with my Catholic faith belief, which holds God dwells within everyone on Earth. His indwelling is regardless of a person's faith or denomination. Regardless of whether they even believe in God. Furthermore, my faith belief is non-Catholics can go to Heaven. I had decided not to judge others in the eyes of God. This reinforced my scientific interest in interfaith meditation and contemplation for all.

The next shift was to examine which faiths have a contemplative tradition. Essentially all major faiths have their own contemplative traditions, especially those based on theistic worldviews. Examples include: Christianity's mysticism, Judaism's Kabbalah,[139,140,141] Islam's Sufism,[142,143,144] and Buddhism's[145] and Hinduism's meditation. Most of these are minority groups within their various faith traditions and denominations. Strangely often these groups are marginalized within their overall faith communities.

As listed each tradition uses a different term but the term contemplation is the most generally accepted by all faiths. That created a challenge. For most faiths, contemplation with a small "c" is a more broadly used term often attributed to an individual's actions. For Christianity Contemplation, with a capital "C" is a gift from God separate from Centering Prayer, which is discussed later. I apologize; sometimes in this discussion I use it both ways and miss the capital letter distinction.

Fr. Thomas Keating encouraged me to practice and later teach Christian Centering Prayer, a form of contemplation. Keating then appointed Kimball Kehoe, a former Jesuit Catholic priest, and me as co-coordinators of the Houston chapter of Contemplative Outreach Ltd. Keating and other Trappist monks founded the organization to teach Centering Prayer worldwide. Since Kimball Kehoe and I are also interested in interfaith dialogue and promoting research, Fr. Keating encouraged us to co-found the nonprofit tax-deductible, interdenominational Christian Contemplative Network (CN). My interest had blossomed and expanded.

The first interfaith effort was with Harvey Gordon, M.D., a Jewish contemplative. Because of the close historical and theological relationship between Judaism and Christianity, we compiled the following historical summary of Judeo-Christian contemplative contemporaries. This was in preparation for our Judeo-Christian presentation at the Houston-Galveston Archdiocesan Church center. The close parallels are fascinating.

C.E.	Christianity	Judaism
-500s	Prophet Ezekiel	Prophet Ezekiel
0–200	Jesus	Akiba & Shimon Yochai
300–600s	The Conferences	Sefer Yetzirah
1100s	Bernard of Clairvaux	Isaac the Blind
1200–1300s	Cloud of Unknowing	Zohar
1400–1500s	John of the Cross/Teresa of Avila	Isaac Luria
1600–1700s	Francis de Sales	Ba'al Shem Tov
1900s	Thomas Merton	Buber & Heschel
2000s	Thomas Keating	Zalman Schachter

Figure 34 Jewish-Christian Contemplative Contemporaries – Table

The words "contemplative" and "mystic" are synonymous. The word "contemplative" is the more universally understood and accepted term among theistic and non-theistic practitioners.

Centuries before the Vatican II Council, the Catholic Church hierarchy didn't understand what the monks and nuns in monasteries and convents were doing in their contemplative prayers. This was partly because they did not have the benefits of modern psychology. Rather than condemn them, the hierarchy wisely told them they could keep praying contemplatively, but it was a mystery to them, hence they called them mystics. Be careful of confusing the term "mystic" with the term "magic," although some do. Unfortunately, the hierarchy at the time instructed the monks and nuns not to tell the laity because they would not understand either.

Though pursuing faith and science in interfaith prayer, I had to start somewhere. The logical beginning was with my Catholic heritage. I explored what Jesus and historical Christians taught about centering and contemplative prayer and applied it to other faith traditions wherever legitimately possible. This was necessary to explore how contemplative prayer, in its broadest religious sense, might help with Confirmation Bias, which is shared by all humans. This became critical to my spiritual journey.

Theology & History – God deeply rooted in past & present

"[The mind] rejects the whole wealth and abundance of thoughts . . . The soul then pours out to God wordless prayers."
St. John Cassian

The very basic question is: "What is prayer?" When asked this question, most people say it is talking to God. That of course is meditation as described earlier. But a better, broader definition is needed. I knew from my journey God wordlessly speaks back; He doesn't just listen. I began researching the fascinating answers many holy men and women over the centuries have given to that question.

The most common answer to what is prayer is "Speaking to God." From the Latin, it is "Entreat" or "Ask God." St. Therese of Lisieux[146] called it "Surge of the heart." St. Augustine of Hippo said prayer is "Nothing but love." Gandhi described it as "Longing of the soul." But my favorite was Fr. Thomas Keating's[147] "Relationship with God." I moved forward focusing on his definition.

The Christian mystics throughout the centuries often gave first-person descriptions of their profound mystical experiences. It is stunning how many there are throughout the centuries, some of whom are listed in the following table.

1st Millennium	2nd Millennium	Modern
Origen	Hildegard of Bingen	Evelyn Underhill
Clement of Alexandria	St. Francis	Friedrich v. Hugel
St. Gregory of Nyssa	St. Dominic	Thomas Merton
St. Basil the Great	St. Catherine of Siena	Jacques Maritain
St. Gregory Nazianzen	Meister Eckhart	John Main
Desert Tradition	Julian of Norwich	Laurence Freeman
St. Paul Evagrius	Cloud of Unknowing	Bede Griffiths
St. Cassian	St. Ignatius of Loyola	William Meninger
St. Augustine of Hippo	St. Teresa of Avila	Basil Pennington
St. Benedict	St. John of the Cross	Thomas Keating

Figure 35 Historical Christian Mystics – Table

I couldn't possibly read them all, but I do have favorites: St. Cassian for the history and methodology; St. Augustine for his link between nature and mysticism; St. Benedict for his influence over present-day monasticism; Meister Eckhart for his amazing understanding and descriptions of mysticism, though he was initially discounted by the Church hierarchy. I especially gravitate to the true giants of mysticism, contemporaries St. Teresa of Avila and St. John of the Cross. I embrace the anonymous author's work *Cloud of Unknowing* for his insight into the subtleties of the practice.

The psychological depth of present-day mystics confirmed this wasn't a subject relegated to ancient history. I had the privilege of meeting and working with Benedictine Fr. Laurence Freeman and Trappists Fr. Thomas Keating, Fr. William Meninger, and Fr. Basil Pennington.

I needed a better idea of how these individuals integrated into my interpretation of the general, historical milestone progressions of Christian mysticism and gain assurance of Christian mysticism's historical and theological validity. Every century had mystics who expanded and clarified the Christian mystical tradition; some shared their experiences more clearly than others.

The first milestone was Jesus, who described mysticism when He answered the question in Matthew 6:6–7, "How do you pray?" I discuss this in the next section with Jesus' answer to the question found in scripture.

The second milestone was St. John Cassian, who wrote the longest work in Christian antiquity, *The Conferences*.[148] He was one of the first Christian news reporters, since his work documented his interviews, or conferences, with the desert fathers and mothers in 4th-century Egypt. They were the precursors to the Christian monastic tradition, which led to present day monks and nuns. St. Benedict was one of the main founders of Western monasticism. He wrote *The Rule of Benedict*[149] based extensively on Cassian's work. Cassian described the lifestyle of those first monastics and in Conferences 9 and 10 he described their prayer life, especially contemplative prayer. Without going through every century, I particularly took note of Pseudo-Dionysius and Gregory in the 6th Century and Bernard of Clairvaux in the 12th century.

The third milestone was *Cloud of Unknowing*[150] by an anonymous 14th-century Benedictine monk in England. In the 20th century, this work was rediscovered and studied by Trappist monk Fr. Meninger.[151] Unfortunately, from the 1500s to the 1960s, the practice of contemplative prayer was pretty much considered abnormal grace and relegated to the cloisters. The hierarchy of the Church didn't understand it, hence the word abnormal.

The fourth milestone was the Vatican II Council encouraging religious orders to rediscover the roots of their founding. These are their charisms, which for the Jesuits[152] is teaching and for the Trappists is prayer. In the late 20th century, this led to the founding of interdenominational Christian contemplative organizations. The Benedictines founded the World Community of Christian Meditation (WCCM), and the Trappists founded Contemplative Outreach Ltd. (COL). When I joined COL, my journey picked up. I was blessed to have its main founder, Fr. Thomas Keating, as a mentor.

The primary theological principle, shared by contemplatives in all the Abrahamic faiths, is God dwells within.

Methodology & Thoughts — God guides us by the right paths

> *"When you pray, go to your inner room, close the door, and pray to your Father in secret. And your Father who sees in secret will repay you . . . do not babble like the pagans, who think that they will be heard because of their many words . . . Your Father knows what you need before you ask him."*
> MATTHEW 6:6–7

To understand the possible scientific implications of contemplative prayer and its interfaith applicability, it was necessary to understand and practice it in my Catholic tradition.

I started with the definitions of Centering Prayer and Contemplative Prayer.[153] Originated by Fr. Thomas Merton, the term Centering Prayer means to "focus on the center of my being," that is the Holy Spirit dwelling within me and everyone on Earth. When I spent time at the Trappist monastery in Gethsemani, Kentucky, Merton was there. Unfortunately, I didn't meet him, since he was a hermit. I learned Centering Prayer at the Trappist monastery in Snowmass, Colorado.

Centering Prayer is something to practice for facilitating Contemplative Prayer. Contemplative Prayer is a pure gift from God, which one may or may not receive, as God wishes. Because all the Abrahamic faiths believe in an indwelling God, Centering Prayer can be taught to all of them. The only proviso in Judaism and Islam is the word Yahweh or Allah is used, respectively, instead of Jesus or the Holy Spirit. After receiving the gift of a mystical experience, I was trained by the Trappist organization, Contemplative Outreach, to teach Centering Prayer. That training and my experience led to the following approach.

Prayer is relationship with God. It can be thought of in four stages analogous with a relationship to a human being and with the Catholic liturgical Mass. This was important to understand since I had been craving and receiving Christ in the Eucharist.

Together the four stages are called *Lectio Divina*, which means reading the Divine in scripture. It was conceived by the 4th-century desert fathers and mothers in Egypt and is practiced today in monasteries and convents. In the 4th-century monastic tradition, the stages are meant to flow together without formal separation. Centuries later, in the Scholastic tradition, the process is described as having more formal intellectualized breaks between each stage. I vastly prefer and follow the monastic tradition, which was described by St. Cassian. When teaching Centering Prayer, I usually ask a volunteer to help demonstrate the analogy between human and Divine relationships. The next figure contains a table, which helps me understand and teach the four stages of prayer.

HUMAN	DIVINE	
PERSONAL	PRAYER*	LITURGY
1 Acquaintanceship	Reading (*Lectio*)	Readings (Scripture)
2 Friendliness	Thinking (*Meditatio*)	Homily (Preaching)
3 Friendship	Speaking (*Oratio*)	Petitions (Prayers)
4 Union	Contemplation (*Contemplatio*)	Communion (Eucharist)

*1–4 *Lectio Divina* (Monastic or Scholastic); some shared by all faiths
 1–3 Discursive (Kataphatic) ACTS e.g. guided meditation
   4 Contemplative (Apophatic) e.g. Centering Prayer (CP)

Figure 36 Prayer as Relationship Analogies – Table

ACQUAINTANCESHIP is when I meet someone. It is more formal with introduction of names. Taking Bill as the name of my volunteer, I ask about his interests and agree to meet again. This is analogous to the first meeting with Jesus when we read the Gospels, *lectio* in Latin. Jesus enjoyed food with friends; that is what happens during the scripture readings at Mass: we get to know Him better.

FRIENDLINESS is my next meeting with Bill when we are less formal and on a first-name basis. We talk about having shared a meal together, since we both enjoy food. This was analogous to thinking, or *meditatio* in Latin, what it would be like to share a meal with Jesus. This is comparable to the homily at Mass immediately after the Gospel reading, which discusses the readings and makes them applicable to contemporary life.

FRIENDSHIP is my next meeting with Bill at which we pretend Bill is very ill. I offer to do anything to help, as I know he would do the same for me. This is like speaking, or *oratio* in Latin, to God. At Mass this is analogous to the prayers of the faithful said after the homily asking for God's help. These first three stages are the discursive, *apophatic*, prayers described earlier. They are sometimes referred to by the acronym ACTS meaning adoration, contrition, thanksgiving, and supplication. The last, supplication, has been the most common for me over the years, the shortest of which is "help."

UNION is my final meeting with Bill when we remain silent and embrace in a heartfelt hug. We know each other so well no words are necessary. In fact, words would get in the way. I experienced this state of deep union with my beloved wife. When I kissed her, not only did I not want to talk, but was physically unable to talk. This is analogous to the Divine union with God called contemplation, *contemplatio* in Latin. Like any human hug, it cannot be forced, it has to be mutual, hence why it is God's gift. At Mass this is the Divine physical and spiritual union with God in the Eucharist in communion and community. I emotionally noted the Latin derivation of those rich words, meaning "with union" and "with unity," respectively.

Reflecting on the two main types of prayer, meditation and contemplation, most of my life I was stuck on meditation, the first three stages. I hadn't heard about, or didn't appreciate the 4th stage, the depth of contemplation, simply listening to God. Both forms are valid and should be continued, but I suddenly realized in the silence, there is no dogma. That is the reason I was able to pursue the interfaith and science of Contemplative Prayer.

Surprisingly even monks sometimes have difficulty practicing *Lectio Divina*. Encouraged by the Vatican II Council, Trappist monks recognized the challenge and decided to investigate its rich Catholic history. This is the reason the Trappists adopted Fr. Thomas Merton's definition of Centering Prayer: it is focused on the God dwelling at the center of all human beings. Trappists priests Thomas Keating, William Meninger, and Basil Pennington[154] worked on a methodology to help monks, nuns and laity facilitate their receptivity of God's gift of contemplation in the 4th stage. After learning the methodology and being commissioned by Contemplative Outreach, I started teaching Centering Prayer.

There are two main aspects to Centering Prayer, relationship with the indwelling God and the discipline required to practice it. In Centering Prayer, a sacred word is chosen as a symbol of the desire to be with God. The word is not meant to generate thoughts in and of itself. It is important to select a word, preferably no more than one or two syllables, that does not stir up spontaneous thoughts or emotions. Obviously, a word like "hate" is avoided, but counterintuitively the word "God" may also be avoided. As a beginner, I used a word. But in teaching, I anecdotally realized 30% to 40% of people use an image or their breath. After much practice, I personally settled on an image. Some of the words I originally considered were *abba*, peace, one, *nil*. Some of the preferably formless images I considered were cloud, star, light, flame.

To further avoid unnecessary distractions, some basic questions were answered by Fr. Keating. When? When relaxed and alert, before meals, for a minimum of 20 minutes twice a day. Where? In a quiet place, with dim lighting and unlikely interruptions, either alone or in a group. What? On a sturdy chair, wearing loose clothing, starting with a short meditative prayer verse and gentle gong, ending with a gentle gong and very slow silent, mental Our Father. How? Straight back, head free, feet flat, eyes closed.

I am going through this lengthy explanation because it was critical in my spiritual journey, my contemplative experience, and my scientific understanding of my prayer life. Please bear with me.

I start Centering Prayer by reciting: "Be still and know that I am God." I repeat it while reducing it: "Be still and know that I am [pause]. Be still and know [pause]. Be still [pause]. Be." I gently sound a gong three times to mark the start.

As learned from the Trappists, *the most important lesson* is to adhere to the following guidelines during the prayer:

1. SACRED SYMBOL
Chosen as intention to consent to God

2. COMFORTABLE POSITION
Introduce symbol of God's presence

3. THOUGHTS & RETURN
When aware of or engaged in thoughts, return to sacred symbol

4. GENTLE READJUSTMENT
Conclude in silence for a couple of minutes

Figure 37 Centering Prayer Guidelines – List

At the end of 20 to 30 minutes, using a quiet timer, I gently sound a gong three times. I mentally recite the Our Father very, very, very slowly. This is in accordance with how Jesus responded when He was asked how to pray in the quote at the beginning of this section.

Inevitably, guideline three gives me the biggest challenge. I am human and have many thoughts. I am not rough on the thoughts, but gently let them go and return to my sacred symbol, which is a symbol of my desire to be with God. I am not trying to make my brain blank or empty of thoughts. I am merely processing the thoughts by gently letting go and returning to God. I do this whenever I become aware of the thoughts or become aware I am engaged with the thoughts. I realize in the process I am not my thoughts. I am much more than my thoughts. The number of thoughts I have is not a measure of how well or how poorly I am doing. The following four "R" principles help. I resist no thoughts. I retain no thoughts. I react to no thoughts. I return, ever so gently, to my sacred symbol.

Regardless of the types of thoughts, I treat them all the same without judgment. I call on my sacred symbol only when I become aware of or engage with my thoughts. I realize my thoughts are of many types, but generally fall into five categories: ordinary imagination, such as did I turn off the lights?; attractions or aversions, such as that person really made me angry; insights or enlightenments, such as now I understand the Trinity better; introspective reflections, such as I am not doing very well at this prayer or I picked the wrong symbol; and unloading of the unconscious, such as I now remember that hurt from my childhood.

The golden nugget in this whole process was the discovery and acknowledgment of the last type of thought, unloading the unconscious. Most of the thoughts are pleasurable or neutral, but not all. Sometimes the unloading of the unconscious is painful. But this too is part of the Divine healer's plan. Thoughts matter![155] For my faith and science spiritual journey, this was important. The unconscious was where my prejudices, habitual sins, and unforgiveness were located.

Unloading Unconscious – God's presence unconsciously there

> *"Until you make the unconscious conscious, it will direct your life and you will call it fate."*
> CARL JUNG

Suddenly I had an epiphany! This was the key to deal with my tendency to rationalize my so-called informed conscience, to release me from Confirmation Bias.

Though I had experienced the gentle love of God in my Centering Prayer practice, I now had to consider what God may or may not do as a result—even though I did not seek anything except to be with Him.

Because of the non-dualism of the physical body and spiritual soul, prayer has effects on both, usually after the prayer. The most frequently reported physical-body effects people experience are lower blood pressure, less melancholy, less suffering, less nervousness, less anger, and less sleep required. The most frequently reported spiritual-soul effects people experience are the gifts of the Holy Spirit described in scripture. They include patience, charity, generosity, love, kindness, chastity, gentleness, joy and peace. Most report experiencing an inner sense of peace.

I realized God's wisdom. He gives the specific fruits of the prayer I most need. God customizes the fruits to my needs. To be clear, the fruits are not necessarily present during the prayer, present instantly, or cause and effect of the prayer. They are not the prayer's purpose, divinely guaranteed, totally predictable, discursive prayer replacements, or just pleasurable. On the other hand, the fruits received are often doorways into personal growth, such as better listening ability and being less judgmental. I also indirectly discovered they lead to improving interpersonal relationships, such as a tendency toward action rather than reaction; my wife noticed this change before I did. Finally, the fruits lead to unconsciously serving others rather than myself. I more spontaneously see God dwelling in others, once I experienced God dwelling within me. I am not saying I am holier, but unconsciously more open to God's influence.

By unloading the unconscious, more and more of the focus is on God's healing. The conscious brain is too busy with life to allow room for the unconscious brain to unload. When practicing Centering Prayer, I am freeing the conscious brain of thoughts and allowing room for the unconscious to unload to the conscious brain. After practicing Centering Prayer for a time, I began seeing the results of this unloading in people I taught. These observations help me appreciate what is happening.

I was so excited to share this experience with Linda. She suffered terribly from bipolar condition, which necessarily consisted of a flood of ruminating thoughts. I taught it to her sitting outside in the backyard. She went so deep that at the end of 20 minutes I didn't want to disturb her. I quietly let her continue for a total of about 45 minutes, at which time she ended her prayer. I silently wept. She obviously was touched by the Divine Healer. She didn't share the details, but I contemplatively knew she experienced God's love within her. She started to read more and more of the lives of the saints. Her favorite was the mystic St. Thérèse of Lisieux who also suffered from depression. She immersed herself in the saint's autobiography.[156]

This was an incredible validation of my F&S ministry, my spiritual journey of love. I was being called to share this with others.

A few months after I taught Centering Prayer to about ten people, I saw one of the participants. When asked how his Centering Prayer was going, he replied outside the prayer practice he became fully aware of what really happened to him in Vietnam. I did not ask for specifics, but it was clear it was a serious PTSD issue. I did ask, "What did you do then?" He replied, "I ever so gently let it go and returned to God." He unconsciously and spontaneously had let go of his thoughts outside of his Centering Prayer practice. Centering Prayer had become a habit assigned to his unconscious brain. Once he became practiced at letting go,[157] the Divine Healer knew he was ready to remember his PTSD moment. He was ready and able to let it go. His unconscious brain protected him from the memory until the conscious brain was ready to deal with it.

I told this true story to a fellow board member at ISH, Jim Lomax, M.D., Ph.D. He is one of the top psychiatrists at Menninger Clinic and is also involved at the Veterans Affairs (VA) hospital in Houston, the second-largest VA hospital in the U.S. He was clearly surprised. He humbly shared psychiatrists were having difficulty treating PTSD patients. The VA hospital had floors and floors of PTSD patients. This led me to teach the VA chaplains Centering Prayer. The head chaplain and I prepared a research proposal for introducing Centering Prayer to volunteer PTSD patients, which I discuss in the Epilogue.

While I was at an international neuroscience conference in Cuba on Disorders of Consciousness, another example occurred. I gave a presentation on a research project studying the effects of prayer on the brain. Our research team included the conference organizer, his daughter, and her husband, all of whom were M.D. neuroscientists. Just before my return home, the daughter asked me to teach Centering Prayer to a few people in her home. One of the people suffered severely from Parkinson's disease. He was slipping into deep depression due to sleep deprivation from nightly freezing episodes.

I met each guest as they calmly arrived, then the family dog entered the room and jumped into everyone's lap. When he leaped into the Parkinson's patient's lap, I will call him Jose, it triggered a severe Parkinson's freeze episode. Jose's outward stretched legs became stiff, his arms were flailing above his head, his fingers and face contorting. His wife swabbed down his body's sweat. The two medical doctors tried to help, but to no avail. I noticed when they tried to help, his freeze seemed to get worse. I concluded he was desperately focused on trying to stop the freeze out of love and concern for his wife's and doctors' attempts to help.

It became apparent I needed to start the prayer; I was running out of time. I mentally fussed with God as to how in the world I could possibly teach under these circumstances. But I began anyway. The husband translated my instructions for fifteen minutes. I suggested one of the possible thoughts all would have to let go of would be concern for Jose and Jose's concern for everyone's reaction. Frankly I had never before been that specific in my instructions. The whole time I was worried Jose's brain was not consciously comprehending the instructions. When practicing Centering Prayer while teaching it, I don't usually go as deep. I want to occasionally open my eyes to see how everyone is doing. Initially all were deep, except Jose.

Within minutes it happened! Jose became totally still, in deep prayer, not sleeping. I had never taught anyone during a Parkinson's freeze episode. Out of catharsis, I buried my head in my hands and quietly wept. After twenty minutes, the timer repeated three gongs. I ended the prayer as quietly and slowly as possible by saying the Our Father, which I do for beginners. I did this to permit Jose to continue in his peaceful state, if he wished. I was stunned he continued to pray for another fifteen minutes.

While Jose remained in prayer, I whispered, "We have just witnessed the infinite loving embrace of God." As Jose's wife's quietly left the room to compose herself, tears rolled down her face. The doctors said they had never seen anything like it. I told the medical doctors they were looking at their next neuroscience research project to help other Parkinson's patients. It was clear God temporarily healed Jose by rewiring his brain through neuroplasticity away from his focus on his freezing episode and toward God's love. There is a difference between healing and cure.

After Jose finished his Centering Prayer, he came within inches of my face and spoke passionately in Spanish. I didn't understand, but listened quietly. The doctor translated. Jose said after the Cuban revolution, as a young child he was taken into the country and purged of his belief in God. He had been searching for God ever since and finally found Him. We embraced and wept on each other's shoulders.

I have had many similar experiences, which anecdotally demonstrate how Centering Prayer facilitates the unloading of the unconscious. The unloading demonstrates it is the seat of buried PTSD experiences and Confirmation Bias. This was a critical epiphany in my faith and science spiritual journey. It meant there is hope for me to come to a truly informed conscience and forgiveness of those who had hurt me.

The Disorders of Consciousness conference I attended exposed me to other altered states of consciousness, not all of which are disorders, as the conference title incorrectly implied.

ALTERED CONSCIOUSNESS — States of God's presence

> *"To whom shall God teach His knowledge? And to whom shall He explain His message? To them who are weaned from the milk and to them who are drawn away from the breasts."*
> ISAIAH 28:9

Contemplative Experiences — God's infused love

> *". . . contemplation is a pure gift. But it must be emphasized that it is a gift that has already been given. Its powers are present but hidden in the unconscious."*
> FR. THOMAS KEATING,[158] Former Monk & Abbot

As a teacher of Centering Prayer, I witness many healing physical and spiritual effects, gifts of the Spirit, which normally take place outside the prayer practice, such as the Vietnam PTSD example. But I have also witnessed some mystical experiences taking place during the prayer, such as the Parkinson's patient. The mystical experiences are consistent with the many reported mystical experiences throughout the centuries when practicing a form of Centering Prayer. They can also happen spontaneously without Centering Prayer as God has gifted them.[159] Mystical experiences are still fairly uncommon.

Fr. Keating told me, in his experience, about 5% to 10% of Centering Prayer practitioners report mild to dramatic forms of mystical experiences. That confirmed my observations of some practitioners when I taught Centering Prayer. It also confirmed my experience.

I had lived through the first two stages of the spiritual journey: the Purgative and Illuminative mentioned earlier. I had been given a taste of what was ascribed to Dionysius as the third and final stage of the spiritual journey. It is the Unitive Stage, a taste of the Divine.

I was surprised when Fr. Keating said, in his experience, monks and nuns have them less than 5% of the time. My surprise lessened when reading the writings of the mystics through the centuries. They said the mystical experiences usually happen to beginners as Divine encouragement. That's what happened to me.

As unusual as mystical experiences are, they are underreported. From my experience, I theorized there are at least five reasons for not reporting them; I call them mystical confidentiality. Not necessarily in order of importance, they are: I don't want people to think I am crazy. Words are inadequate to describe the experience. The recollection fades quickly so I am unable to remember the depth of the experience. I am concerned people will try to have the same experience, not realizing it is true gift from God, not anything I am doing. I worry people will think I am holy when I was really in the state of serious sin at the time of the mystical experience.

A fortunate meeting with Dr. Bernard McGinn taught me even more about the many mystics[160] throughout the centuries[161] and their writings about their mystical experiences.[162] For me, the most informative have been the doctors of the Church St. Teresa of Avila and St. John of the Cross. They tended to use poetry to overcome the inadequacies of words. But in the final analysis, most mystics shared the following four attributes of mystical experiences, which continue today in the overall population. These attributes are: *Spaceless*, since there is a form of ecstasy or out-of-body experience; *Timeless*, since the prayer seems shorter than it really is; *Wholeness*, since there is often a sense of perfection or peace; *Oneness*, since there is a sense of unity with God and the Universe.

As fortune would have it, or more accurately, the synchronistic intervention of the Holy Spirit, I met Calixto Machado, M.D., Ph.D. He is the organizer of the Disorders of Consciousness conference and one of the world's experts in recovering people from comatose states. Upon my inquiry, he described his many patients who told him about their near-death experience (NDE). My interest was piqued.

Near-Death Experiences – God at the gate for us

"I've told my children that when I die, to release balloons in the sky to celebrate that I graduated. For me, death is a graduation."
   Dr. Elisabeth Kubler-Ross, Physician

My learning took a detour. I didn't expect to pursue the faith and science of NDEs. They had been going on for millennia, but physicians had initially dismissed them. That is, until, in some cases, they themselves had an NDE. A couple of famous examples include Raymond Moody, M.D.,[163] and Melvin Morse, M.D.[164] Neuroscientists began to acknowledge NDEs are real even though the experience cannot be studied while happening. It started to be taken more seriously when some subjects, especially children, reported seeing and knowing things they could only know if they were having a real out-of-body experience.[165] They were initially underreported, just like mystical experiences, often for the same reasons. Of the hundreds ultimately reported, a couple of cases are especially interesting.

Eben Alexander, M.D., a Harvard-educated neurosurgeon, wrote *Proof of Heaven*. By his own admission, he thought the title of his book, pushed by his publishers, was misleading. He also came under criticism from his colleagues challenging the possibility his experience was medication induced, since he was not clear on what was administered to him while he was unconscious. But his story is nonetheless similar to hundreds published by others—except he is a neurosurgeon, who previously believed consciousness is located solely in the brain. After his experience he believed the brain did not produce consciousness as he previously thought, but consciousness came from outside the brain. As he put it:

... the brain itself doesn't produce consciousness. That it is instead a kind of reducing valve or filter, sifting the larger, nonphysical consciousness that we possess in the nonphysical world down into a more limited capacity for the duration of our mortal lives.[166]

This is not just consistent with experiences of the unloading of the unconscious brain but goes beyond to some direct sharing of a broader consciousness by the conscious brain. The brain is actually a filter to limit the input to protect the brain. Alexander described his experiences including seeing multiple Universes. This is consistent with my study: Being separate from our Universe by definition necessitates not being limited by space and time. There is an intense union with the non-physical realities of creation. The core of the experience is a union with the Source, Love, God. This is an incredible epiphany of the awe of God's deep love.

A more recent example of NDEs describes what happened to Mary Neal, M.D.,[167] an orthopedic spine surgeon. She died in frigid waters in a river accident; she was without oxygen for thirty minutes. After being resuscitated, she reported leaving her body and being greeted by loved ones with joy not describable in Earthly words. She was told about the future death of her oldest son. She was told she must return to finish her work. She was a fact-based scientist, which furthered her curiosity. Her experience is yet another case study of a scientist meeting and needing faith. Yes, her son did die later, but she was at peace.

NDEs have four main attributes in common: *Paranormal*, since they were out-of-body, ecstasy; *Cognitive*, since they happened in a short time; *Affective*, since there was a sense of total peace; *Transcendent*, since they involved a sort of Divine encounter of angels, love, etc.

I was starting to see a pattern. I had observed similar attributes for mystical experiences. This was inexorably leading me to the exciting scientific comparison of NDEs and mystical experiences. I enthusiastically moved on to more of God's awe.

Transcendent Events – Nature is giving us its map to God

"The devout Christian of the future will either be a 'mystic,' one who has experienced something, or he will cease to be anything at all."
Fr. Karl Rahner, Theologian

If I was to scientifically compare NDEs and mystical experiences, I needed a more universally accepted term for mystical. As mentioned, the term contemplative is synonymous with mystical and more broadly accepted between faiths. Because contemplative experiences are not restricted to self-proclaimed religious, but also the more generic, self-proclaimed spiritual practitioners, a modifier was needed. I coined the term Spiritual Contemplative Experience (SCE) for my scientific research. It has the visual advantage of comparison to the three-letter NDE. I consciously chose not to use the broader published term Spiritually Transformative Experience (STE), because it could refer to many altered states of consciousness including both NDE and SCE.

Before I went to the next scientific step, I realized my awakening was mind-blowing. In the earliest chapter in my journey, "Physics to Creation," I concluded with the attributes of the Singularity at the beginning of the Big Bang, which I asked you to remember for later. Well, later is now.

My epiphany? The three transcendent events, NDE, SCE and the Singularity, all have common attributes. The following table summarizes those attributes with line-by-line comparisons, footnoted with the sources, which I describe later.

NDE*	SCE**	SINGULARITY***
1 PARANORMAL -	1 SPACELESS -	1 DIMENSIONLESS -
Out-of-body	Ecstasy	Non-material
2 COGNITIVE -	2 TIMELESS -	2 TIMELESS -
Timeless	Short Prayer	No Light
3 AFFECTIVE -	3 WHOLENESS -	3 ORDERED -
Peace	Perfection	Zero Entropy
4 TRANSCENDENT -	4 ONENESS -	4 UNIFIED -
Divine-Religious	With Universe	Four Forces

* Dr. Moody described NDE attributes in 1975 and Bruce Greyson developed a scale for attributes.
** Dr. W. James described mystical (SCE) attributes in *The Varieties of Religious Experience*, 1902.
*** Einstein's theories led to Singularity attributes at the beginning of the Big Bang.

Figure 38 Transcendent Events - Table

I have not seen the consistency of these attributes between the three events published before, although they may have been. They were independently, with synchronicity, discovered on my spiritual journey. I shouldn't have been surprised. All three states are at the juncture between Heaven and Earth, this life and the next. Words cannot describe these states. To call them common moments implies time, of which they are independent. To call them common places implies space, of which they are independent. I was being given a glimpse of the Divine. Of God again as Awe! I was not going to dismiss this lightly. I continued on my discovery of God as Awe, to the point of changing His Omnibenevolent name to Awe of Oneness.

In some ways others had alluded to this, including Cannato.[168] My true inspiration for taking this very seriously came from an incident that occurred while I was teaching Centering Prayer.

At the end of a twenty-minute Centering Prayer session of a group of five first-time practitioners, three of them launched into a discussion. They had just relived their previous NDE. Until that moment I was not aware of their NDE history. I was mesmerized as I listened to the three of them describe how their NDEs repeated themselves, in real time, as SCEs. For an hour they proceeded to describe, in detail, to each other their profound reliving of their NDE.

The brain activity of an NDE during a meditative state had been studied by Beauregard.[169] But no one ever compared the brain activity of NDE and SCE. This inspired Calixto Machado, M.D., Ph.D., and me to complete a research project comparing the brain scans of subjects remembering their NDE and SCE. Though I was initially skeptical, Calixto convinced me remembering an event was a neuroscientifically acceptable approach in circumstances where you cannot catch the subjects in the act of either NDE or SCE. The research used quantitative electroencephalography (EEG) tomography (QEEGt), continuous EEG (CEEG), and continuous anatomical assessment (CAA) measuring heart rate (HR) and HR variability (HRV). The results showed a clear neural and emotional correlation between NDE and SCE. I describe the research in more detail in the Epilogue.

We were entering into the relatively uncharted waters of neuroscience and neurotheology.

NEUROSCIENCE & NEUROTHEOLOGY – Earth & Heaven

> *"The uncertainty principle is oddly like St. John of the Cross. As God in the highest eludes the grasp of concepts, so in the ultimate constitution of matter . . . Heisenberg shows . . . a fabulous new concept of nature with ourselves in the midst of it and destroys the simple illusion of ourselves as detached and infallible observers."*
> Fr. Thomas Merton, Trappist monk

Early psychologists were some of the first to recognize consciousness and its spiritual implications. I was inspired by William James's classic work,[170] which is referenced in the previous figure. He was one of the first psychologists to scientifically recognize and discuss mystical experiences. The attributes he gave them are similar to what I had observed: Language is inadequate; the knowledge is non-conceptual; it is of brief duration; and it happens passively without volition. Ornstein's classic work,[171] *The Psychology of Consciousness*, also postulates the importance of both intuition and reason being required to understand consciousness.

With the emergence of improved brain scanning tools, it didn't take long to move from psychology to neuroscience. Those scientists on the path included Andrew Newberg[172] and Kevin Nelson.[173] Those of faith on the path included theologians and philosophers such as Edward Kelly[174] and Ken Wilson.[175]

Unfortunately, the available brain scanning tools are somewhat limited. Generally speaking, they don't simultaneously provide both accurate spatial and temporal measurements of the brain. In studying first-person experiences, there is a more fundamental scientific problem. Even though I accepted many first-person accounts as real, they could not be objectively studied with the normal objective scientific method. As a hard scientist, not a psychiatrist, I could no longer objectively and quantitively measure a subjective experience.

I remained resolute. I did not forget my belief God reveals Himself through faith and science. As Merton alluded to in his quote above, I proceeded with inductive science.

Neuroplasticity Scans – God looks at us from within

> "... neuroplasticity means that emotions such as happiness and compassion can be cultivated in much the same way that a person can learn through repetition to play golf and basketball or master a musical instrument, and that such practice changes the activity and physical aspects of specific brain areas."
> ANDREW WEIL, M.D.

The same error Einstein initially made thinking the Universe was static was also made by neuroscientists thinking the brain was static. Neuroscientists had to change their thinking when they discovered the brain has neuroplasticity. It is not static, but changes including with meditative and contemplative practices. Most of the excellent brain scan research on contemplatives, called meditators by Buddhists, was done by Richie Davidson[176] on Tibetan Buddhist monks.

The dramatic results of that research reinforced my Catholic faith. I believe the Holy Spirit dwells within everyone on Earth, so I was not surprised He also acts within the brains of non-believers. We are all non-dualistic, God and man. We are meant for each other.

After Davidson's work, there has been an increase in brain-scan research on theistic contemplatives with one of the earlier ones done by Andrew Newberg.[177] He performed MRI brain scans on Franciscan nuns who practiced Centering Prayer. He demonstrated their brains were being rewired by the Divine Healer. Further studies used other brain scan tools.[178]

Newberg went on to describe the various parts of the brain associated with God. He believed the brain is hard wired for faith. Referring to the map of the brain at the beginning of the last chapter, "Biology to Consciousness," his observations allowed me to personalize my faith. Though these anatomical parts of the brain apply to other things, I was most intrigued by their functions relative to God.

The occipital-parietal identifies God as object. The parietal-frontal gives the relationship with God. The frontal integrates the intellectual and religious understanding of God. The thalamus provides a holistic and emotional sense of God. The amygdala can lead to an emotional fear of God. The striatum can lead to emotional security in God. The anterior cingulate can lead to a loving God.

Ecstasy Proposition – Taste of the Divine presence

> "... our contemplation of Him [God] is a participation in His contemplation of Himself."
>
> Fr. Thomas Merton, Trappist Monk

Two earlier researchers, D'Aquili and Newberg,[179] probed the biology of mystical experiences. In addition to the many previously mentioned dualisms of the brain, neuroscientists were starting to consider an additional one: a "sense of selfhood" and a "sense of embodiment."

Several authors offered a possible neuroscientific explanation for an out-of-body experience. The belief is the right temporoparietal junction is involved. Its activation correlates with feelings commonly associated with spirituality, including interfaith empathy, compassion, and a sense of transcendence. That sense of higher self-transcending material existence can lead to an out-of-body experience. Neuroscientists believe the brain is electrically wired with base-2 communication receptors.[180]

I was a little concerned I was getting lost in the weeds of neuroscience, which was still young and not very definitive. Yet I had to ask: How has God touched me? How does He touch the many others on our spiritual journeys?

When combined with wormhole entanglement,[181] the brains' base-2 communication receptors may provide a Divine route for directly informing the conscious brain of the Oneness of the Universe from anywhere, everywhere, anytime, every-time; unrestricted by space and time in the Universe. That could explain why some NDEs and SCEs report learning details of some future event or the intimate details of something or even someone in the past. God and man, body and soul are indeed non-dualistic. God lovingly dwells within us including within our synapses. God is truly Omnibenevolent.

Many like Kripal[182] document cases of confirmed predictions of the future, though there never seems to be so much information that it violates free will. The hints are also too subtle to imply predetermination. God is the Gatekeeper; He gives us glimpses of the future without depriving us of our free will.

Many have documented confirmed cases of intimate union with someone from the past. The sense of union can be so strong they believe they actually were that person, equivalent to that person, which some ascribe to reincarnation. I humbly offer a different interpretation. If there is true relational loving Oneness, our empathy for a previous soul can be so strong we can feel one with them, to the point of thinking we are that soul, just occupying a different body. In other words, dualism between body and soul belies that reincarnation interpretation. My non-dualistic faith means a loving relationship, not an equivalent selfhood.

For some the sense of Divine union is so strong they believe we can become God. Someone who believes this recently challenged me to submit my application for being the Messiah, since he believed we all become God. I laughed and answered, "If and when I am able to create another universe, I will invite you there and submit my application to become the Messiah." God forgive my sarcasm. My conclusion is a mystical experience gives us only a taste of the Divine Oneness. A taste of that Oneness is unconstrained by space and time. Our prison of space and time can lead us to a false interpretation we are becoming Divine.

I believe the reason there are some differences in reported memories of NDE and SCE is the memories of the experiences fade and our flawed unconscious fills in the details when we return. While still in the mystical experience, we are all embraced by the same God in the *Cloud of Unknowing*.

This was mind boggling. I launched into exploring God as the One Consciousness, the Oneness.

Collective Oneness – The relational Body of Christ

> "... our present consciousness is only one out of many worlds of consciousness that exists, [which] worlds must contain experiences which have a meaning for our life."
> WILLIAM JAMES, Psychologist

We all have experienced some sort of collective consciousness and conscience in our daily lives, but never identified it as that. Collective consciousness exists as generally accepted medical and scientific knowledge not just information, for example the Earth is round. It is amazing there are always some outliers like the current Flat Earth Society. Collective conscience exists as generally accepted religious and civil norms, for example murder is wrong. There too it is amazing there are outliers who don't make moral distinctions between murder and killing, such as fundamentalist cults like the one that led to the Jonestown massacre and masochistic dictatorships like the one that led to the Holocaust.

How collective consciousness and conscience evolved is intriguing. Some scientists turned to the animal kingdom for guidance in collective consciousness. One somewhat dismissed idea is the so-called Hundred Monkey Effect. It is based on an experiment in which potatoes were thrown onto an island beach. Some monkeys were observed washing the sand off the potatoes before eating them. The young learned it first, then it spread to the adults as if the young were teaching them. The argument is once the behavior reached a critically figurative 100, the consciously learned process jumped instantaneously to monkeys on another island. Since the monkeys couldn't swim, it is attributed to collective consciousness between the monkeys on the two islands.[183]

Though intriguing, I was interested in God's communication through consciousness in NDE, SCE, the lives of the saints, mystics, and elsewhere.

Some drew analogies between sociological evolution and spiritual evolution in terms of Christ Consciousness. This yielded some interesting perspectives, one of which follows.

The Anthropic Principle of God's conception of humans 13.7 billion years ago, before humans' actual arrival, compared to conception, 9 months before birth. The first human's consciousness some 6 million years ago compared to the supposed ability to know right from wrong by about 7 years old. Collaborative agrarian society about 10,000 years ago compared to teenage adolescence when humans interact socially with friends. Christ's incarnation about 2,000 years ago compared to focus less on self and more on others in the Body of Christ when more mature in the ages of twenties and thirties. Contemporary interconnectivity through travel and internet compared to more compassionate relational maturity in midlife. Humanity's Divine union drawn by God compared to a mystical experience later in life. In Teilhard de Chardin's classic *The Phenomenon of Man*,[184] he discusses the concept of the final step of our journey to the Omega point, God.

Instead of relying only on someone else's postulations to describe collective consciousness, I reviewed the chapter-by-chapter lessons learned on my faith and science journey. I wanted to reflect on them and draw my own conclusion.

My "Physics to Creation" journey showed the immensity of the Universe came from a single point of energy, the Singularity. At that point, the forces forming the Universe were unified, unrestrained by space and time and perfectly ordered. The Big Bang started the Universe with the express, preconceived, intelligent purpose of later life, including my life. God is continually creating the Universe in an exponential expansion. There is a universal, natural attraction between all bodies in the Universe. The Universe is curved back on itself, which enables subatomic informational connections between the present, the past, and the future. Before creating the Universe, God conceived of me personally. I was escaping from trust in humans and seeking God as awe in the Universe. My travels spanned the world and the Universe seeking His awe in natural wonders. My awe of the Universe led back to life itself. My name for the Omnipotent God became Awe of Nature.

My "Chemistry to Life" journey taught the atoms, which arose at the very beginning of the Big Bang, became part of the stars. Those same atoms from the stars became part of my body. Just as I was getting excited about what science was teaching, science itself determined the very design of the Universe made it impossible to understand it completely. Yet that same Divine design enabled God to intervene without me scientifically knowing it. All life contains common DNA molecules making me one with all other life, especially other human beings. My escape from human hurts is impossible. Each cell contains DNA, and each DNA contains a full map of the body. Evolution is both physical and spiritual. Biological life has a tendency toward more complexity, but at the same time more relational love. Humans are made to be both the whole and part of the whole of the DNA body of life and the Body of Christ. Instant communication throughout the Universe is possible between the present and both the past and the future. I was being drawn inexorably to God as ultimate Life. Travel took me worldwide seeking God's Awe in His infinite examples of life in nature. My preferred name for this Omnipresent God started to shift to Awe of Life.

My "Biology to Consciousness" journey showed the uniqueness of humanness. What distinguishes humans from the animals is heightened consciousness, conscience, and free will with the help of the loving indwelling Holy Spirit. Travel took me worldwide seeking God's Life in manmade examples of the results of His love. My science focus was shifting to more of a mixture of science and faith because evolutionary theory alone couldn't explain the arrival of man. It could not show why evolution resulted in the monkeys not landing on the moon or building skyscrapers, even though they share 97% DNA with humans. The true explanation had to include the ability of humans to choose love or evil. I cannot judge others' culpability in the eyes of God since, scientifically, I cannot climb inside their brain. My brain has both conscious and unconscious capability, so I can learn from mistakes. I can experience unconscious learning, which includes faith itself. I have virtues and vices stored in the unconscious brain. Science taught the human tendency of Confirmation Bias, which is the closest scientific equivalent term for my faith's term, original sin. It is preferential repetition of habitual sin, which is an obstacle to union with God. Yet scientific research also shows it is possible to experience physical and spiritual healing simply by my theistic faith, liturgical attendance, and frequent prayer. That healing effect has been scientifically observed in forgiveness and love. The brain may be wired such that it can process instantaneous quantum entangled information from present, past, and future. My preferred name for this Omniscient God shifted to Awe of Love.

My "Psychology to Mysticism" journey showed I can open myself to God's gift of mystical love through prayer, particularly for me, Centering Prayer. God dwells within, is available to, and desires union with everyone on Earth. There are at least three transcendent events between God and humans: mystical experience, near-death experience, and the Singularity moment of the Big Bang. My journey was cycling back to the Universe showing the Oneness of God's plan. I was made to be one with God. He was, and always is, there for me. When I experience the God within me, I more spontaneously and unconsciously see and experience the God dwelling within everyone. I share a oneness with God that bridges my ability to perceive Him and to hold onto Him. I am loved intensely and completely. There is a relational quality to sharing the Divine in others. God can share some of His Divine collective

Oneness, including past and present events, only if humans listen to His synchronistic silent messages with the conscious brain. God relentlessly calls me to the mystical union of His love. Travel took me worldwide seeking God's Love in manmade interfaith examples of the results of His love. I was inclined to change the name of this Omnibenevolent God to Awe of Oneness.

Review of my journey shows the recurring message is evolutionary love, oneness, procreation, relationship, Divine union. When I was a teenager I read Teilhard de Chardin's postulated noosphere,[185] from the Greek word for mind "*noo*." It is the incandescent glow of consciousness, the defining factor in God's relentless call to mystical love, toward God the Omega point.

Endless world travels to find the Omnipotent God's Awe in Nature, the Omnipresent God's Awe in Life, the Omniscient God's Awe in Love, the Omnibenevolent God's Awe in Oneness took me around the world and the Universe. I suddenly realized what I was searching for everywhere actually resided within me. My endless wonderings and wanderings were described perfectly by one of my favorite mystics, Meister Eckhart: "God is at home, it's we who have gone out for a walk."[186]

My ever-changing names for God were becoming impulsive attempts at control, at knowing the unknowable, the ineffable. The Holy Spirit within made me realize God's real name was the Unknowable,[187] No-Thing, Nothing. The names often used by the mystics. All along by giving Him names, I had been creating God in my image. I had to allow Him to create me in His or Her image by accepting God as the ultimate unknowable.

My unconscious learning is faith with a small "f." My true Faith is a mystical union with God with a capital "F." I had to surrender my search to true Faith, which is not empirical but unseen. God's relentless call to mystical love had come through science, but led back to Faith.

I have been given a glimpse of how Jesus non-dualistically conquered sin and death, which enhances the more important knowledge of why He did so. I honor those who shared God's love in my spiritual journey of discovery and have gone before me. Abbot Joseph Boyle, Fr. Thomas Keating, Monk Theophane, and most importantly my beloved wife, Linda.

The night before my wife died, she said to me, "I love you so deeply I can't put it into words." I cannot recall these loving words without simultaneously weeping in grief and in joy. Linda was sharing with me the Divine Oneness of love that goes beyond words. It is not her farewell in body I carry with me, but her eternity of Spirit. Death is not the end, but the beginning. I say to her, "I love you," not "I loved you." I am in union with God and Linda to this day.

I am reminded of God's relentless call to all humans in the interfaith words of the famous Sufi mystic, Rumi: "Goodbyes are only for those who love with their eyes. Because for those who love with heart and soul there is no such thing as separation."[188] I am reminded of God's relentless call from my Catholic mystic mentor, monk Fr. Keating.

> There is the possibility that there is only one Self. There is only God. There is only one Self, or one consciousness in fact. And in the light of scientific discoveries, if there is one consciousness, it is the infinite unlimited consciousness of God, which is shared with every creature according to its capacity.[189]

I had reached the point in my ever-spiraling journey where I had to cycle back and reflect on the moment I received the precious mystical gift from God. I now humbly wish to share it with you.

7
CALLED TO SERVE

Figure 39 Monk Theophane at Trappist Monastery, Colorado – Photo

"Together we'll go into the heart of God."

Theophane the Monk

RUMINATING THOUGHTS – The Devil made me do it

I am transported back to the monastery at my first contemplative retreat where this book started.

There were twenty-six retreatants, eighteen women and eight men, living in hermitages, sleeping two in each. The hermitages were close to the prayer chapel. Every day we had three hours of Centering Prayer in the chapel. It consisted of three twenty-minute sets each hour with a circular walk between each set. There was no speaking during the day. We could make the thirty-minute walk to the monastery across the valley for daily liturgy of the hours and Mass. Only after Mass on Sunday were we allowed to speak to a couple of the monks in the bookstore. We never knew which monks would be there, but everyone looked forward to the conversation.

One Sunday was a special blessing. Abbot Joseph and Theophane, the Monk[190] were there to greet us. Theophane published only one book, *Tales of a Magic Monastery*, which I discovered and read much later. The book truly captured his spirit of holy playfulness.

This particular Sunday was the Abbot's birthday. Theophane decided to sing a happy-birthday song dedicated to the Abbot. With Theophane, one never knew what to expect. He belted out the words to the hilarious old song "Cigarettes, Whiskey, and Wild, Wild Women" made famous by Buck Owens. The following stanzas were in the same catchy melody with words applicable to the Abbot. We were all doubled over in laughter. The contrast between the stereotypical monk, pictured at the beginning of this chapter, combined with the words and melody was hilarious. The Abbot was seriously embarrassed, blushing intensely. I will never forget that delightful moment done with love and humor. It was just like Theophane.

We didn't wear out our welcome. We had our next prayer set in the chapel, a thirty-minute walk away. When we arrived, I started Centering Prayer as usual, but this time, I was really struggling. I was new at letting go of my thoughts, but nothing had prepared me for this struggle. Let me tell you, if the words "Cigarettes, Whiskey, and Wild, Wild Women" repeated themselves once in my thoughts, they repeated themselves a thousand times.

I could not, for the life of me, get them out of my mind. It was funny at first, but I was getting seriously annoyed.

At the end of the first twenty-minute set, I did something contrary to my training even though I knew I shouldn't. I stopped letting go of my thoughts and got angry at God. "Why won't You help me? I am truly trying and I get no help from You. What the hell are You doing? Why aren't You helping me?"

LOVING ECSTASY – God brings me home

Then it happened!

I was caressed out of my body and lifted up. I knew my feet were still touching the ground, but it was as if I were on ice skates. As I hovered above everyone, there was no friction or sense of leg movement. At that moment, the wind rushed into the chapel; the windows were open due to the heat. Papers were flying everywhere. Everyone in the room stopped their prayer and scrambled to pick them up. Though I was aware of the activity, I was completely disengaged from it. I felt totally secure being held in His arms without a care in the world. I can't exactly describe it as joyful, though it certainly was. It was more absolute peace, knowing I was infinitely loved and caressed.

I barely remember getting up from my chair between the second and third prayer sit and walking the thirty-foot circumference of the chapel; I was still detached from my body. The prayer session ended; everyone left the chapel. I was the only one in the room. I was still floating. I never wanted to leave His embrace. When that desire became a thought is when the ecstasy, ever-so-gradually, started to leave me. I knew I was not supposed to hold onto it because then I was putting myself back in control, which left God out of control. His gift was leaving. It was a pure dilemma!

I struggled to hold on, but couldn't. I slowly came to realize I would inevitably have to let go and return. I tried to retain the memory; I wanted to relive it later. But the memory of the experience was fading. It was too much for my brain to grasp purely on its own. I could remember only a small fraction of it.

I strained to get up and leave the prayer chapel. An hour and a half had passed, but it felt like five to ten minutes. I could hardly walk. Every muscle in my body felt like it was torn. It was as if I had played consecutive games of baseball and football, as I had in high school, and got two muscle cramps in each leg. While my brain was elsewhere, my disconnected body was apparently struggling for signals to its muscles, but to no avail. It is as if my muscles were having spasms, but I didn't realize it until later.

The joy I felt drove the need to share this with someone who would understand. The first people I told were Sarah and her mother, Pat. Pat cooked for the retreatants. But she was so much more. Over many years, she had seen every contemplative moment pass through that prayer room. She was a mentor and spiritual companion to many. She knew suffering well. Pat's daughter, Sarah, accidentally fell when she was an infant, which caused severe retardation the rest of her life. Mentally Sarah was only a few months old. At thirty-two she couldn't speak. While Pat cooked, Sarah laid on the table during every retreat.

It was logical to tell Sarah first. God was in her silent smile. She couldn't talk, but when I told her, she understood immediately. I knew God was speaking to me through her eyes and beautiful smile. In addition to losing some of the memory, I realized I had no words capable of describing the experience. Sharing my feelings with Sarah, and have her respond without words, fulfilled the experience completely.

I turned to Sarah's blessed mother for a private talk. Pat is a true contemplative. She knew what I was describing and gave assurance and encouragement just by listening.

RECOVERY & EVALUATION – Love is what it's about

I was completely unprepared for what had happened. I went to my hermitage and randomly cracked open my Bible, letting my finger land on a reading. I will share that later.

I was walking around in a stupor. I made an appointment for an unusual private meeting with the Abbot. Surely he would know what was going on. After doing my best to describe the experience, I looked to him for wisdom, but his response was not what I expected. He said God was encouraging me for difficult times ahead. God knew I needed encouragement for my future spiritual journey, but I wasn't ready for that message yet. Over time, I eventually came to appreciate the Abbot's wisdom.

I felt an increased burst of energy. Behind the prayer chapel was Bernie's mountain. Bernie was a monk who had died some years earlier. He was apparently a simple person, who loved God simply, and thus with a level of purity the more educated monks noticed right away. Keating clearly learned that simple love from him. He would refer to Bernie in an interestingly sweet and tender way. The monks named the mountain after Bernie because it is where he would go to find God in nature. I decided to hike up the mountain, about a 7,500-foot elevation. I have asthma and was seriously out of shape. I barely made it to the top, but the view was spectacular. I practiced Centering Prayer while up there. On the way down, I suffered a nasty sprained ankle.

The next prayer sit was excruciatingly painful. I remembered something Keating had said. To use the pain as my sacred image. I did, even though it was difficult. It was almost a symbolic premonition of what the Abbot had predicted.

I thought long and hard about sharing this story. I prayed. And lest there be any misunderstanding, it is *not* an indication of being holy. Quite the contrary. At the time, I was in the state of serious sin. I was a novice on my spiritual journey. I didn't seek the experience. Though I would love to have it happen again, it is not necessary. What God did for me will last a lifetime. I know with absolute certainty God loves me. And He loves us all beyond our wildest imagination. I knew I needed to share my experience with others so they may know God loves them too, beyond their wildest imagination.

This is the passage my finger came to rest on after my wind-swept contemplative experience in the chapel.

> "Do not be amazed that I told you, 'You must be born from above.' The wind blows where it wills, and you can hear the sound it makes, but you do not know where it comes from or where it goes; so it is with everyone who is born of the Spirit."
> JOHN 3:7–8

EPILOGUE

Figure 39 Mahar Aung Mye Bon San Monastery, Myanmar – Photo

"There is almost a sensual longing for communion with others who have a large vision. The immense fulfillment of the friendship between those engaged in furthering the evolution of consciousness has a quality impossible to describe."

Fr. Teilhard de Chardin, Paleontologist

I had been transformed in my spiritual journey to see God in others and to experience His peace in communion with, and service to others. As the Abbot had predicted, I would share in the suffering of many and counterintuitively experience true joy. This even affected my travels. I saw God in cindered cities from Masada in Israel to Hiroshima in Japan. I saw Him in penalizing prisons from Auschwitz in Poland to the maximum-security Michael unit in Palestine in Texas.

In this Epilogue, I offer my personal experiences with specific ministries and resources to which I was drawn. I do not mean for this to be a spiritual travelogue or a complete rendering, nor necessarily applicable to everyone's spiritual journey. I only hope it will give some insight into the potential ministerial opportunities and resources for loving service through faith and science.

MINISTRIES & SEMINARIES – Relational love

> *"Even the other sciences and their development help the church in its growth in understanding . . . The thinking of the church must recover genius and better understand how human beings understand themselves today, in order to develop and deepen the church's teaching."*
> Pope Francis

> *"The love of God cradles us unceasingly."*
> Thomas Keating, Monk and Former Abbot

The following are just a few ministries I have found benefit from F&S.

MARRIAGE PREPARATION MINISTRY – As a deacon, I facilitated couples in marriage preparation. Having been married for 45 years and received all seven sacraments, like most permanent deacons, I have a perspective most priests lack.

There is normal family pressure to get Catholic marriage preparation, but less interest from the youthful couples who are more secular than religious. Based on my anecdotal, non-scientific experience, approximately 25% of the couples were cohabitating. Here is an example of my approach.

My introduction is to explain my only purpose is to help the couple have a long-lasting marriage, which they always wholeheartedly accept and agree with. If I determine they are cohabitating, after a couple of meetings, I present the early sociological statistical studies on cohabitation described in Chapter 5. In this way I avoid the preachiness of Church teaching, to which they are often not open. Those studies showed couples who cohabitated have a 50% increased likelihood of divorce if they get married; in Europe it was 80%. I remind them the divorce rate is over 60% and rising. I also remind them our original agreement for my involvement is for me to help them have a long marriage. Anecdotally, I found about 50% of the cohabitating agree to live separately until after marriage. Of course, I have no way of knowing if they actually did that.

BIBLE STUDY MINISTRY – I know contemplatives have pointed out for centuries scripture has a contemplative dimension,[191] which is often overlooked in Catholic Bible study. I am delighted to continually learn the breadth of scripture has a natural component of God's revelation. In light of a hermeneutic approach, the following is an example of that dimension.

Ancient stories of the origin of life often use a myth genre, which provides wonderful stories that cannot be interpreted literally, but contain central truths. One of the main applications of this is Genesis. Unfortunately, fundamentalists have hijacked this approach. Applying what I learned about consciousness, there is a refreshing approach to Genesis, which remains consistent with, and reinforcing of, the central theological truths. It revolves around using scientific definitions to unpack the text. For example, consciousness is part of what distinguished the first human. His nakedness is part of the gift of consciousness that is self-awareness. Death is not new physically, but Adam and Eve become conscious of their inevitable death. The fruit is the gift of free will and conscience to choose. Original sin is our natural human tendency toward Confirmation Bias. Free will means we are not automatons, but can sin or worship. Love is not genuine, if not freely chosen and shared. Suffering involves our consciousness moving the pain from physical to emotional. Evolution is not mankind's fall, but the emergence of falling upward toward God.[192]

HOMILETIC MINISTRY – Priests and deacons regularly give homilies. I discovered, due to the increased scientific training of parishioners, they are more open to scientific reinforcement of scriptural truths. This is especially true in the technical composition of the population of Houston, since it has the largest medical center in the world and is the energy capital of the world. Additionally, the spread of contemplative prayer in the lay community caused an increased awareness of the contemplative dimension of the gospel, which has been written about extensively.[193,194,195] So I started incorporating science in my homilies. It is not unusual for teenagers to awaken from their usual state of boredom. Scientific reinforcement is a powerful tool to increase understanding of the scriptural readings.

I offer the following brief excerpt from a homily I gave on the 30th Sunday Ordinary Time, Year "B" as an example. The readings are Jeremiah 31:7–9, Hebrews 5:1–6, and Mark 10:46–52. The Gospel is the main reference in the homily, which I repeat here for clarity before the homily excerpt.

> Gospel Reading [Mark 10:46–52] - They came to Jericho. And as he was leaving Jericho with his disciples and a sizable crowd, Bartimaeus, a blind man, the son of Timaeus, sat by the roadside begging. On hearing that it was Jesus of Nazareth, he began to cry out and say, "Jesus, son of David, have pity on me." And many rebuked him, telling him to be silent. But he kept calling out all the more, "Son of David, have pity on me." Jesus stopped and said, "Call him." So they called the blind man, saying to him, "Take courage; get up, he is calling you." He threw aside his cloak, sprang up, and came to Jesus. Jesus said to him in reply, "What do you want me to do for you?" The blind man replied to him, "Master, I want to see." Jesus told him, "Go your way; your faith has saved you." Immediately he received his sight and followed him on the way.

Sight vs. Insight [Homily]—In Mark's Gospel today, blind Bartimaeus begs for his sight and is healed instantly and completely by Jesus's word. But interestingly enough, two chapters earlier another nameless blind man is healed, but initially he is only given his physical sight. Bartimaeus is immediately given his eyesight, but more importantly, insight. There seems to be a natural progression in Mark's Gospel from just physically having sight by Jesus's touch to having insight by Jesus's word.

EPILOGUE

Scripture contains a number of stories about healing the blind. Blindness was very common in biblical times. In contrast, starting in the 18th century until now, there have been very rare occasions when modern medicine has restored sight to someone blind since early childhood. And in all cases, there were similar complications, but only now are we starting to realize what was happening.

You may have heard the story of Michael May. When he was a baby he totally lost his sight through a freak explosion. At age 46, May had his sight restored by a rare and miraculous medical procedure. He is one of only a few who have had their sight restored after a lifetime of blindness; he is also the only person whose experience has been thoroughly studied. The medical results of that neurological study were published the summer of 2003.

It turns out even though the operation fully restored his visual capabilities, after years his brain still could not completely interpret and understand those signals. May still saw the world like an abstract painting. He couldn't recognize objects in three dimensions, make sense of complex landscapes, recognize faces, or interpret facial expressions. He struggled with nearness and distance, such as why one couldn't touch trees in the distance. He could catch a ball, but he couldn't recognize his wife's face. He could tell a cube is a cube only if it were moving. He recognized colors perfectly, but he often couldn't distinguish the shadows from the trees. Basically May had physical sight, but lacked the learned mental wiring for insight.

So what relevance does this study have when we hear Jesus say to Bartimaeus, "What do you want me to do for you?" If viewed only superficially, the question is almost insulting. The man is obviously blind, he wants to see! But if we go deeper, Jesus was not being insulting. He was calling Bartimaeus to conversion—asking him if he wanted the insight of God's love for him. In asking the question, Jesus is essentially confirming to Bartimaeus, and by extension to all of us, we have freedom to choose. Bartimaeus gets the point. And how do we know he gets the point? Because in answering the call of Jesus, Bartimaeus not only emphatically says, "Master, I want to see!" but he "throws aside his cloak." This is a big deal! For a beggar, the cloak is his bed by night and his way of collecting coins by day. The beggar throws aside what little security he has. Clearly he is asking for insight, not just eyesight. When he is cured and can see, he chooses to go with Jesus.

Bartimaeus gets full insight because he addresses Jesus as "Son of David," a title reserved for the Messiah, as was prophesized in the Old Testament. So unlike Michael May, who couldn't recognize his wife's face, Bartimaeus could recognize Jesus. We cannot see the spiritual world; we can only have insight into it. So for Bartimaeus the miracle is complete and is a much more wonderful miracle than we could possibly have imagined by superficial thinking! If only May could have had that. Bartimaeus had both sight of and insight into God's love. As with Bartimaeus, God gives us insight into His love in many ways.

HOSPITAL CHAPLAINCY – There is a better chance of understanding if the more natural approach to the logical development of moral theology is explained. The patients and their families will better understand non-judgmentalism, double-effect evaluation, and love. Teaching Centering Prayer often encourages people to not fear death, especially when I describe our research showing correlation between NDE and SCE. I taught Centering Prayer to health professionals at M.D. Anderson Cancer Center, the largest in the world. I also taught it directly to patients in their rooms via closed-circuit TVs at Methodist Hospital.

PRISON MINISTRY – In 1988 Fred Eckart, Kimball Kehoe's and my predecessor Coordinator for the Houston chapter of COL, taught Centering Prayer in prisons. He authored a brochure[196] entitled *Locked Up and Free*. He did this to support COL's international prison ministry, which he founded and managed.

I have firsthand experience realizing how popular this ministry is. Prisoners have more need of unconscious unloading and forgiveness of others, especially of themselves, than the general population.[197] There is a higher rate of mental illness in prisons. Due to my wife's suffering, I can relate to those suffering from depression. They also have plenty of time alone to practice Centering Prayer. This is a very enriching ministry for many.

It is a ministry that has become enriching in my later life. I have been involved in Catholic ACTS retreats at parishes. ACTS in this context is an acronym standing for Adoration, Community, Theology, and Service. My brother John invited me to join in a Kolbe retreat, which is an ACTS retreat adapted for prisons. I serve in various capacities on several retreats at the Michael Unit, a maximum-security prison in Palestine, Texas. Sometimes the retreat is delayed due to an execution in the morning, which brings the reality of the situation starkly into focus.

On the bright side, I discovered the inmates already practice Centering Prayer at the Michael Unit. Their leader is lovingly referred to by fellow inmates as the Abbott. He is a blessed soul. I attend these retreats to serve the men, but in the end, they serve me immensely in my spiritual journey. I find God in the suffering and dignity of each of them.

I am struck with a sense of profound irony. I was originally self-imprisoned without love; I became liberated with love. It happened in a prison through the selfless love of so-called prisoners.

SEMINARIES' CURRICULUM traditionally has not included F&S courses. My journey to learn this was a bit circuitous. After being ordained a permanent Catholic deacon, I was asked by Fr. Donald Nesti to organize and co-teach a graduate course on F&S. He is founder and head of the Center for Faith and Culture (CFC) at the University of St. Thomas in Houston. Upon his retirement, the CFC now bears his name, Donald S. Nesti, CSSp, CFC. The F&S course is part of the curriculum for a master's degree in faith and culture, which is a subject first promoted by the Vatican II Council. Not surprisingly, I suggested organizing the topics in the same order and scope as chapters two through six in this book, except non-autobiographical in genre.

We had some clergy and seminarians sign up for the course. They never had training in F&S as part of their formation and degrees before ordination. I was asked to give presentations for the master's degree specifically in F&S at several seminaries including the Pontifical University, Regina Apostolorum, in Rome; the Seminario de San Carlos y San Ambrosio in Havana, Cuba; and closer to home, St. Mary's Seminary in Houston. None of the seminaries in Havana and Houston taught an F&S course to their seminarians studying for the priesthood. In fact, such a course is rarely taught at Catholic seminaries, even though God revealed Himself, not just in scripture and tradition, but also in nature. That information launched me into trying to understand this phenomenon better.

In 1990, out of 125 U.S. public and private universities surveyed, only 3 had courses on spirituality and health. By 2000 that number increased to 72 universities. This was a precursor movement to the more specific topic of my interest in F&S in seminaries.

Fortunately, more and more seminaries began adding F&S courses to their curricula. This is partly due to funding by the Templeton Foundation, which by 2018 had funded F&S courses in 31 Catholic seminaries. Doris Donnelly at John Carroll University had been one of the principal proponents of this movement. But overall, seminaries in some of the largest U.S. cities failed to incorporate F&S in their curricula.

The argument I often hear is the amount of curriculum time needed for philosophy and theology leaves no time for anything else. Additional challenges include the need for interdepartmental collaboration, interdisciplinary agreement on terminology, and multiple science disciplines. Often the failed attempt is to teach F&S strictly as a philosophy or history of science course, which includes relitigating of past conflicts. Sadly, that leaves out the recent exponential increase in scientific discoveries and major paradigm shifts in theories, both of which are leading to an asymptotic convergence of F&S.

A temporary solution has been to add F&S to ongoing education courses for clergy and lay ministers. I was asked to give F&S courses to permanent deacons at six different dioceses worldwide from South Africa to Cuba. Priests are increasingly interested in attending.

This lengthy background assessment is important because it helped guide my journey to serve others. If clergy and lay ministers are not trained in F&S, they will not see its application to existing or even new ministries.

CONFERENCES & RESEARCH – Meeting with God

> *"The first gulp from the glass of natural sciences will turn you into an atheist, but at the bottom of the glass God is waiting for you."*
> WERNER HEISENBERG, Physicist

I got involved in numerous conferences relevant to my faith and science journey. To my shock, there is little or no cross-fertilization between the

EPILOGUE

general categories of these conferences. There is a clear, crying need for them to communicate with each other, but academia is very siloed, isolated, and not often open to it. The following is a list of some available, relevant resources but certainly not all. These are the ones in which I had some involvement. The titles of the categories are my general descriptions and within each category conferences are listed in the chronological order they were founded. Due to an observed need of cross-fertilization, Kimball Kehoe and I co-founded the non-profit Contemplative Network as a vehicle to bridge the gap.

FAITH & SCIENCE CONFERENCES consist of two major categories, theistic and non-theistic. Numerous theistic conferences are sponsored by the Pontifical Academy of Sciences (PAS). The non-theistic conference is sponsored by the Mind and Life (M&L) Institute.

- PAS was founded in 1936 by the Catholic Church and is dedicated to interdisciplinary, interfaith science. Its president is appointed by the pope. It holds conferences around the world. I attended one on palliative care held in the Texas Medical Center (TMC).

- M&L was co-founded in 1991 by the Dalai Lama Tenzin Gyatso, primarily for and by Buddhists. It is dedicated to interdisciplinary science with special emphasis on neuroscience. Its leader, the Dalai Lama, invited Fr. Keating with the intent to broaden M&L's faith diversity. At his request, I was Fr. Keating's advance-man to assess the legitimacy of the science. Their science is sound and ahead of its time. It shows the healing benefits of non-theistic meditation mainly by research on Tibetan Buddhist monks.

MEDICINE & RELIGION CONFERENCES fall into two general categories, national and international. National includes the George Washington Institute for Spirituality & Health (GWISH) and the Institute for Spirituality and Health (ISH). International includes the Conference on Medicine & Religion (CMR) and the European Conference on Religion, Spirituality & Health (ECRSH). The academic community surprisingly has only recently rediscovered the centuries-old healing benefits of faith, liturgy, and prayer, which were abandoned about 200 years ago. The following conferences disseminate that research.

- ISH was founded in 1955 by the Methodist Church in the TMC. Its original name was Institute for Religion and Health. It is the oldest such organization in the U.S. dedicated to interfaith and interdisciplinary science. It was the first to train hospital chaplains in the U.S. I presented at its annual Psychotherapy and Faith conference, which has been in existence since 1995. ISH is led by Rev. John Graham, M.D., D.Min. I am retired vice chairman and currently on the faculty.

- GWISH was founded in 2001 by George Washington University. It is dedicated to interfaith and interdisciplinary science and is led by Christina Puchalski, M.D. I attended one conference.

- ECRSH was founded in 2008 by the Research Institute for Spirituality & Health and is dedicated to interfaith and interdisciplinary science. I have presented at its biennial conferences, which have numerous, primarily European, university sponsors.

- CMR was founded in 2012 by the University of Chicago (UOC) and is dedicated to interfaith and interdisciplinary science. Co-sponsors with UOC include: Harvard University, St. Louis University, Baylor University, Loma Linda University, Notre Dame, Ohio State University, Oregon State University, Duke University, and ISH. While on the ISH board and after giving presentations at several conferences, I approached Harvard and UOC with the idea of holding the conference, co-sponsored by ISH, in the TMC. They agreed; the conference was held there for two consecutive years.

SPIRITUAL & SCIENCE CONFERENCES listed are interdenominational theist and non-theist, based on spiritual experiences and interdisciplinary science. They include the Scientific & Medical Network (SMN) and the Institute of Noetic Sciences (IONS). To my knowledge, I am the only Catholic clergy to give a presentation sponsored by both organizations.

EPILOGUE

- SMN was founded in 1973 by academically accomplished individuals from broad backgrounds, many of whom had spiritual experiences. They seek to engage science in a better understanding of those experiences. The program director is David Lorimer. In 2017 SMN founded the Galileo Commission (GC), which is dedicated to developing an interdisciplinary network for research projects. Its leaders are David Lorimer and Harald Walach.

- IONS was founded in 1973 by Edgar Mitchell, the sixth astronaut to walk on the moon. While on the moon he had a profound experience, which led him to create IONS. It is dedicated to studying spiritual experiences through valid science. Its CEO is Claire Lachance.

CONTEMPLATIVE PRAYER CONFERENCES listed are interdenominational Christian, dedicated to worldwide, religious, and spiritual Christian contemplative prayer. Their organizers fall into two categories. The larger consists of the World Community for Christian Meditation (WCCM) and Contemplative Outreach Ltd. (COL). The smaller consists of the Center for Action and Contemplation (CAC) and Contemplative Network (CN).

- WCCM was founded in 1975 by Catholic Benedictine monk Fr. John Main and is led by Benedictine monk Fr. Laurence Freeman[198] using a prayer methodology similar to Centering Prayer. It normally has annual conferences. I attended a recent one at the University of St. Thomas where I am adjunct professor.

- COL was founded in 1986 by Catholic Trappists Fr. Basil Pennington, Fr. William Meninger, and Fr. Thomas Keating. It has annual conferences and was led by Fr. Keating until his passing in 2018. In 2004, Kimball Kehoe, a former Jesuit, and I became co-coordinators of COL's Houston chapter. We are both commissioned presenters of Centering Prayer. I attend many COL conferences.

- CAC was founded in 1986 by Catholic Franciscans. It is led by Fr. Richard Rohr. I attended a recent conference in Santa Fe, New Mexico.

- CN was founded in 2008 by Kimball Kehoe and me. It is virtual and does not have annual conferences. At the time, COL was only interested in teaching Centering Prayer, even though Fr. Keating's personal interests included scientific research and interfaith dialogue. Houston is the most religiously diverse city in the U.S. and includes the TMC, the largest medical center in the world. When I met with Fr. Keating, he encouraged us to form the non-profit CN. It is dedicated to teaching Centering Prayer and promoting both research and interreligious dialogue. It is primarily interdenominational Christian with an interfaith board with minority representation by non-Christian contemplatives. Kimball Kehoe is chairman of the board and I am president. It is through this organization cross-fertilization between the other conferences was implemented.

ALTERED CONSCIOUSNESS CONFERENCES are in two major categories: altered states and disordered states of consciousness. The altered states of consciousness conferences are sponsored by The Science of Consciousness (TSC) and International Association for Near-Death Studies (IANS). The disordered states of consciousness conference is sponsored by Brain Death and Disorders of Consciousness (BDDC). These conferences disseminate the research on the cutting edge of science, primarily neuroscience.

- TSC was founded in 1994 by the University of Tucson and is dedicated to worldwide interfaith, interdisciplinary research on consciousness. It is the largest and longest-running interdisciplinary conference on consciousness. Key areas of interest include the philosophy of mind, cognitive science, neuroscience, anthropology, biology, physics, computer science, and mathematics. I presented at its 2019 conference and had the opportunity to meet Roger Penrose[199] and Stuart Hameroff M.D., the conference organizers. Though others had proposed a relationship between consciousness and quantum mechanics,[200] they are collaborating to combine Penrose's quantum theory and Hameroff's microtubules theory to explain consciousness. Honestly, I only understood about a half percent of what they were saying. I mention it here

EPILOGUE

to show the intensity of the scientific research, with which those of faith are not keeping up.

- IANS was founded in 1981 and is dedicated to worldwide interfaith and interdisciplinary research on near-death experiences. It is led by Yvonne Kason, M.D. This is on my radar screen for future attendance.
- BDDC was founded in 2003 by the Institute of Neurology and Neurosurgery in Cuba and is dedicated to interdisciplinary science on death and disorders of consciousness. It is led by Calixto Machado, M.D., Ph.D., who conducts a biannual international conference. Calixto heard me give a presentation on prayer and neuroscience at a conference I organized at the Catholic seminary in Havana. We became friends. He invited me to organize an entire day at his 2015 BDDC conference dedicated only to research on faith and science. The result of that effort is an example of the power of integrating faith and science at a conference, which for years was only atheistic. It was the first time since the revolution religion had been presented at a public university in Cuba. It is best described by the following excerpts from an article[201] in the *Texas Catholic Herald*.

> CUBA — On Dec. 9, 2015 a historic event took place in Cuba when religion was presented to the University of Havana, via the School of Medical Science, for the first time in over 50 years since the revolution. It was also historic because the Archdiocese of Havana and the University of Havana jointly sponsored the event with Jaime Cardinal Ortega of Havana present at the opening session. Calixto Machado, M.D., Ph.D. of the Institute of Neurology and Neurosurgery, of the University of Havana's School of Medical Science ... was interested in the neurotheology and neuroscience of prayer since he was himself an internationally respected neuroscientist specializing in brain death and near-death. As president of the International Symposium on Brain Death & Disorders of Consciousness, he invited Deacon Hesse to organize a one-day session on spirituality and health at his planned VII symposium on Dec. 8 to 11, 2015 at the TRYP Habana

Libre Hotel. Two world-renowned keynote-prerecorded speakers lovingly offered their time: Harold Koenig, M.D., Duke University Medical Center, is one of the world's experts on medicine and religion and editor of "The Handbook of Religion and Health," and Ken Pargament, Ph.D., Bowling Green State University and adjunct professor The Menninger Department of Psychiatry, is one of the world's experts on psychotherapy and spirituality and Editor-In-Chief of the 2013 two-volume "APA Handbook of Psychology, Religion and Spirituality" ... plus a professor from the Pontifical University, Regina Apostolorum.

The Spirituality and Health Session covered the large and growing body of scientific research that shows that belief in a higher power, religion and spirituality all promote healing. It started with general medical research ... It concluded with teaching Centering Prayer, a form of contemplative prayer, to both believers and atheists. Some participants immediately testified to its potential neuroscientific benefits.

FAITH & SCIENCE RESEARCH is of two types, both of which are valid and show healing effects. One shows the healing benefits of non-theistic meditation mainly with research on Tibetan Buddhist monks. The other shows the healing benefits of theistic faith, liturgical attendance, and frequent prayer, primarily discursive, not contemplative.

The obvious question: If both heal, why not get "double bang for the research buck" by conducting research on theistic contemplation? I started by promoting that philosophy at the disparate conferences just described. The following research projects are examples of what resulted from the power of God's hand in combining F&S.

- NDE & SCE research is now conducted comparing the two transcendent states as described. It sprang from my friendship with neuroscientist Calixto Machado and my contemplative experience and interest as a deacon and scientist. He has access to the NDE subjects, I have access to SCE subjects.

EPILOGUE

The research shows scientific correlations between remembering a near-death experience (NDE) and spiritual contemplative experience (SCE) a.k.a. mystical experience. It is these results I presented at the 2019 TSC conference in Switzerland where I met other researchers. For a more detailed overview, the following is a draft abstract of presentations and a soon-to-be-published paper on the results of that study.

> With age, fear of dying can be detrimental to spirituality and health. Faith's wisdom literature over centuries describes the normal peace of an NDE and separately a mystical experience not associated with death, which we call a spiritual contemplative experience (SCE). While teaching contemplative Centering Prayer (CP), contemporary first-person SCEs were reported as relived NDEs, which provided insight and incentive for this study. Neuroscience has never made a direct comparison of NDE and SCE even though the Greyson Scale confirms four similar attributes: *cognitive timelessness, affective peace, transcendent oneness,* and *paranormal out-of-body.*
>
> Separate NDE and SCE subjects were asked to maintain a resting state and then remember their experience. We recorded and processed neural and anatomical correlates using quantitative electroencephalography (EEG) tomography (QEEGt), continuous EEG (CEEG), and continuous anatomical assessment (CAA).
>
> QEEGt and CEEG showed neural correlations between NDE and SCE across broad frequency ranges. There was higher neural activity for SCE consistent with fact subjects were not dying. CAA measuring heart rate (HR) and HR variability (HRV) showed emotional correlation between SCE and those reporting pleasant NDEs. There was no correlation with those reporting anxious NDEs. Some subjects changed their Greyson Scale score, perhaps explainable by conflicting NDE memories between painful dying and pain-free, out-of-body experience.
>
> Our preliminary research shows QEEGt and CEEG were the best tools for such a study and the number of subjects should be

increased for more statistically significant results. Meanwhile CP should be taught to willing patients in palliative and hospice care, since it can lead to an SCE thus lessening fear of death and NDE. CP is a silent form of prayer without dogma thus applicable to the approximate 87% of the population believing in God and an afterlife.

- PTSD research was inspired by my experience with practitioners of Centering Prayer, especially the example in an earlier chapter. I met the head chaplain, Rev. Steven Smith, Ph.D., a Baptist minister, at the VA hospital in Houston, the second largest in the US; he invited me to teach Centering Prayer to all his chaplains. Because of their positive experience and his need for a dissertation topic for his second doctorate, we agreed to collaborate. He prepared a research proposal explaining I would teach Centering Prayer to VA patient volunteers suffering from PTSD. He would evaluate the results in collaboration with the VA psychiatrists.

    We anticipated participating in Centering Prayer would reduce some PTSD symptoms among members of the study group and generally promote mental and spiritual healing. Reducing these symptoms would imply Centering Prayer could be used as one treatment modality for those veterans suffering with PTSD. Because it is based on religion, the VA would allow it only for volunteers. Moreover, successful findings would have implications for a wider application of Centering Prayer to non-VA PTSD patients with a possible new theistic-based therapy. That therapy would be complementary to existing non-theistic Mindfulness-Based Stress Reduction (MBSR), Dialectical Behavior Therapy (DB), Mindfulness-Based Cognitive Therapy (MBCT), and Acceptance and Commitment Therapy (ACT).[202] Unfortunately, Rev. Smith was transferred and the proposal languished due to a lack of another VA employee to implement it.

INTERRELIGIOUS DIALOGUE – God within everyone

"Dialogue between faith and science also belongs to the work of evangelization."
POPE FRANCIS

Many interreligious functions start with a prayer by one of the participants. Inevitably words like Allah, God, Buddha, etc., though sincere, would get in the way of true dialogue. Because essentially all faiths have a contemplative tradition, and most theistic faiths, certainly the Abrahamic faiths, believe God dwells within everyone, there is a better way to start interreligious dialogue. I have had some success in getting pre-agreement from participants to start in silent prayer because, in silence, there is no dogma. This almost invariably sets the tone for a more meaningful verbal dialogue to follow.

A good example was a dialogue at the University of St. Thomas. I called my co-panelist and friend, Zen Master Tsan Miao, to plot our approach. When the meeting began, we said we were going to practice contemplation in silence for three minutes. I hit the gong and we began. Since they had not been trained on how to handle their thoughts, the audience was restless. At the end, I hit the gong again. The Zen Master and I explained what we were each doing during the contemplation. It worked wonderfully and the people were ready to listen.

The photo at the beginning of this Epilogue symbolically captures the spirit of that dialogue approach. When I took the picture, the first monk looked at me in peace and silence.

There is an additional opportunity to discuss how God reveals himself through nature without having to immediately discuss sacred texts or traditions. My interest in F&S has provided me with that opportunity on numerous occasions; other faiths have similar interests.[203] I have experienced the success of this approach at numerous conferences.

Acknowledgments

To the Holy Spirit for inspiring and encouraging me, with synchronicity through so many people. To my beloved wife, Linda, and my children, Kristin Cavazos and Chris Hesse, for teaching me how to love. To my brother, Paul Hesse, whose editorial comments kept my journey real and honest. To my brother, John Hesse, who kept me connected with nature through our many trips to the country. To Fr. Tom for allowing me to forgive. To Fr. (Msgr.) Joe Grosthwait and Fr. Daokim Nguyen for welcoming and encouraging me in my return to the Church. To Carolyn Rogas and Deacon Pat Camerino, theologian and Ph.D. biochemist, for their helpful advice. To Conor McCarthy for early editing. But most especially to Jan Masterson for encouraging and helping me with professional editorial advice. Without her help, this book would not have been possible.

About the Author

Figure 40 Robert J. Hesse, Ph.D. – Photo

Robert Hesse, Ph.D., is a permanent Catholic deacon. He is Co-founder and President of Contemplative Network, dedicated to interdenominational Christian contemplative prayer teaching, scientific research and interfaith dialogue. He was inspired by Trappist monk Fr. Thomas Merton, while on retreat at Gethsemani Trappist monastery. Later he was appointed by Trappist Fr. Thomas Keating, Commissioned Presenter of Contemplative Outreach Ltd. (COL) and Keating's emissary to the first COL dialogue with the Mind & Life Institute, in response to an invitation by The Dalai Lama to Keating. He is retired Vice Chairman and current faculty member of the interfaith Institute for Spirituality and Health, the oldest such organization in the U.S.A. located in the Texas Medical Center, the largest in the world. He is also Adjunct Professor at the University of St. Thomas and faculty member of the Magis Center and Spiritual Direction Institute at the Emmaus Spirituality Center. He has given numerous international and interfaith presentations, retreats, and courses on contemplative prayer and Faith and Science, having degrees in both.

Contemplative Network: www.contemplative.net
Presentations: www.youtube.com/ContemplativeNetwork

Robert Hesse is available for interviews, presentations and seminars. Contact him at rjh@contemplative.net.

ABOUT THE EDITOR

Jan Masterson is a sassy senior woman, widow, mother, grandmother, nana, friend, confidant. She has an English degree with a minor in social science, but more importantly, she is a student of life with an open mind and an open heart. She has an insatiable curiosity about the world and is always listening, learning, growing, sharing, reading, and writing.

Jan has edited books on faith and science, travel stories and faith and culture. She writes a quarterly column, *The Garrulous Grandma*, and is the interviewer, feature writer and copy editor for the *Eagle Vista* newsletter. She facilitates a memoir writing seminar. She is currently writing her memoirs. She is Managing Editor and copywriter for the online newsletter, *News and Views from the Contemplative Network* and Director of Communications for the *Contemplative Network* organization. You can contact Jan at: editor@contemplative.net.

Glossary

The following are definitions generally accepted by students of faith[204] and science. In some cases where there are multiple definitions, I have chosen the ones applicable to this book. I have taken the liberty of abbreviating them in my own words for easier access by the reader.

Faith

- Faith – Strong intuitive belief without proof
- Fundamentalism – strict literal interpretation of doctrines or texts
- Miracle – Extraordinary, unexpected event providing a message
- Epistemology – How we know things
- Ontology – What things exist
- Metaphysics – Epistemology & Ontology
- Conscience – Internal moral guide
- Consciousness – Comprehension of external reality
- Meditation – Discursive prayer using the imagination
- Contemplation – Silent gift of union with God
- Centering Prayer – Method of reducing obstacles to contemplation
- Mysticism – Synonym for contemplation
- *Apophatic* – Resting in God beyond concepts
- *Kataphatic* – Engaging the imagination to pray
- Ecstasy – Temporary full or partial out-of-body union with the Divine
- Divine Therapy – Paradigm of spiritual journey as psychotherapy
- Divine Union – Experience or transformation in union with God

- Transformation – Conviction of ongoing abiding presence of God
- *Lectio Divina* – Reading Divine in the words of scripture

Science

- Science – Systematic study of physical and natural world
- Reason – Power of brain to form judgment by logic
- Scientism – Excessive belief in the power of scientific knowledge
- Logic – Codification of principles of proof
- Principles – Fundamental proposition for systematizing
- Proposition – Assertion that expresses opinion
- Theories – System supposition to explain observations
- Supposition – An uncertain belief
- Postulates – Assumed truth as basis for reasoning
- Assumptions – Accepted as truth without proof
- Axioms – Proposition regarded as self-evident
- Cosmology – Study of Universe's origin

Figures

Cover Photo: Penguins, Half Moon Island, Antarctic – Photo. xi

Figure 2 Michelangelo's Sistine Chapel, Vatican – Painting/Photo. xxi

Figure 3 My Young Family, Norway – Photo. 1

Figure 4 Mandelbrot Fractal Mathematics of Chaos – Image 11

Figure 5 Light Echo V838 – Photo. 23

Figure 6 Solar System Relative Sizes – Image 27

Figure 7 Nearby Stars' Relative Sizes – Image 28

Figure 8 Birth & Death of Stars – Photos 29

Figure 9 Milky Way Galaxy – Image. 29

Figure 10 Galaxies Ultra-Deep Field – Photo. 30

Figure 11 Gravity in General Relativity – Image 35

Figure 12 Light Bent in General Relativity – Image 36

Figure 13 Einstein's Space-Time Thought Experiment – Image 39

Figure 14 Wormhole Theory in Space-Time – Image 40

Figure 15 Visible Spectrum – Image 41

Figure 16 Electromagnetic Spectrum – Image. 42

Figure 17 Meeting of Fr. Lemaitre & Einstein – Photo 46

Figure 18 Expanding Universe Creation Process – Image. 48

Figure 19 DNA Helical Molecule Viewed Axially – Image 53

Figure 20 Hadron Collider Map and Tunnel, Switzerland – Photos. 55

Figure 21 Hydrogen and Complex Atomic Models – Images 57

Figure 22 Hydrogen Electron Probability Density – Image 59

Figure 23 Mandelbrot Fractals from Chaos – Images 61

Figure 24 DNA Molecule, Watson & Crick – Photo 68
Figure 25 Evolution Overview – Image 72
Figure 26 Primate Evolution – Image................................ 73
Figure 27 Abstract Conscious Brain Art – Image..................... 79
Figure 28 Brain Map of Functions – Image........................... 81
Figure 29 Universe Network & Brain Circuitry – Images.............. 82
Figure 30 Multi-Stable Stimuli: Cup or People? – Image............. 85
Figure 31 Phineas Gage Injury – Photo & Image 91
Figure 32 Free-Will Model – Diagram................................ 103
Figure 33 Abstract Mystical Brain Art – Image 113
Figure 34 Jewish-Christian Contemplative Contemporaries – Table ... 116
Figure 35 Historical Christian Mystics – Table 117
Figure 36 Prayer as Relationship Analogies – Table................. 120
Figure 37 Centering Prayer Guidelines – List....................... 123
Figure 38 Transcendent Events - Table.............................. 132
Figure 39 Monk Theophane at Trappist Monastery, Colorado – Photo . 143
Figure 39 Mahar Aung Mye Bon San Monastery, Myanmar – Photo .. 149
Figure 40 Robert J. Hesse, Ph.D. – Photo 169

Timeline

The purpose of this timeline is to give the reader some perspective on the explosion of scientific discoveries over the last 120 years relative to previous years and notable faith events. The main source is the *The Timetables of History*.[205] It is not meant to be totally comprehensive or equally balanced between faiths. It does not include details, only signposts of titles for the reader to explore deeper if so desired.

B.C.	FAITH	SCIENCE
5000–4000		Egyptian Calendar 360 Days/12 Mo/30 Days/Mo
4000–3000		Egypt Alloys, Sumerian Gold & Silver
		1st numerals
3000–2000	Egypt: Pharaoh God King	1st Systematic Astronomy
		1st Iron; Egypt Calendar 365 Days
2000–1000	Stonehenge Worship	Geometry, Surgery, Mercury, Water Clock, Pythagorean Theorem, Polar Axis, Iron Age
	Moses 10 Commandments	
1000–500	Paganism, Pantheism, Brahminism, Atmanism, Elijah, Amos, Hosea, Isaiah, Zoroastrianism, Buddha, Old Testament Tradition	Fabric Dyes, Iron, India Medical Training, Spoked Wheels, Canals & Tunnels, Soldering, Predicted Solar Eclipse, Veins & Arteries
500–400	Confucius, Vardhamana, Socrates, Torah, Plato	Hippocrates, Surgery, Astronomy
400–300	Pentateuch, Aristotle	Euclidian Geometry
300–200	Septuagint	Mathematics, Eratosthenes
		Earth Around Sun
200–100	Maccabaeus, Book of Daniel, Rosetta Stone	Gears, Water Wheel, First Globe
100–0	Jesus's Birth (4 B.C.)	Asclepiades Physician Nature Healing
A.D.	FAITH	SCIENCE
0–100	Christ's Life, Paul's Ministry, Gentile Christians, Buddhism to China	Roman Soap
100–200	St. Ignatius of Antioch Letters, Docetism, Mayan Monuments	Ptolemy Maps, Greek Medicine, Pi Calculated

FAITH and SCIENCE

200–300	Christian Persecution, India Sanskrit, St. Anthony Monasticism	1st Algebra Book, Compass, Mechanical Machines
300–400	Christian Persecution Ends, China Buddhism Grows, 5M Christians, Teotihuacan, *Lectio Divina*	Books Replace Scrolls
400–500	St. Augustine Hippo, Pelagianism, Shinto Shrines, NT in Greek	Alchemy, Power & Roots of Numbers
500–600	St. Benedict Monasticism, Oldest Pagoda China, St. Sophia Basilica, Muhammad Born, Buddhism Japan	Black Plague Killed half of Europe, Decimals, Book Printing in China, Smallpox
600–700	Muhammad Dies	China Porcelain
700–800	Germany Evangelized, Islam Splits	Acids, Wind Organs
800–900	Angkor in Cambodia, Rheims Cathedral	Persian Algebra
900–1000	Yucatan Mayans, First Canonization of Saints	Paper Manufacture, Peru Potatoes & Corn, Gunpowder
1000–1100	Strasbourg, Chartres, & Wurzburg Cathedrals, East-West Schism, Muslims Capture Jerusalem	Gothic Structural Design
1100–1200	Celibate Priesthood, Rules for Canonization, Carmelites, Jerusalem Falls in Crusades	Decline of Islamic Science, Italy Seat of Medicine, University of Paris Founded
1200–1300	East-West Schism, Transubstantiation, Chartres Cathedral, Inquisition	Fr. Roger Bacon, Sorbonne University, Glass Mirrors
1300–1400	Dante's Divine Comedy, Milan Cathedral, German Jews Persecuted	Sawmill, Weaving, Mechanical Clock, Great Wall
1400–1500	Pope Schism Ends, *Imitatio Christi*, Blue Mosque, Sikhism, Indulgences	Encyclopedia, Insane Hospital, Printing Press
1500–1600	Sistine Chapel, Luther, Inquisition, Seminary System, Jesuits, Mystical Saints	Da Vinci, Magellan, Surgery Manual, Magnetic Pole, Copernicus, Decimals
1600–1700	Passion Play, Protestant Spinoffs, Trappists, American Bible, Salem Trials	Kepler, Galileo, Telescopes, Descartes, Newton, Calculus, Moon Map
1700–1800	Jesuits Dissolved, Kant Reason Alone, Lives of the Saints, Secularism, Inquisition Ends, 1st US Bishop	Electrical Conductivity & Capacity, Fahrenheit, Halley's Comet, Hydrodynamics, Dalton, Steam Engine, Chemistry, Hypnosis, Electricity, Industrial Revolution

TIMELINE

1800–1900	Jesuits Reestablished, Mormons, US Anti-Catholicism, Immaculate Conception, Lourdes, Social Justice	Electromagnetism, Submarine, Urea Synthesis, Atom, Ohm's Law, Darwin, Kelvin, Neanderthal Skull, Telephone, Crude Oil, Light Speed, Transatlantic Cable, Periodic Table, Bacteria, Genes, Pasteurization, Camera, Edison, Inheritance
1900–2020	Pope Condemns Modernism, Pastoral Reforms, Canon Law, Pope Condemns Communism & Nazism, Encyclicals: *Humani Generis, Mystici Corporis, Divino Afflante Spiritu, Mater et Magistra, Pacem in Terris,* & *Humanae Vitae, Laudato Si* Teilhard de Chardin, Vatican II, Mother Teresa, Charismatic Renewal, Catholic-Lutheran-Methodist Justification Agreement, Neurotheology	THEORIES etc.: Gravitational, Quantum, Special Relativity, General Relativity, Equivalence, Wormhole, Quantum Entanglement, Chaos, Evolution, Morphogenesis, Uncertainty, Unified Forces, Anthropic, Pangea, String, Membrane, P-Brane, BVG DISCOVERIES: Gravity, 4 Forces, Milky Way Dimensions, Galaxies, Black Holes, Expanding Universe, Magnitude & Age, Pangea, Cambrian Explosion, Subatomic, Molecules, Amino Acids, RNA & DNA, Penicillin, Viruses, Neuroscience, Neuroplasticity, Brain Functions & Dualities, Unconscious Learning, Faith-Liturgy-Prayer Healing, Computer Learning, Altered Consciousness, NDE, SCE, Confirmation Bias INNOVATIONS: Automobile, Airplane, Television, Motion Pictures, Organ Transplants, Computers, Particle Accelerators, Hydrogen & Atomic Bombs, Artificial Hearts, Men on Moon, Mars Landing, Communication Satellites, Internet, Hubble Telescope

Bibliography

Alexander, Eben. *Proof of Heaven: A Neurosurgeon's Journey into the Afterlife.* (New York: Simon & Schuster, 2012).

Aquinas, Thomas. *The Summa Theologica*, trans. Fathers of the English Dominican Province. (London: Burns, 1947).

Ashley, Benedict, and Deely, John. *How Science Enriches Theology.* (South Bend, IN: St. Augustine's Press, 2012).

Ayala, Francisco J. *Darwin's Gift to Science and Religion.* (Washington, DC: Joseph Henry / National Academies Press, 2007).

Baer, Ruth A., ed. *Mindfulness-Based Treatment Approaches.* (San Diego: Academic Press, 2006).

Baldwin, Philip, Boelens, Peter, et al. "Neural Correlates of Healing Prayers, Depression and Traumatic Memories: A Preliminary Study." (*Complementary Therapies in Medicine* 27, 2016).

Bao, Ning, et al. *Traversable Wormholes as Quantum Channels: Exploring CFT Entanglement Structure and Channel in Holography.* (University of California–Berkeley: arXiv:180.05963v2 [hep-th], November 12, 2018).

Barbour, Ian *Neuroscience, Artificial Intelligence, and Human Nature: Theological and Philosophical Reflections—Neuroscience and the Person.* (Vatican City: Vatican Observatory Publications, 2002).

———. *Religion and Science: Historical and Contemporary Issues.* (San Francisco: HarperCollins, 1990).

———. *When Science Meets Religion: Enemies, Strangers or Partners?* (New York: HarperCollins, 2000).

Barnhill, D., and Gottlieb, R., eds. *Catholicism and Deep Ecology.* (Albany: SUNY Press, 2001).

Barks, Coleman, trans. *The Essential Rumi.* (San Francisco: Harper, 1995).

Barron, Robert. *Letter to a Suffering Church.* (Park Ridge, IL: Word on Fire, 2019).

Beauchamp, Tom, and Childress, James. *Principles of Biomedical Ethics.* (New York: Oxford University Press, 1997).

Beauregard, Mario, Courtemanche, Jerome, and Paquette, Vincent. "Brain Activity in Near-Death Experiences during a Meditative State." (*Resuscitation Journal* 80, 2009: 1006–1010).

Blanke, Olaf, Faivre, Nathan, and Dieguez, Sebastian. "Leaving Body and Life Behind: Out-of-Body and Near-Death Experience." (In *The Neurology of Consciousness*, 2nd ed., 2015, 323–348).

Boelens, Peter, and Boelens, Eleanor. *Released to Soar: A Medical Study Shows the Power of Healing Prayer.* (Pella, IA: Write Place, 2010).

Bonsor, Jack A. *Athens and Jerusalem: The Role of Philosophy in Theology.* (New York: Paulist, 1993).

Boslough, John. *Stephen Hawking's Universe.* (New York: Quill / William Morrow, 1985).

Bradley, Gerard, and DeMarco, Don, eds. *Science and Faith.* (South Bend, IN: St. Augustine's Press, 2001).

Bronowski, J. *The Ascent of Man.* (Boston: Little, Brown and Company, 1973).

Bruteau, Beatrice. *God's Ecstasy: The Creation of a Self-Creating World.* (New York: Crossroad, 1997).

Buckley, William. *Nearer My God.* (New York: Harcourt Brace & Co., 1997).

Cairns-Smith, A. G. *Evolving the Mind: On the Nature of Matter and the Origin of Consciousness.* (New York: Cambridge University Press, 1996).

Cannato, Judy. *Radical Amazement: Contemplative Lessons from Black Holes, Supernovas, and Other Wonders of the Universe.* (Notre Dame, IN: Sorin Books, 2006).

Cassian, John. *The Conferences.* (New York: Newman Press, 1997).

Catechism of the Catholic Church. (Washington, DC: US Conference of Catholic Bishops, 2000).

Chittister, Joan. *The Rule of Benedict.* (New York: Crossroad, 2003).

Chodron, Thubten. *Buddhism for Beginners.* (Ithaca, NY: Snow Lion, 2001).

CIA. *Fertility Data by Country.* (https://www.cia.gov/the-world-factbook/field /total-fertility-rate/country-comparison).

Clark, Kenneth. *Civilization.* (New York: Harper & Row, 1969).

Corbett, Lionel. *The Sacred Cauldron.* (Wilmette, IL: Chiaron Publications, 2011).

Coyne, George V., and Omizzolo, Alessandro. *Wayfarers in the Cosmos: The Human Quest for Meaning.* (New York: Crossroad, 2002).

BIBLIOGRAPHY

D'Aquili, Eugene, and Newberg, Andrew. *The Mystical Mind: Probing the Biology of Mystical Experience.* (Minneapolis: Fortress, 1999).

D'Arcy, Paula. *When People Grieve.* (New York: Crossroad, 2013).

Dalai Lama. *In My Own Words.* (New York: Hay House, 2008).

Darwin, Charles. *On the Origin of Species.* (New York: Random House, 1975).

Davidson, Richard. *The Emotional Life of Your Brain.* (London: Penguin, 2013).

Delio, Ilia. *Christ in Evolution.* (New York: Orbis, 2008).

———. *The Unbearable Wholeness of Being: God, Evolution, and the Power of Love.* (New York: Orbis, 2013).

De Mello, Anthony. *Taking Flight: A Book of Story Meditations.* (New York: Doubleday, 1990).

Diamond, Jared. *Guns, Germs, and Steel.* (New York: W. W. Norton & Company, 1999).

Douglas-Klotz, Neil, trans. *Prayers of the Cosmos.* (New York: HarperCollins, 1990).

Drees, Willem. *Religion, Science and Naturalism.* (Cambridge: Cambridge University Press, 1997).

Dupre, Louis, and Wiseman, James A., eds. *Light from Light: An Anthology of Christian Mysticism.* (New York: Paulist, 2001).

Eagleman, David. *Incognito.* (New York: Random House, 2011).

Eckart, Fred. *Locked Up and Free.* (Houston: Contemplative Network, 1988).

Eckhart, Meister. *Sermons and Treatises.* (London: Element Books, 1992).

Ecklund, Elaine. *Why Science and Faith Need Each Other.* (Grand Rapids: Brazos, 2020).

Edelson, Edward. *Gregor Mendel—and the Roots of Genetics.* (New York: Oxford University Press, 1999).

Ehman, J. W., et al. "Do Patients Want Physicians to Inquire about Their Spiritual or Religious Beliefs If They Become Gravely Ill?" (*Archives of Internal Medicine*, 1999).

Fins, Joseph. *Rights Come to Mind.* (New York: Cambridge University Press, 2015).

Flynn, Eileen. *Issues on Health Care Ethics.* (Upper Saddle River, NJ: Prentice-Hall, 1997).

Fraden, S., Epstein, I., and Ermentrout, B. "Testing Turing's Theory of Morphogenesis in Chemical Cells." (*Proceedings of the National Academy of Sciences*, March 25, 2014).

Francis (pope). *Laudato Si': On Care for Our Common Home.* (Vatican: Encyclical Letter, May 24, 2015).

Freeman, Laurence. *Jesus the Teacher Within.* (New York: Continuum, 2000).

Funk, Mary. *Thoughts Matter: The Practice of the Spiritual Life.* (New York: Continuum, 2002).

Galilei, Galileo. *The Collected Works of Galileo Galilei.* (Hastings, UK: Delphi Publishing, 2017).

Gamow, George. *One Two Three . . . Infinity.* (New York: Dover Publications, 1988).

Ganss, George, trans. *The Spiritual Exercises of Saint Ignatius.* (Chicago: Loyola Press, 1992).

Gleick, J. *Chaos: Making a New Science.* (New York: Penguin, 1988).

Goldin, Stan. "The Human Soul: Can It Survive in an Age of Neuroscience?" (Harvard Medical School, Cognitive Rhythms Collaborative, For the November 19, 2014 Cambridge Roundtable).

Goleman, Daniel, and Davidson, Richard. *Altered Traits: Science Reveals How Meditation Changes Your Mind, Brain, and Body.* (New York: Penguin Random House, 2017).

Goodenough, Ursula. *The Sacred Depths of Nature.* (New York: Oxford University Press, 1998).

Green, Arthur, and Barry Holtz. *Your Word Is Fire: The Hasidic Masters on Contemplative Prayer.* (Woodstock, VT: Jewish Lights, 2006).

Green, Michael. *Who Is This Jesus?* (Nashville: Thomas Nelson, 1992).

Greene, Brian. *The Fabric of the Cosmos.* (New York: Random House, 2004).

Gregory of Nyssa. *The Life of Moses.* (New York: Paulist, 1978).

Grun, Bernard. *The Timetables of History.* (New York: Simon & Schuster, 1991).

Gulen, Fethullah. *Key Concepts in the Practice of Sufism.* (Fairfax, VA: The Fountain, 1999).

Hackett, Conrad, and McClendon, David. *Christians Remain World's Largest Religious Group, but They Are Declining in Europe.* (Washington, DC: Pew Research Center, 2015).

Hahn, Scott. *A Father Who Keeps His Promises.* (Ann Arbor, MI: Servant Publications, 1998).

Haisch, Bernard. *The Purpose-Guided Universe.* (Franklin Lakes, NJ: New Page Books, 2010).

BIBLIOGRAPHY

Haught, J. F. *God after Darwin: A Theology of Evolution*. (Oxford: Westview Press, 2000).

Hawking, Stephen. *A Brief History of Time*. (New York: Bantam, 1988).

———. *Brief Answers to the Big Questions*. (New York: Bantam, 2018).

Hazen, Robert M. *Genesis: The Scientific Quest for Life's Origins*. (New York: Joseph Henry Press, 2005).

Hendra, Tony. *Father Joe*. (New York: Random House, 2005).

Henshaw, S., Singh, S., and Haas, T. "The Incidence of Abortion Worldwide." (*International Family Planning Perspectives* 25 Supplement, January 1999: S30–S38).

Hesse, Hermann. *Siddhartha*. (New York: Bantam, 1951).

Hewlett, Martinez J. *A God for Evolution*. (Pontifical University of the Holy Cross, Rome, March 1–2, 2001, Ninth Annual Conference, "God and Nature").

Hillis, Daniel. *The Pattern on the Stone: The Simple Ideas That Make Computers Work*. (New York: Basic Books, 1998).

Hoffman, Dominic M. *The Life Within: The Prayer of Union*. (New York: Sheed and Ward, 1966).

Holder, Rodney, and Mitton, Simon, eds. *Georges Lemaitre: Life, Science and Legacy*. (Berlin: Springer-Verlag, 2012).

Holy Bible. *The New American Bible*. (New York: Oxford University Press, 1990).

Howe, Mary. *Sitting with Sufis: A Christian Experience of Learning Sufism*. (Brewster, MA: Paraclete Press, 2005).

Inge, W. R. *Christian Mysticism*. (New York: Meridian Books, 1956).

James, William. *The Varieties of Religious Experience: A Study in Human Nature*. (1902; USA: Seven Treasures, 2009).

John Paul II. *Faith Can Never Conflict with Reason*. (Vatican: Pontifical Academy of Sciences, November 4, 1992).

———. *The Human Person Must Be the Beginning, Subject and Goal of All Scientific Research*. (Rome: Pontifical Academy of Sciences, November 9, 1994).

———. *Magisterium Is Concerned with Question of Evolution, for It Involves Conception of Man*. (Vatican: Pontifical Academy of Sciences, November 24, 1986).

———. *The Problems of Science Are the Problems of Man*. (Rome: European Physical Society, March 30, 1979).

———. *Science and Faith in the Search for Truth*. (Cologne: University Students, November 15, 1980).

———. *Science and Human Values.* (Vatican: Marcel Grossman Meeting on Relativistic Astrophysics, June 21, 1985).

———. *Science and Religion Can Renew Culture.* (Rome: Symposium Pontifical Academy of Sciences and the Pontifical Council for Culture, 1991).

———. *Science Serves Humanity Only When It Is Joined to Conscience.* (Padua: International Conference on Space Research, January 11, 1997).

———. *Scientists and God.* (Vatican: General Audience, July 17, 1985).

———. *A Thought on the Faith of the Scientist.* (Vatican: Pontifical Statement, July 17, 1985).

———. *The Value of Cosmology for Our Vision of Ourselves.* (Vatican: Vatican Observatory on the Subject: The Frontiers of Cosmology, July 6, 1985).

Johnston, William. *Mystical Theology: The Science of Love.* (New York: Orbis, 1995).

Johnston, William K., ed. *The Cloud of Unknowing.* (New York: Doubleday, 1973).

Kaku, Michio. *Hyperspace.* (New York: Anchor Books Doubleday, 1994).

Kant, Immanuel. *Religion within the Limits of Reason Alone.* (New York: Harper Torchbooks, 1960).

Kavanaugh, Kieran, and Larking, Erneste E., eds. *John of the Cross, Selected Writings.* (New York: Paulist, 1987).

Keating, Thomas. *Awakenings.* (New York: Crossroad, 1990).

———. *The Daily Reader for Contemplative Living.* (New York: Continuum, 2006).

———. *The Human Condition.* (Mahwah, NJ: Paulist, 1999).

———. *Intimacy with God.* (New York: Crossroad, 1994).

———. *Invitation to Love.* (New York: Continuum, 1992).

———. *Manifesting God.* (New York: Lantern Books, 2005).

———. *Open Mind, Open Heart.* (New York: Continuum, 1992).

———. *The Parables of Jesus.* (New York: Crossroad, 2010).

———. *Reawakenings.* (New York: Crossroad, 1992).

———. *Reflections on the Unknowable.* (Brooklyn: Lantern Books, 2014).

———. *That We May Be One: Christian Non-Duality.* (West Milford, NJ: Contemplative Outreach Publication, 2019).

Kehoe, Nancy. *Wrestling with Our Inner Angels: Faith, Mental Illness, and the Journey to Wholeness.* (San Francisco: Jossey-Bass, 2009).

Kelly, Edward, Crabtree, Adam, and Marshall, Paul. *Beyond Physicalism: Toward Reconciliation of Science and Spirituality.* (Lanham, MD: Rowman & Littlefield, 2015).

BIBLIOGRAPHY

Kennedy, Robert. *Zen Gifts to Christians.* (New York: Continuum, 2004).

———. *Zen Spirit, Christian Spirit.* (New York: Continuum, 1995).

Koenig, H., King, Dana, and Carson, Verna, eds. *Handbook of Religion and Health.* (Oxford: Oxford University Press, 2012).

Komonchak, J., Collins, M., and Land, D., eds. *The New Dictionary of Theology.* (Collegeville, MN: Liturgical Press, 1990).

Kreeft, Peter, and Tacelli, Ronald. *Handbook of Christian Apologetics.* (Downers Grove, IL: InterVarsity Press, 1994).

Kripal, Jeffrey. *Comparing Religions.* (Chichester: Wiley & Sons, 2014).

———. *The Flip.* (New York: Bellevue Literary Press, 2019).

———. *Roads of Excess, Palaces of Wisdom.* (Chicago: University of Chicago Press, 2001).

Krummel, Richard. *Fear, Control, and Letting Go: How Psychological Principles and Spiritual Faith Can Help Us Recover from Our Fears.* (Bloomington, IN: WestBow, 2013).

Kuhn, Thomas L. *The Structure of Scientific Revolutions.* (Chicago: University of Chicago Press, 1996).

Kung, Hans. *The Beginning of All Things: Science and Religion.* (Grand Rapids: Eerdmans, 2007).

Kurtz, Ernest, and Ketcham, Katherine. *The Spirituality of Imperfection.* (New York: Bantam, 1992).

Kushner, Harold S. *How Good Do We Have to Be?* (New York: Little, Brown and Company, 1996).

———. *When Bad Things Happen to Good People.* (New York: Avon, 1983).

Kushner, Lawrence. *Honey from the Rock: An Introduction to Jewish Mysticism.* (New York: Harper & Row, 2000).

———. *The Universe in a Single Atom: The Convergence of Science and Spirituality.* (New York: Morgan Road, 2005).

Landa, Fray Diego de. *An Account of the Things of Yucatan.* (Mexico: Monclem Ediciones, 2000).

Landis, B., and Gottlieb, R., eds. *Deep Ecology and World Religions: New Essays on Sacred Ground.* (New York: State University of New York Press, 2001).

Lederman, Leon. *The God Particle: If the Universe Is the Answer, What Is the Question?* (New York: Dell, 1994).

Leonardini, Ray. *Toxic Shame and Contemplative Prayer: From Hiding to Healing.* (Folsom, CA: Prison Contemplative Fellowship, 2019).

Levin, Jeff. *God, Faith, and Health: Exploring the Spirituality-Healing Connection.* (New York: John Wiley & Sons, 2001).

Levy, David. *Gray Matter: A Neurosurgeon Discovers the Power of Prayer.* (Carol Stream, IL: Tyndale House, 2011).

Lewis, C. S. *A Grief Observed.* (San Francisco: HarperCollins, 1961).

———. *Mere Christianity.* (San Francisco: HarperCollins, 2001).

———. *The Problem of Pain.* (New York: Simon & Schuster, 1996).

Lienhard, John. *The Engines of Our Ingenuity.* (New York: Oxford University Press, 2000).

———. *How Invention Begins.* (Oxford: Oxford University Press, 2006).

———. *Inventing Modern.* (New York: Oxford University Press, 2003).

Linn, Dennis, and Linn, Matthew. *Healing Life's Hurts.* (New York: Paulist, 1977).

Linn, Matthew, Linn, Sheila, and Linn, Dennis. *Understanding Difficult Scriptures in a Healing Way.* (New York: Paulist, 2001).

Losee, John. *A Historical Introduction to the Philosophy of Science.* (New York: Oxford University Press, 2001).

Lu, Chao-Yang, et al. "First Object Teleported from Earth to Orbit." (*MIT Technology Review*, July 10, 2017).

Luisi, Pier Luigi. *The Emergence of Life: From Chemical Origins to Synthetic Biology.* (Cambridge: Cambridge University Press, 2006).

Machado, Calixto, et al. "A Reason for Care in the Clinical Evaluation of Function on the Spectrum of Consciousness." (Functional Neurology, Rehabilitation, The Spectrum of Consciousness and Ergonomics, 2017).

Madrid, Patrick. *Surprised by Truth 2.* (Manchester, NH: Sophia Institute Press, 2000).

Manning, Brennan. *Ruthless Trust.* (New York: HarperCollins, 2002).

Marinelli, Anthony. *Conscience and Catholic Faith.* (Mahwah, NJ: Paulist, 1991).

Matt, Daniel. *God and the Big Bang: Discovering Harmony between Science and Spirituality.* (Woodstock, VT: Jewish Lights, 2006).

Matt, Daniel. *The Essential Kabbalah.* (New York: Harper One, 1979).

———, trans. *Zohar.* (Woodstock, VT: Skylight Paths, 2007).

Matthews, Dale. *The Faith Factor: Proof of the Healing Power of Prayer.* (New York: Penguin, 1998).

McGinn, Bernard. *Christian Mysticism.* (New York: Random House, 2006).

McGinn, Bernard, ed. *Christian Mysticism: The Essential Writings.* (New York: Modern Library, 2006).

McGinn, Bernard, and McGinn, Patricia. *Early Christian Mystics.* (New York: Crossroad, 2003).

McNeil, J. A., et al. "American Pain Society Questionnaire of Hospitalized Patients." (*Journal of Pain and Symptom Management* 16, no. 1 [1998]: 29–40).

"Meditation." *Business Week* (August 30, 2004).

Meninger, William. *The Loving Search for God: Contemplative Prayer and the Cloud of Unknowing.* (New York: Continuum, 1995).

———. *The Process of Forgiveness.* (New York: Continuum International, 2004).

Merton, Thomas. *The Ascent to Truth.* (New York: Harcourt Brace & Co., 1981).

———. *Dialogues with Silence.* (San Francisco: HarperCollins, 2001).

———. *Mystics and Zen Masters.* (New York: Farrar, Straus and Giroux, 1967).

———. *New Seeds of Contemplation.* (New York: New Directions, 1961).

———. *The Seven Storey Mountain.* (Orlando: Harcourt Brace & Company, 1948).

———. *A Year with Thomas Merton.* (San Francisco: HarperCollins, 2004).

Miller, L., et al. "Neuroanatomical Correlates of Religiosity and Spirituality in Adults at High and Low Familial Risk for Depression." (*JAMA Psychiatry*, 2014).

Moody, Raymond. *Life after Life.* (New York: Doubleday Dell, 1975).

Moore, Lauren, and Greyson, Bruce. "Characteristics of Memories for Near-Death Experiences." (*Consciousness and Cognition*, May 2017).

Moore, Thomas. *Care of the Soul.* (New York: Harper Perennial, 1992).

Morris, M., Thorne, K., and Yurtsever, U. "Wormholes, Time Machines, and the Weak Energy Condition." (American Physical Society: *Physical Review Letters* 61, no. 13, September 26, 1988).

Morse, Melvin, and Perry, Paul. *Closer to the Light: Learning from the Near-Death Experiences of Children.* (New York: Ivy Books, 1990).

Neal, Mary. *To Heaven and Back: A Doctor's Extraordinary Account of Her Death, Heaven, Angels, and Life Again.* (Colorado Springs: WaterBrook Press, 2012).

Nelson, Kevin. *The Spiritual Doorway in the Brain.* (New York: Penguin Group, 2011).

Newberg, Andrew. *Neurotheology: How Science Can Enlighten Us about Spirituality*. (New York: Columbia University Press, 2018).

Newberg, Andrew, and Waldman, Mark. *Born to Believe*. (New York: Simon & Schuster, 2006).

———. *How God Changes Your Brain*. (New York: Bantam Books, 2009).

Nietzsche, Friedrich. *Sprach Zarathustra: Ein Buch für Alle und Keinen*. (Mannheim: Ernst Schmeitzner, 1883–1891).

Nouwen, Henri. *Clowning in Rome*. (New York: Doubleday, 1979).

———. *The Only Necessary Thing*. (Crossroad, 1999).

———. *The Return of the Prodigal Son*. (New York: Doubleday, 1992).

———. *The Way of The Heart*. (New York: HarperCollins, 1981).

O'Leary, Denyse, and Beauregard, Mario. *The Spiritual Brain: A Neuroscientist's Case for the Existence of the Soul*. (New York: HarperCollins, 2007).

O'Murchu, Diarmuid. *Quantum Theology: Spiritual Implications of the New Physics*. (New York: Crossroad, 1997).

O'Neill, John. *The Fisherman's Tomb: The True Story of the Vatican's Secret Search*. (Huntington, IN: Sunday Visitor Publishing, 2018).

Origen. *An Exhortation to Martyrdom*. (New York: Paulist, 1979).

Ornstein, Robert. *The Psychology of Consciousness*. (New York: Penguin, 1972).

Palmieri, Arianna, et al. "'Reality of Near-Death-Experience Memories: Evidence from a Psychodynamic and Electrophysiological Integrated Study. (*Human Neuroscience*, June 19, 2014).

Pargament, Kenneth. *Spiritually Integrated Psychotherapy: Understanding and Addressing the Sacred*. (New York: Guilford, 1999).

Peacock, Arthur. *The Sound of Sheer Silence: How Does God Communicate with Humanity: Neuroscience and the Person*. (Vatican City: Vatican Observatory Publications, 2002).

Peck, M. Scott. *The Road Less Traveled*. (New York: Simon & Schuster, 1998).

Pennington, Basil M. *Centering Prayer: Reviewing an Ancient Christian Prayer Form*. (New York: Doubleday, 1980).

———. *True Self—False Self*. (New York: Crossroad, 2000).

Penrose, Roger. *The Emperor's New Mind: Concerning Computers, Minds, and the Laws of Physics*. (New York: Penguin Books, 1991).

———. *Fashion, Faith, and Fantasy*. (Princeton, NJ: Princeton University Press, 2016).

Polkinghorne, John. *Belief in God in an Age of Science*. (New Haven, CT: Yale University Press, 1998).

———. *The Quantum World*. (Princeton, NJ: Princeton University Press, 1989).

———. *Quarks, Chaos & Christianity*. (New York: Crossroad, 1997).

Price, John. *Revealing Heaven*. (New York: HarperCollins, 2013).

Pseudo-Dionysius, The Complete Works. (New York: Paulist, 1987).

Rahner, Karl. *On Prayer*. (Collegeville, MN: Liturgical Press, 1967).

Rohr, Richard. *Everything Belongs: The Gift of Contemplative Prayer*. (New York: Crossroad, 2002)

———. *Falling Upward: A Spirituality for the Two Halves of Life*. (San Francisco: Jossey-Bass, 2011).

Rolheiser, Ronald. *Forgotten among the Lilies*. (New York: Doubleday, 2005).

———. *The Holy Longing*. (New York: Doubleday, 1999).

Rosenblum, Bruce, and Kuttner, Fred. *Quantum Enigma: Physics Encounters Consciousness*. (New York: Oxford University Press, 2011).

Russell, Jeffrey B. *Inventing the Flat Earth: Columbus and Modern Historians*. (New York: Praeger, 1991).

Schachter-Shalomi, Zalman. *Jewish with Feeling*. (New York: Penguin, 2005).

Schroeder, Gerald. *Genesis and the Big Bang*. (New York: Bantam, 1992).

———. *The Hidden Face of God: How Science Reveals the Ultimate Truth*. (New York: Simon & Schuster, 2001).

———. *The Science of God*. (New York: Simon & Schuster, 2009).

Sheldrake, Rupert. *Morphic Resonance: The Nature of Formative Causation*. (Rochester, VT: Inner Traditions International, 2009).

Sheldrake, Rupert, McKenna, Terence, and Abraham, Ralph. *Chaos, Creativity, and Cosmic Consciousness*. (Rochester, VT: Inner Traditions International, 2001).

Smith, Huston. *Why Religion Matters*. (New York: HarperCollins, 2001).

———. *The World's Religions*. (San Francisco: HarperCollins, 1961).

Southgate, Christopher. *God, Humanity and the Cosmos: A Textbook in Science and Religion*. (New York: T&T Clark, 2011).

Spitzer, Robert. *New Proofs for the Existence of God: Contributions of Contemporary Physics and Philosophy*. (Cambridge: Eerdmans, 2010).

———. *The Soul's Upward Yearning*. (San Francisco: Ignatius Press, 2015).

Steiner, Rudolf. *Mystics after Modernism*. (Great Barrington, VT: Anthroposophic Press, 2000).

Suzuki, D. T. *The Zen Doctrine of No-Mind*. (Boston: Weiser Books, 1969).

Swimme, Thomas, and Tucker, Mary. *Journey of the Universe*. (New Haven, CT: Yale University Press, 2011).

Teasdale, Wayne. *The Mystic Heart: Discovering a Universal Spirituality in the World's Religions*. (Novato, CA: New World Library, 1999).

Teilhard de Chardin, Pierre. *The Phenomenon of Man*. (New York: Harper & Row, 1975).

Teresa of Avila. *The Book of My Life*. (Boston: Shambhala, 2007).

———. *The Way of Perfection*. (New York: Doubleday, 1964).

Texas Catholic Herald. "Houston Deacon Presents Healthy Benefits of Prayer." February 21, 2016.

Theophane the Monk. *Tales of a Magic Monastery*. (New York: Crossroad, 2001).

Therese of Lisieux. *The Autobiography of Saint Therese of Lisieux: The Story of a Soul*. (New York: Doubleday, 1957).

Tocqueville, Alexis de. *Democracy in America*. (New York: Random House, 2000).

Tsan, Miao. *Living Truth: The Path of Light*. (Houston: Bright Sky Press, 2014).

Wallace, B. Alan. *Genuine Happiness*. (Hoboken, NJ: John Wiley & Sons, 2005).

Ward, Benedicta, trans. *The Desert Fathers: Sayings of the Early Christian Monks*. (London: Penguin, 2003).

Watts, Fraser. *Cognitive Neuroscience and Religious Consciousness: Neuroscience and the Person*. (Vatican: Vatican Observatory Publications, 2002).

Wicks, Robert. *Crossing the Desert*. (Notre Dame, IN: Soring Books, 2007).

Wilber, Ken. *A Theory of Everything*. (Boston: Shambhala, 2000).

———. *Integral Psychology: Consciousness, Spirit, Psychology, Therapy*. (Boston: Shambhala, 2000).

———. *The Marriage of Sense and Soul: Integrating Science and Religion*. (New York: Broadway Books, 1999).

Wilson, Ken. *Mystically Wired: Exploring New Realms in Prayer*. (Nashville: Thomas Nelson, 2009).

Wiseman, James A. *Theology and Modern Science: Quest for Coherence*. (New York: Continuum, 2002).

BIBLIOGRAPHY

Woods, Thomas. *How the Church Built Western Civilization*. (New York: Regnery History, 2005).

World Life Expectancy. *Life Expectancy Fertility Rate*. (https://ourworldindata.org/life-expectancy).

Worthington, Everett, Jr., ed. *Handbook of Forgiveness*. (New York: Taylor & Francis Group, 2005).

Zammattio, Carlo, et al. *Leonardo the Scientist*. (New York: McGraw-Hill, 1980).

Zubay, G. *Origins of Life on the Earth and in the Cosmos*. 2nd ed. (New York: Academic Press, 2000).

Index

A

abba, 122
Abbot Joseph, 144
abortion, 100
Abrahamic faiths, 119, 120, 165
accelerator, 55, 56, 177
Acceptance and Commitment Therapy, 164
acids, 65–66, 69, 176, 177
acronyms, 92
ACT. *See* Acceptance and Commitment Therapy
ACTS (adoration, contrition, thanksgiving, supplication), 121, 154–55
addiction, 106
adenosine triphosphate, 69
adoration, 8, 121
adult formation, xx
affective peace, 97, 163
Africa, 54, 70, 74, 156
afterlife, 13, 15
AI. *See* artificial intelligence
alchemy, 176
Alco Standard, 24, 62
Alexander, Eben, 130
algebra, 176
Allah, 120, 165
altered consciousness, 128, 177
altered states, 98, 128, 132, 160
alternating current, 56
Amos (OT book), 175
amplitude modulation, 42
amygdala, 135
anecdotal, 90, 150
Angkor Wat, 104
anterior cingulate, 135

Anthropic Principle, 51, 52, 138, 177
anthropomorphism, 77
antibiotics, 101
anxiety, 109, 110
apes, 54, 72
apologetics, xx
apophatic prayer, 108, 120, 121,
Aquinas, Thomas, 94, 99, 101, 156
Arctic Ocean, 25
Argentina, 25, 80
arteries, 175
artificial intelligence, 83, 84
Asclepiades, 175
aspiration, 102
Association for Near-Death Studies, 160
assumptions, 13, 31,
astronomy, 175
asymptotic convergence, xxi, 16, 156
atheists, 114, 162
atherosclerosis, 106
Atmanism, 175
atmosphere, 36, 67
atom bomb, 33
Atomic Model, 57
atoms, 33, 46, 50, 52, 54, 57–60, 63, 65, 81, 177
attributes, 19, 66, 98, 129, 131, 134
Augustine of Hippo, 14, 61, 90, 102, 117
Auschwitz, 150
Australia, 74
awe, 25, 31, 45, 46, 52, 77, 105, 133, 139, 141
axioms, 172

B

Bacon, Roger, 21, 176

bacteria, 74, 177
Baldwin, Philip, 109
Barbour, Ian, 65, 70
Bartimaeus, 152, 153
Baylor College of Medicine, 109
Baylor University, 158
BDDC. *See* Brain Death and Disorders of Consciousness
Beauregard, Mario, 133
Benson, Herbert, 110
Bernard of Clairvaux, 118
biases, 111
Bible, 14, 146
Big Bang Theory, 43, 45, 46, 47, 48, 49, 50, 52, 54, 57, 98, 114, 132, 139, 140
bioethics, 97, 98, 101, 102
biology, xx, 79, 136
bipolar condition, 2 77, 81, 93, 125
black holes, 34, 50, 177
Black Plague, 176
blood pressure, 106, 124
Blue Mosque, 113, 176
body, 16, 17, 69, 91, 105, 106, 129, 130, 131, 136, 145, 146, 162,
Body of Christ, 69, 138
Boelens, Peter, 109
Bohr, Niels, 57, 59
bombs. *See* atom bomb; hydrogen bomb
Borde, Arvin, 52
Boson, 56
Bowling Green State University, 162
Boyle, Joseph, 141
Brahminism, 175
Brain Death and Disorders of Consciousness, 160, 161
brain, xx, 33, 52, 76, 79–92, 94–99, 108, 111, 123, 125, 126, 130, 131, 133, 135, 136, 145, 146, 161
brain disorders, 90
brain hemispheres, 84
brain waves, 82
Brazil, 25

Bruteau, Beatrice, 77
Buddha, 165, 175
Buddhism/Buddhists, 17, 88, 114, 115, 135, 157, 162, 175, 176
Burma, 17
Butterfly Effect, 61
BVG Proof, 52, 177

C

Ca atom (calcium), 63
CAC. *See* Center for Action and Contemplation
calculus, 176
calendar, 175
Cambodia, 176
Cambrian explosion, 54, 70, 71, 177
canals, 175
cancer, 7, 8, 20, 106
Cannato, Judy, 133
canon (biblical), establishment of, 15, 16
canonization of saints, 176
Canon Law, 177
carbon, 49, 66, 69, 80
cardiovascular health, 106
Carmelites, 176
Carson, Ben, 80
Cassian, John, 117, 118, 120
cats, DNA of, 75
catatonic state, 87
Catechism of the Catholic Church, 103
Catholic Church, xxi, xxiv, 2, 8, 14, 76–77, 98, 99, 116, 157. See also *Catechism of the Catholic Church*
celestial bodies, 56
cells, 51, 54, 67, 69, 70, 71, 76, 82
Center for Action and Contemplation, 159
Center for Faith and Culture, 155
Centering Prayer, 8, 115, 119, 120, 122–29, 133, 135, 140, 144, 147, 154, 155, 159, 160, 162, 164
centrifugal force, 34

INDEX

CFC. *See* Center for Faith and Culture
chaos, 11, 58, 60, 61, 62, 76
chaos theory, 60, 61, 62
chaplains, hospital, 99, 105, 126, 158, 164
Chartres Cathedral, 176
chemistry, xx, 2, 12, 22, 32, 48, 49, 50, 52, 65, 66, 67, 80
chemotherapy, 8
Chile, 75
chimpanzees, DNA of, 75
China, 74, 100, 175, 176
chirality, 66
cholesterol, 106
Christ, 4, 27, 45, 67, 69, 73, 76, 104, 106, 120, 137, 138, 139, 175
Christianity, 15, 99, 111, 114, 115–16
Church of the Holy Sepulchre, 104
classism, 93
clergy, xx, 156
Clockmaker Theory, 62
clocks, 39, 44, 54
Cloud of Unknowing, 118
CMR. *See* Conference on Medicine & Religion
CN. *See* Contemplative Network
cognition, as NDE attribute, 95, 110, 132
cognitive timelessness, 163
cohabitation, 107, 150, 151
COL. *See* Contemplative Outreach
collective consciousness, 138
Columbus, Christopher, 38
coma, 82
communism, 177
compass, 176
compassion, 100, 135, 136
computers, 60, 80, 83, 84
condensation trail, 56
conductivity, 177
Conference on Medicine & Religion, 157, 158
Conferences, The, 118
confession, 4, 6

Confirmation Bias, 110, 111, 114, 115, 116, 124, 140, 177
Confucius, 175
conscience, 13, 17, 89, 90, 94, 96, 98, 103, 104, 110, 114, 124, 128, 137, 138, 140, 151
conscious, 77, 82, 84, 86, 87, 92, 93, 94, 97, 100, 101, 102, 104, 111, 124, 125, 126, 131, 136, 140, 141, 151
consciousness, xx, 33, 70, 77–80, 82, 86, 89, 97, 98, 99, 103, 104, 113, 128, 130, 131, 132, 134, 137–42, 149, 151, 160, 161
conservation of matter, 32
contemplatio, 108, 114, 121
contemplation, 82, 108, 110, 111, 115, 121, 122, 128, 136, 159, 162, 165,
Contemplative Network, xii, 115, 157, 159, ,
Contemplative Outreach, 115, 119, 120, 122, 154, 159, 160
contemplative prayer, 116, 118, 119, 122, 152, 159, 162
continuous anatomical assessment, 133, 163
contrition, 121
convergence, xxi, xxii
Copernicus, 176
coronary artery disease, 106
Corpus Callosum, 85
Craster, Katherine, 87
creation, xx, 15, 25, 26, 33, 43, 46, 48, 52, 63, 66, 70, 73, 76, 77, 82, 98, 131
Crick, Francis, 68
crude oil, 177
Crusades, 176
Cuba, 126, 127, 155, 156, 161
culpability, 93, 94, 95, 96, 100, 140
culturalism, 93
cultures, 75, 99, 100
cyclotron, 56

D

Dalai Lama, 157
Dalton, John, 57
Daniel (OT book), 175
D'Aquili, Eugene, 136
dark energy, 31, 32, 34
dark mass, 32
dark matter, 31, 32, 34
Darwin, Charles, xxii, 71, 72, 177
Da Vinci, Leonardo, xxii, 176
Davidson, Richie, 135
daydreaming, 39, 82
DB. *See* Dialectical Behavior Therapy
deacons, 150, 151, 156
death, culture of, 100
death certificate, 101
decimals, 176
deductive logic, 19–20, 59
Delio, Ilia, 77
depression, 2, 53, 58, 62, 77, 106, 109, 110, 125, 126, 154,
Descartes, Rene, 176
diabetes, 106
Dialectical Behavior Therapy, 164
dialogue, xx, 160, 165
dimensions, 26, 38, 47, 58, 63
dinosaurs, extinction of, 54
Dionysius, 25, 94, 129
direct current, 56
disorder, 50, 97
Disorders of Consciousness, 126, 128, 130, 160
dissipative structures, 76
dissonance, 17
Divine Healer, 126
Divine, 15, 16, 35, 67, 73, 97, 103, 104, 120, 121, 124, 126, 129, 131, 133, 135–42, 176
divinity, 12, 18
divorce, 107, 151
DNA, 12, 53, 54, 65, 67, 68, 69, 73, 75, 77, 139, 140, 177

dogs, DNA of, 75
Donnelly, Doris 156
doppler effect, 44
Double Effect Principle, 102
dualism, 84, 87, 89
Dyson, Freeman, 49

E

Eagleman, David, 87, 88
earth, 20, 25–28, 30–38, 45, 51, 54, 63, 66–72, 75, 77, 98, 115, 119, 134–35, 140, 175
East-West Schism, 176
echo, 44
Eckart, Fred, 154
Eckhart, Meister, 118, 141
economism, 93
ECRSH. *See* European Conference on Religion, Spirituality & Health
ecstasy, 8, 77, 129, 131, 136, 145
Edison, Thomas, 177
EEG. *See* electroencephalography
Einstein, Albert, xxii, 11, 12, 14, 19, 26, 28, 32, 33, 35–41, 43, 45, 46, 47, 49–52, 56, 63, 64, 135
electroconvulsive therapy (ECT), 3
electroencephalography, 82, 133, 135, 163
electromagnetic energy, 42, 43, 44, 46, 58, 63, 81, 82, 177
electron microscopes, 43, 58
electrons, 57, 58, 59, 60, 62, 63
Elijah (OT book), 175
embodiment, 136
emotion, 83, 86, 110, 113, 122, 135
empathy, 110, 136, 137
enantiomers, 66
energy, 32, 33, 34, 36, 39, 41, 43, 44, 49, 51, 56, 58, 59, 64, 67, 69, 81, 139, 147
engineering, 12, 24, 62, 83, 100
England, 15, 71, 118
entanglement, 64, 65, 177
entropy, 50, 52, 65, 76

environmental protection, 102
enzymes, 69
epilepsy, 85
Equivalence Principle, 36, 177
Eratosthenes, 175
ethics, 98
Ethiopia, 73, 74
Eucharist, 3, 4, 8, 121
Europe, 74, 100, 107, 151, 176
European Conference on Religion, Spirituality & Health, 157
euthanasia, 98
Evolutionary Theory, 71
exothermic reaction, 33
expert systems, 83
extraterrestrials, 44

F

faith, xxi, xxii, xx, 12, 16–19, 21, 22, 25, 41, 45, 46, 51, 53, 57, 61, 62, 65, 69, 72, 73, 78, 83, 84, 88, 89, 90, 93, 94, 96, 98–101, 103–9, 114, 115, 116, 124, 128, 130, 131, 134, 135, 139, 140, 141, 150, 152, 155–58, 161, 162, 165, 175
Faraday, Michael, 56
fertility rate, 100
fission, 33
Flat Earth Society, 37, 137
fMRI (functional magnetic resonance imaging), 109
force, 22, 32, 33, 34, 45, 46, 47, 50, 51, 64, 91, 121
forgiveness, xxiv, 5, 6, 107, 109, 128, 140, 154
four forces, 47, 48, 51
fractals, 11, 61
Francis (pope), 96, 150, 165
Franciscans, 135, 159
Franklin, Rosalind, 68
freedom, 16, 95
Freeman, Laurence, 117, 118, 159
frequency modulation, 41–42
free will, 84, 89, 90, 103, 104, 136, 140, 151
frontal lobes, 81, 91, 135
Fr. Tom, 2, 4, 5, 6, 24, 93
fruit fly, DNA of, 75
F&S (faith and science), xxi, xxii, xx, 150, 156, 165
fudge factor, 46
Fuegian Indians, 75
functional magnetic resonance imaging (fMRI), 109
fundamentalism, 16
fusion, 33
fuzzy logic, 83

G

Gage, Phineas, 90, 91, 94
Galapagos Islands, 71
galaxies, 29, 30, 31, 34, 40, 44, 49, 50, 82
Galileo Commission, 159
Galileo Galilei, xxii, 176
Gamow, George, 12
gears, 175
Gene Theory, 72
General Relativity, 35, 36, 37, 40, 41, 177
genes, 177
Genesis (OT book), 43, 45, 110, 151
genomics, 75
geometry, 175
George Washington Institute for Spirituality & Health, 157, 158
Germany, 54, 74, 176
Gethsemani (Abbey of), 7, 113, 119
Gandhi, Mahatma, 117
Giffords, Gabby, 97
glass, 176
globe, first, 175

God, xxi, xxii, xxiii, 1, 3, 6, 7, 8, 13–21, 23, 25, 26, 27, 31, 33, 43, 45, 55, 56, 58, 63, 65, 67, 70, 71, 77, 80, 86, 89, 90, 94, 95, 96, 98, 104, 106, 107, 108, 110, 114, 117, 119, 120–26, 128, 130, 131, 132, 134, 135, 136, 140, 145, 146, 147, 150, 151, 156, 165
"God is dead," 58
God Particle, 55, 56
Goldin, Stan, 82
gong, 122, 123, 165
Gordon, Harvey, 115
Gothic structural design, 176
Graham, John, 158
gravity, 33–37, 45, 50, 51, 177
Great Wall, 80, 176
Gregory of Nyssa, 117
grief, xxiv, 8, 142
gunpowder, 176
Guth, Alan, 52
GWISH. *See* George Washington Institute for Spirituality & Health

H

Hadron Collider, 55, 56
Haldane, John, 67
HamA, 109
HamD, 109
Hameroff, Stuart, 160
Handbook of Religion and Health, 105, 162
Harvard University, 158
Hawking, Stephen, 83, 114
healing research, 104–11
healings, 18
Heaven, 3, 5, 18, 51, 98, 133, 134
Heisenberg, Werner, 58, 62, 134, 156
Heisenberg Uncertainty Principle, 58
hermeneutic approach, 13, 14, 151
Hermitage Museum, 80
Hesse, Kristin (Cavazos), 62
Hesse, Linda, 2, 3, 8, 24, 58, 62, 77, 102, 125, 158

Higgs, Peter, 56
Hinduism, 114, 115
hippocampus, 82
Hippocrates, 175
Hiroshima, 33
HIS. *See* Institute for Spirituality and Health
Holocaust, 138
homiletics, 151–54
hominids, 54
Hoover Dam, 80
HOPE LOT, 109
Hosea (OT book), 175
hospital chaplaincy, 154
hostility, 110
Hubble telescope, 30, 177
Hugo, Victor, 18
humans, 15, 52, 54, 72–77, 81, 83, 84, 87, 93, 100, 115, 116, 138, 139, 140
Hundredth Monkey Effect, 138
hybrids, 73
hydrocarbons, 49, 56, 66, 80
hydrodynamics, 177
hydrogen, 33, 48, 57, 59, 62, 69, 80
hydrogen bomb, 33
hypnosis, 82, 177
hypotheses, 19, 21, 69

I

IANS. *See* International Association for Near-Death Studies
Iceland, 80
Ignatius of Antioch, 176
illuminative stage, 94, 129
immigration, 100
incarceration, 96
incarnation, 138
indeterminacies, 62, 76
inductive reasoning, 19, 20, 59
indulgences, 176
Industrial Revolution, 177

indwelling, 94, 103, 104, 115, 120, 122, 140
inheritance, 177
insomnia, 110
Institute for Spirituality and Health, 104, 105, 109, 126, 157, 158
Institute of Neurology and Neurosurgery, 161
Institute of Noetic Sciences, 158, 159
integration, xxii
intelligent life, 54
intercessory prayers, 108
interfaith (interreligious) dialogue, xx, 115, 160, 165
interfaith empathy, 136
interfaith meditation, 115
interfaith prayer, 114, 116, 119, 122
interfaith science, 157, 158
Interlukin-6, 106
International Association for Near-Death Studies, 160, 161
internet, 24, 138, 177
intubation, 102
intuition, 86
invisible, 31–34, 82
IONS. *See* Institute of Noetic Sciences
iron, 175
Isaiah (OT book), 128, 175
ISH. *See* Institute for Spirituality and Health
Islam, 115, 120, 176
Israel, 150
Italy, 176
IV medications, 109

J

James, William, 134, 137
Japan, 88, 150, 176
Jerusalem, 176
Jesus, 3, 14, 16, 17, 18, 27, 32, 98, 99, 116, 118, 120, 121, 123, 141, 152, 153, 175
John Carroll University, 156

John Cassian, 117, 118
John of the Cross, 8, 118, 129, 134
John Paul II, xxii, 11, 13, 14, 16, 17, 19, 21
Jonestown massacre, 138
Judaism, 15, 114, 115, 120
judgmentalism, 95, 154
Jungfrau mountain, 80
justice, 96, 102
just war theory, 102

K

Kabbalah, 115
Kason, Yvonne, 161
kataphatic prayer, 108
Keating, Thomas, 8, 67, 73, 115, 117, 118, 122, 128, 147, 150, 160
Kehoe, Kim, 115, 154, 159, 160
Kelly, Edward, 134
Kelvin, 177
Kennedy, Jacqueline, 101
keplar, 176
ketamine, 3
kinetic energy, 51
knowledge, xxi, 5, 13, 15, 16, 45, 95, 128, 134, 137
Koenig, Harold, 105, 162
Kripal, Jeffrey, 136
Kubler-Ross, Elisabeth, 130

L

Lachance, Claire, 159
languages, xxii, 14, 89
Laws of Inheritance, 73
Lectio Divina, 120, 122
Lemaitre, Georges, xxii, 43, 46
Lewis, C. S., xxi
life, xx, 2, 7, 8, 17, 28, 33, 38, 51, 52, 54, 65–71, 85, 87, 95, 99, 101, 106, 118, 124, 125, 133, 137, 145
life expectancy, 106

light, 22, 23, 26, 27, 28, 30, 34, 36, 39–43, 45, 47, 49, 50, 63, 64, 65, 75, 77, 122, 142, 151, 177,
light-years, 26
limbic system, 87
linguistics, 96
liturgy, 39, 105, 106, 120, 140, 144, 158, 162
logic, 16, 19, 20, 39, 59, 83, 114,
Loma Linda University, 158
Lomax, Jim, 126
Lorimer, David, 159
Louvre, the, 80
love, xxiv, 3, 9, 17, 18, 27, 31, 35, 43, 45, 65, 70, 89, 98, 111, 117, 125, 128, 140, 144, 147, 150, 154
lupus, 106
Luther, Martin, 14, 176

M

Maccabaeus, 175
Machado, Calixto, 97, 129–30, 133, 161, 162
machines, 176
Machu Pichu, 80
Magellan, Ferdinand, 176
magnetic field, 56
magnetic resonance, 80
Maimonides, 43
Main, John, 159
Mandelbrot, Benoit, 11, 61
marriage preparation, 150
Masada, 150
Mass, 144
massage, 109
mathematics, xxii, 11, 12, 83, 160, 175
matter, 17, 32–36, 39, 41, 50, 51, 61, 79, 82, 86, 101, 124, 134
May, Michael, 92, 94, 154
Mayans, 75, 176
MBCT. *See* Mindfulness-Based Cognitive Therapy

MBSR. *See* Mindfulness-Based Stress Reduction
McGinn, Bernard, 129
McMath, Jahi, 97
M.D. Anderson Cancer Center, 154
medicine, 92, 102, 153 157, 176
medicine and religion conferences, 157–58
meditatio, 108, 121
meditation, 82, 108, 109, 115, 117, 122, 157, 159, 162
Membrane Theory, 47, 177
memory, 3, 82, 126, 145, 146
Mendel, Gregor, xxii, 72, 73
Mendeleev, Dmitri, 60
Mendelian heredity, 73
Meninger, William, 117, 118, 122, 159
Menninger Clinic, 126
Menninger Department of Psychiatry (Baylor College of Medicine), 162
Mercury, 175
Merton, Thomas, 1, 7, 8, 9, 114, 119, 122, 134, 136
microbes, 54, 69
microwaves, 43–46
Milan Cathedral, 176
Milky Way, 26, 29, 30, 34, 177
Miller, Harold, 66, 67
Miller, Lisa, 106
Mind and Life Institute, 157
Mindfulness-Based Cognitive Therapy, 164
Mindfulness-Based Stress Reduction, 164
ministries, xxiii, 150–54
miracles, 14, 154
Mitchell, Edgar, 159
M&L. *See* Mind and Life Institute
mnemonic devices, 92
Moebius curve, 37, 38
molecules, 33, 43, 52, 54, 65–70, 80, 139, 177
momentum, 58
monasteries, 7, 8, 108, 119, 143, 144, 149

monasticism, 176
monks, 17, 115, 116, 118, 122, 129, 135, 144, 147, 157, 162
Mont Saint-Michel, 104
Moody, Raymond, 130
moon, the 33, 36, 77, 140
Moore, Thomas, 18
morals, 2, 81, 89–99, 154
Mormons, 177
morphogenesis, 71, 177
Morse, Melvin, 130
Moses, 175
MRI (magnetic resonance imaging), 135
Muhammad, 176
Muir Woods, 54
Müller, Gerhard Ludwig, 96
multiple-stable stimuli, 85
Muslims, 93, 100, 114, 176
Myanmar, 17, 149
mystery, 15, 116
mystical confidentiality, 129
mysticism, xx, 51, 62, 82, 110, 111, 115, 118
mystics, 8, 13, 116, 117, 118, 125, 129, 131, 142
myth, 151

N

nationalism, 93
natural death, 100, 101
naturalism, 93
natural selection, 71
nature, xxi, xx, xxiv, 13, 14, 15, 18, 19, 21, 22, 25, 27, 34, 37, 39, 58, 60–66, 68, 71, 76, 79, 88, 90, 103, 110, 118, 134, 139, 147, 151, 155, 165
Nazism, 177
NDE. *See* Near Death Experiences
Neal, Mary, 131
Neanderthals, 177
Near Death Experiences, 97, 98, 130–33, 136, 137, 138, 140, 154, 162, 163, 177

Nelson, Nelson, 86, 134
neocortex, 87
nerves, 82
Nesti, Donald, 155
neurons, 82
neuroplasticity, 135, 177
neuroscience, 13, 91, 96, 100, 126, 127, 133–36, 157, 160, 161, 162, 177
neurotheology, 133, 161, 177
Neuschwanstein castle, 80
Newberg, Andrew, 134, 135, 136
New Testament, 14
Newton, Isaac, 33–34, 35, 37, 176
Newtonian mechanics, 59
Ngorongoro Crater, 54
Nguyen, Daokim, 6–7
Nicene Creed, 27, 77
Nietzsche, Friedrich, 20
NMR. *See* nuclear magnetic resonance
Nobel Prize, 44, 55, 76, 79
non-dualism, 15–18, 69, 84, 99, 124, 135
non-local universe, 63–65
non-theism, 108, 116, 157, 162, 164
noosphere, 141
North America, split in, 75
North Pole, 25
Nouwen, Henri, 4
nuclear force, 47, 102
nuclear magnetic resonance, 80
nuclear reaction, 33
nucleus, 57, 58, 59, 81
nuns, 2, 24, 116, 118, 122, 129, 135

O

occipital-parietal region, 135
Ohio State University, 158
Old Testament, 14, 154, 175
Omega point, 76, 138, 141
omnibenevolence, 133, 136, 141
omnipotence, 52, 139, 141
omnipresence, 77, 139, 141
omniscience, 98, 140, 141

oneness, 77, 82, 129, 133, 136, 137, 140, 141, 142
ontology, 171
Oparin, Aleksandr, 67
orbit, 27, 34, 57, 58, 59
ordination, 7, 111, 155
Oregon State University, 158
Origen, 117
original sin, 151
Ornstein, Robert, 134
Ortega, Jamie, 161
Our Savior on Spilled Blood Cathedral, 104
outside space, 38, 49, 131
outside time, 50
Ozarks, 25

P

paganism, 175
pain, 99, 101, 109, 110, 147, 151
palliative care, 157
Pangea, 54, 70, 71, 177
pantheism, 175
paradigm, 19, 35, 37, 38, 46, 52, 59, 60, 64, 156
paranormal, 98, 131
Pargament, Ken, 107, 162
parietal-frontal region, 135
parietal lobes, 92
Parkinson's disease, 126–27, 128
particle, 41, 56, 57
pasteurization, 177
Paul (apostle), 93
P-Brane Theory, 47, 177
peace, 8, 18, 97, 122, 125, 129, 131, 145, 149, 165
Pelagianism, 176
penicillin, 177
Pennington, Basil, 117, 118, 122, 159
Penrose, Roger, 52, 80, 83–84, 160
Penzias, Arno, 44
periodic table, 60, 177

permanent deacon, 94, 110
Peterhof Palace, 80
Phenomenon of Man, The (Teilhard de Chardin), 76, 138
philosophy, xxii, 13, 24, 156, 160, 162
photons, 39, 41, 49, 51, 63
physics, xx, 43, 52
pi, calculation of, 176
Planck, Max, 55, 79
planets, 20, 21, 27, 30, 54, 66
Plato, 175
Poland, 74, 150
polar axis, 175
polarity, 55, 56
political voting, 102
politicism, 93
Pontifical Academy of Sciences, 157
Pontifical University, xxi, 96, 155, 162
post-traumatic stress disorder, 93, 109, 126, 128, 164
postulates, 172
potential energy, 51
prayer, xii, 7–8, 105, 108–10, 113, 114. *See also* Centering Prayer; Contemplative Prayer
prefrontal cortex, 81, 86
prejudice, 93, 110, 111, 124
premenstrual syndrome, 110
Prigogine, Ilya, 76
principles, 13, 16, 17, 18, 21, 71, 84, 98, 99, 101, 102, 123
prioritization, 101
prison, 3, 7, 137, 154, 155
procreation, 141
proposition, 172
protons, 57
Pseudo-Dionysius, 118
psychology, xx, 90, 111, 116, 134
Ptolemy maps, 176
PTSD. *See* post-traumatic stress disorder
purgative, 25, 129
Pythagorean theorem, 175

Q

QEEGt (quantitative EEG tomography), 133, 163
quantum entanglement, 63, 64, 136, 140
quantum leaps, 59
quantum mechanics, 59, 63
quantum physics, 20, 41, 55, 59, 60, 63, 64, 76, 79, 140, 160
quantum theory, 55, 59, 60
quarks, 57

R

racism, 93
radar, 43, 44, 161
radio, 43
rapid eye movement, 83
rationalization, 2, 4, 5, 89, 95, 110, 124
reason, xxii, 13, 16, 17, 19, 34, 47, 86, 88, 94, 134, 177
red shift, 44, 45, 46
redundancy, 86
reincarnation, 17, 88, 137
relational love, 73, 137, 139, 140
relationship, 6, 56, 115, 120, 122, 135, 141
religion, xxi, 11, 15, 16, 55, 105, 161, 162
religionism, 93
REM. *See* rapid eye movement
resilience, 86
retreats, 7, 8, 144, 146, 155–56
revelation, 13
Rheims Cathedral, 176
rheumatoid arthritis, 106
rhythmic waves, 83
RNA, 68, 69, 177
Rohr, Richard, 159–60
Rosetta Stone, 175
Rule of Benedict, 118
Rumi, 142
Rumi Mosque, 113
Russia, 74, 100
Rutherford, Ernest, 57

S

sacraments, 2, 150
Sanazaro, Ernie, 6
satellites, 34
SCE. *See* Spiritual Contemplative Experience
Schachter-Shalomi, Zalman, 114
Schroeder, Gerald, 45
science, v, xxi, xxii, xx, 11, 12, 13, 16–19, 21, 22, 24, 25, 26, 28, 32, 34, 37, 40, 41, 43, 52, 54, 55, 58, 59, 63, 69, 71, 72, 74, 77, 78, 81, 83, 84, 89, 90, 93, 96, 97, 99, 101–5, 115, 116, 122, 124, 128, 130, 134, 139, 140, 141, 152, 156, 157, 158, 160, 161, 165
Scientific & Medical Network, 158, 159
scientific method, 21, 134
scientific notation, 21, 26
scientism, 16, 20, 93
scripture, xxi, 13, 14, 15, 18, 32, 42, 83, 99, 118, 120, 121, 125, 151, 155
secularism, science and, 2–3
secular science (scientists), 25, 102–3
secular world, 25, 56, 99, 108
self-awareness, 86, 89, 151
selfhood, 136
seminaries, xxi, 2, 4, 6, 7, 16, 24, 155, 156, 161
Seminario de San Carlos y San Ambrosio, 155
Septuagint, 175
Serengeti Park, 54
sexers, 88
sexism, 93
Sheldrake, Rupert, 71
Shell, 24
Shinto Shrines, 176
Sikhism, 114, 176
sin, xxiv, 2, 4, 95, 96, 147, 151
singularity, 48, 49, 50, 51, 76, 98, 132, 139, 140
Sistine Chapel, xxi, 176

sleep, stages of, 82
smallpox, 176
Smith, Smith, 164
SMN. *See* Scientific and Medical Network
smoking, 107
soap, 175
social justice, 177
Socrates, 20, 175
solar eclipse, 175
solar system, 27, 29, 49, 51
Song of Solomon (OT book), 18, 33
Sorbonne University, 176
soul, 4, 16, 17, 18, 69, 76, 77, 84, 103, 104, 105, 117, 124, 137, 142, 155
South America, 70, 71, 75, 100
space, 35–41, 49, 50, 51, 62, 65, 114, 133, 136, 137, 139
space-time continuum, 40
Spain, 74
Special Relativity, 38, 39
spectrum, 42, 44, 68
speed of light, 26, 32, 39, 40, 63, 64
Spirit, 3, 5, 7, 14, 15, 67, 73, 94, 104, 119, 120, 125, 128, 129, 135, 140, 141, 142, 147,
spiritual and science conferences, 158–59
Spiritual Contemplative Experience, 129, 132, 133, 136, 137, 138, 154, 162, 163, 177
spiritual direction, xx
spirituality, 17, 105, 136, 156, 161, 162
Spirituality of Imperfection, 90
Spiritually Transformative Experience, 132
Spitzer, Robert, 51
statistics, 19, 100
St. Benedict, 118, 176
St. Cassian, 118, 120
STE. *See* Spiritually Transformative Experience
steam engine, 177
St. Louis University, 158
St. Mary's Seminary, 155

Stonehenge, 15, 175
St. Peter's Basilica, 104
Strake, George 104
String Theory, 47, 177
strong nuclear force, 46
subatomic particles, 41, 47, 48, 52, 54, 55, 56, 57, 64, 65, 69, 76, 139, 177
subprograms, 83
Sufism, 115
suicide, 16, 17, 96, 100
sun, 15, 27, 28, 35, 39
Sun, the, 26, 28, 33, 35, 75, 175
supplication, 121
surgery, 8, 175, 176
Switzerland, 39, 55, 163
syllogism, 20
symbols, 26, 64
synapses, 78, 81
synchronicity, 3, 133
synchronization, 17
synchrotron, 55, 56
Syneidesis, 89

T

Teilhard de Chardin, Pierre, 76, 77, 138, 141, 149, 177
telephone, 177
telescope, 30, 43, 44, 176
temperatures, 48, 49, 56
Temple Mount, 104
Templeton Foundation, 156
Ten Commandments, 175
Teotihuacan, 176
Teresa of Avila, 8, 116, 117, 118, 129
Teresa of Calcutta, 177
Texas Catholic Herald, 161
Texas Medical Center, 105, 157
TFR. *See* total fertility rate
Thailand, 54
thalamus, 135
thanksgiving, 121

INDEX

The Institute for Rehabilitation and Research (TIRR), 97
Theophane the Monk, 141, 143, 144
theory, 18, 19, 34, 35, 36, 37, 39, 41, 43, 45, 47, 49, 52, 61, 63, 65, 71, 72, 76, 102, 140, 156, 160
Theory of Morphogenesis, 71
Therese of Lisieux, 117, 125
thermodynamics, 50, 76
The Science of Consciousness, 160, 163
Thomas Aquinas. *See* Aquinas, Thomas
Thomson, J. J., 57
thoughts, 7, 8, 37, 108, 117, 122–27, 144, 145, 165
time, 4–7, 32, 35, 37, 38, 39, 45–48, 50, 56, 70, 76, 80, 92, 95, 96, 99, 111, 121, 131, 133, 144, 147, 154, 156, 161, 162
timeline, xxii, 52, 54, 71, 175
Timetables of History, The (Grun), 175
Torah, 175
total fertility rate, 100
tradition, xxi, 14, 15, 99, 108, 115, 118, 119, 120, 155, 165, 175
transcendence, 15, 49, 51, 136
transcendent, 97, 98, 131, 132, 140, 162
Trappists, 7, 8, 108, 113, 115, 119, 120, 122, 123, 143, 159, 176
traumas, 93
triatum, 135
Trinity, 12, 124
Tsan Miao, 165
TSC. *See* The Science of Consciousness
Turing, Alan, 71

U

Ultra-Deep Field, 30
uncertainty, 58, 59, 60, 62, 76, 134, 177
Uncertainty Principle, 58, 59, 62
unconscious, 26, 80, 82, 86–89, 92, 93, 97, 103, 104, 110, 111, 124, 125, 126, 128, 130, 131, 137, 140, 141, 154
Unified Forces, 177

Unified Theory, 45, 46, 47, 48, 49, 50
Unitive Stage, 129
universe, 15, 20, 21, 22, 26, 28, 31, 32, 34, 35, 37, 38, 40, 42–54, 56, 58, 62, 63, 65, 76, 77, 80, 82, 87, 129, 131, 135, 136, 139, 140, 141, 177
University of Chicago, 158
University of Notre Dame, 158
University of Paris, 176
University of St. Thomas, 155, 159, 165
Unparticle Force, 64
Uranium 235, 33
Urey, Stanley, 66
Urey-Miller experiment, 66

V

vagus nerve, 3
Vardhamana, 175
variability, 71
Vatican II, 4, 116, 119, 122, 177
vegetative state, 102
veins, 175
Venezuela, 25
Versailles, 80
Veterans Affairs, 126
Vietnam, 6, 126, 128
Vilenkin, Alexander, 52
viruses, 177
visible, 25, 28, 29, 31, 32, 38, 42, 43, 44, 56, 82

W

Walach, Harald, 159
water clock, 175
water wheel, 175
Watson, James, 68
waves, 41, 42, 43, 44, 45, 82
WCCM. *See* World Community of Christian Meditation
weak nuclear force, 46
wellbeing, 106, 107
Western Wall, 113

wheels, 175
Whitman, Walt, 84
Wilson, Ken, 134
Wilson, Robert, 44
Windsor Castle, 80
World Community of Christian Meditation, 119, 159
wormhole entanglement, 136
wormholes, 40, 64, 65, 177
Wormhole Theory, 40

Worthington, Everett, Jr., 107

X

X-ray crystallography, 68
X-rays, 43

Z

Zohar, 116
Zoroastrianism, 15, 175

Endnotes

1 Public domain

PREFACE

2 Barbour, Ian. *When Science Meets Religion: Enemies, Strangers or Partners?* (New York: HarperCollins, 2000).
3 Wilber, Ken. *The Marriage of Sense and Soul: Integrating Science and Religion.* (New York: Broadway Books, 1999).
4 Galilei, Galileo. *The Collected Works of Galileo Galilei.* (Hastings, UK: Delphi Publishing, 2017).
5 Darwin, Charles. *On the Origin of Species.* (New York: Random House, 1975).
6 Holder, Rodney, and Mitton, Simon, eds. *Georges Lemaitre: Life, Science and Legacy.* (Berlin: Springer-Verlag, 2012).
7 Edelson, Edward. *Gregor Mendel—and the Roots of Genetics.* (New York: Oxford University Press, 1999).
8 Losee, J. L. *A Historical Introduction to the Philosophy of Science.* (New York: Oxford University Press, 2001).
9 Coyne, George V., and Omizzolo, Alessandro. *Wayfarers in the Cosmos: The Human Quest for Meaning.* (New York: Crossroad, 2002).
10 Barbour, Ian. *Religion and Science: Historical and Contemporary Issues.* (San Francisco: HarperCollins, 1990).
11 Grun, Bernard. *The Timetables of History.* (New York: Simon & Schuster, 1991).
12 Zammattio, Carlo, et al. *Leonardo the Scientist.* (New York: McGraw-Hill, 1980).
13 Kreeft, Peter, and Tacelli, Ronald. *Handbook of Christian Apologetics.* (Downers Grove, IL: InterVarsity Press, 1994).
14 Southgate, Christopher. *God, Humanity and the Cosmos: A Textbook in Science and Religion.* (New York: T&T Clark, 2011).

1 — MOTIVATED TO LOVE

15 Nouwen, Henri. *The Return of the Prodigal* Son. (New York: Doubleday, 1992).

2 – REVELATION TO PRINCIPLES

16 Merton, Thomas. *The Seven Storey Mountain*. (Orlando: Harcourt Brace & Company, 1948).
17 Dupre, Louis, and Wiseman, James A., eds. *Light from Light: An Anthology of Christian Mysticism*. (New York: Paulist, 2001).
18 Keating, Thomas. *Open Mind, Open Heart*. (New York: Continuum, 1992).
19 Avila, Teresa of. *The Way of Perfection*. (New York: Doubleday, 1964).
20 Kavanaugh, Kieran, and Larking, Erneste E., eds. *John of the Cross, Selected Writings*. (New York: Paulist, 1987).
21 Credit: Courtesy Frances Griffin.
22 Gamow, George. *One Two Three . . . Infinity*. (New York: Dover Publications, 1988).
23 *Catechism of the Catholic Church*. (Washington, DC: US Conference of Catholic Bishops, 2000).
24 Drees, Willem. *Religion, Science and Naturalism*. (Cambridge: Cambridge University Press, 1997).
25 Rolheiser, Ronald. *The Holy Longing*. (New York: Doubleday, 1999).
26 Ecklund, Elaine. *Why Science and Faith Need Each Other*. (Grand Rapids: Brazos, 2020).
27 Ashley, Benedict, and Deely, John. *How Science Enriches Theology*. (South Bend, IN: St. Augustine's Press, 2012).
28 Moore, Thomas. *Care of the Soul*. (New York: Harper Perennial, 1992).
29 Kuhn, Thomas L. *The Structure of Scientific Revolutions*. (Chicago: University of Chicago Press, 1996).

3 – PHYSICS TO CREATION

30 Nietzsche, Friedrich. *Sprach Zarathustra: Ein Buch für Alle und Keinen*. (Mannheim: Ernst Schmeitzner, 1883–1891).
31 Credit: NASA.
32 Swimme, Thomas, and Tucker, Mary. *Journey of the Universe*. (New Haven, CT: Yale University Press, 2011).
33 Credit: Alexaldo/Dreamstine.com.
34 Credit: Mark Garlick.
35 Credit: NASA.
36 Public domain. Nick Risinger (text) and Robert Hesse (captions).
37 Credit: NASA.
38 Credit: Nicolas Douillet, with text and captions by Robert Hesse.

ENDNOTES

39 Credit: Nicolas Douillet, with text and captions by Robert Hesse.
40 Credit: Gwen Shockey/Science. Source with text and captions by Robert Hesse.
41 Morris, M., Thorne, K., and Yurtsever, U. "Wormholes, Time Machines, and the Weak Energy Condition." (American Physical Society: *Physical Review Letters* 61, no. 13, September 26, 1988).
42 Credit: Veronika Oliinyk / Dreamstine.com, with text and captions by Robert Hesse.
43 Credit: Veronika Oliinyk / Dreamstine.com.
44 Schroeder, Gerald L. *The Hidden Face of God: How Science Reveals the Ultimate Truth*. (New York: Simon & Schuster, 2001).
45 Public domain.
46 Kaku, Michio. *Hyperspace*. (New York: Anchor Books Doubleday, 1994).
47 Credit: NASA Image Collection / Alamy Stock Photo.
48 Haisch, Bernard. *The Purpose-Guided Universe*. (Franklin Lakes, NJ: New Page Books, 2010).
49 *The Soul's Upward Yearning*. (San Francisco: Ignatius Press, 2015), 310–311.

4 — CHEMISTRY TO LIFE

50 Credit: Science Photo Library.
51 Hazen, Robert M. *Genesis: The Scientific Quest for Life's Origins*. (New York: Joseph Henry Press, 2005).
52 Credit: CERN, Grantotufo, Dreamstime.com.
53 Credit: CERN, Dmfrancesco, Dreamstime.com.
54 Lederman, Leon. *The God Particle: If the Universe Is the Answer, What Is the Question?* (New York: Dell, 1994).
55 Credit: Lonely11 / Dreamstine.com.
56 Hawking, Stephen. *A Brief History of Time*. (New York: Bantam, 1988).
57 Credit: Author Geek3.
58 Gleick, J. *Chaos: Making a New Science*. (New York: Penguin, 1988).
59 Credit: Courtesy Frances Griffin.
60 Sheldrake, Rupert, McKenna, Terence, and Abraham, Ralph. *Chaos, Creativity, and Cosmic Consciousness*. (Rochester, VT: Inner Traditions International, 2001).
61 Keating, Thomas. *Reflections on the Unknowable*. (Brooklyn: Lantern Books, 2014).
62 Greene, Brian. *The Fabric of the Cosmos*. (New York: Random House, 2004).
63 Lu, Chao-Yang, et al. "First Object Teleported from Earth to Orbit." (*MIT Technology Review*, July 10, 2017).

64 Morris, M., Thorne, K., and Yurtsever, U. "Wormholes, Time Machines, and the Weak Energy Condition." (American Physical Society: *Physical Review Letters* 61, no. 13, September 26, 1988).

65 Barbour, Ian. *Religion and Science: Historical and Contemporary Issues*. (San Francisco: HarperCollins, 1990).

66 Luisi, Pier Luigi. *The Emergence of Life: From Chemical Origins to Synthetic Biology*. (Cambridge: Cambridge University Press, 2006).

67 Zubay, G. *Origins of Life on the Earth and in the Cosmos*. 2nd ed. (New York: Academic Press, 2000).

68 Credit: Barrington Brown / Science Source.

69 Fraden, S., Epstein, I., and Ermentrout, B. "Testing Turing's Theory of Morphogenesis in Chemical Cells." (*Proceedings of the National Academy of Sciences*, March 25, 2014).

70 Sheldrake, Rupert. *Morphic Resonance: The Nature of Formative Causation*. (Rochester, VT: Inner Traditions International, 2009).

71 Hazen, Robert M. *Genesis: The Scientific Quest for Life's Origins*. (New York: Joseph Henry Press, 2005).

72 Ayala, Francisco J. *Darwin's Gift to Science and Religion*. (Washington, DC: Joseph Henry / National Academies Press, 2007).

73 Haught, J. F. *God after Darwin: A Theology of Evolution*. (Oxford: Westview Press, 2000).

74 Credit: Andree Valley, University of Wisconsin–Madison.

75 Bronowski, J. *The Ascent of Man*. (Boston: Little, Brown and Company, 1973).

76 Chardin, Teilhard de. *The Phenomenon of Man*. (New York: Harper & Row, 1975), 63.

77 Manney, Jim. "Papal Praise for Teilhard." (https://www.ignatianspirituality.com/papal-praise-for-teilhard/).

78 Delio, Ilia. *Christ in Evolution*. (New York: Orbis, 2008).

79 Delio, Ilia. *The Unbearable Wholeness of Being: God, Evolution, and the Power of Love*. (New York: Orbis, 2013).

80 Bruteau, Beatrice. *God's Ecstasy: The Creation of a Self-Creating World*. (New York: Crossroad, 1997).

5 – BIOLOGY TO CONSCIOUSNESS

81 Credit: Sergey Khakimullin / Dreamstine.com.

82 Credit: Rob3000 / Dreamstime.com.

83 Goldin, Stan. "The Human Soul: Can It Survive in an Age of Neuroscience?" (Harvard Medical School, Cognitive Rhythms Collaborative, For the November 19, 2014 Cambridge Roundtable).
84 Credit: NASA.
85 Credit: Benjamin Arenkiel.
86 Penrose, Roger. *The Emperor's New Mind: Concerning Computers, Minds, and the Laws of Physics*. (New York: Penguin Books, 1991).
87 Credit: Bryan Derksen.
88 Davidson, Richard. *The Emotional Life of Your Brain*. (London: Penguin, 2013).
89 Cairns-Smith, A. G. *Evolving the Mind: On the Nature of Matter and the Origin of Consciousness*.(New York: Cambridge University Press, 1996).
90 Eagleman, David. *Incognito*. (New York: Random House, 2011).
91 Craster, Katherine (1841–1874). Attributed as author.
92 Eagleman, David. *Incognito*. (New York: Random House, 2011), 57–58.
93 Kung, Hans. *T The Beginning of All Things: Science and Religion*. (Grand Rapids: Eerdmans, 2007).
94 Kurtz, Ernest, and Ketcham, Katherine. *The Spirituality of Imperfection*. (New York: Bantam, 1992).
95 Public domain.
96 Credit: Science Photo Library.
97 Holy Bible. *The New American Bible*. (New York: Oxford University Press, 1990).
98 Aquinas, Thomas. *The Summa Theologica*, trans. Fathers of the English Dominican Province. (London: Burns, 1947).
99 Hesse, Robert. "Letter to Cardinal Müller on Sin." (Rome: Congregation for the Doctrine of the Faith, September 19, 2014).
100 Fins, Joseph. *Rights Come to Mind*. (New York: Cambridge University Press, 2015).
101 Machado, Calixto, et al. "A Reason for Care in the Clinical Evaluation of Function on the Spectrum of Consciousness." (Functional Neurology, Rehabilitation, The Spectrum of Consciousness and Ergonomics, 2017).
102 Machado, Calixto. "Jahi McMath: A New State of Disorder of Consciousness." (*Journal of Neurosurgical Sciences* 2021, doi:10.23736/S0390-5616.20.04939-5).
103 Moody, Raymond. *Life after Life*. (New York: Doubleday Dell, 1975).
104 Beauchamp, Tom, and Childress, James. *Principles of Biomedical Ethics*. (New York: Oxford University Press, 1997).
105 Flynn, Eileen. *Issues on Health Care Ethics*. (Upper Saddle River, NJ: Prentice-Hall, 1997).
106 Aquinas, Thomas. *The Summa Theologica*, trans. Fathers of the English Dominican Province. (London: Burns, 1947).

107 Henshaw, S., Singh, S., and Haas, T. "The Incidence of Abortion Worldwide." (World Life Expectancy. *Life Expectancy Fertility Rate.* (https://ourworldindata.org/life-expectancy).

108 World Life Expectancy. *Life Expectancy Fertility Rate.* (*http://www.worldlifeexpectancy.com/fertility-rate-by-country*)

109 Aquinas, Thomas. *The Summa Theologica*, trans. Fathers of the English Dominican Province. (London: Burns, 1947).

110 Landis, B., and Gottlieb, R., eds. *Deep Ecology and World Religions: New Essays on Sacred Ground.* (New York: State University of New York Press, 2001).

111 Francis (pope). *Laudato Si': On Care for Our Common Home.* (Vatican: Encyclical Letter, May 24, 2015).

112 *Catechism of the Catholic Church.* (Washington, DC: US Conference of Catholic Bishops, 2000), 900).

113 O'Neill, John. *The Fisherman's Tomb: The True Story of the Vatican's Secret Search.* (Huntington, IN: Sunday Visitor Publishing, 2018).

114 Levin, Jeff. *God, Faith, and Health: Exploring the Spirituality-Healing Connection.* (New York: John Wiley & Sons, 2001).

115 Koenig, H., King, Dana, and Carson, Verna, eds. *Handbook of Religion and Health.* (Oxford: Oxford University Press, 2012).

116 Ehman, J. W., et al. "Do Patients Want Physicians to Inquire about Their Spiritual or Religious Beliefs If They Become Gravely Ill?" (*Archives of Internal Medicine* [1999]: 803–806).

117 Miller, L., et al. "Neuroanatomical Correlates of Religiosity and Spirituality in Adults at High and Low Familial Risk for Depression." (*JAMA Psychiatry* 71, no. 2 [2014]: 128–135).

118 Koenig, H. G., Cohen, H. J., et al. "Attendance at Religious Services, Interleukin-6, and Other Biological Parameters of Immune Function in Older Adults." (*International Journal of Psychiatry Medicine* 27, no. 3 [1997]: 233–250, doi: 10.2190/40NF-Q9Y2-0GG7-4WH6. PMID: 9565726).

119 Worthington, Everett, Jr., ed. *Handbook of Forgiveness.* (New York: Taylor & Francis Group, 2005).

120 Pargament, Kenneth. *Spiritually Integrated Psychotherapy: Understanding and Addressing the Sacred.* (New York: Guilford, 1999).

121 Meninger, William. *The Process of Forgiveness.* (New York: Continuum International, 2004).

122 Meninger, William. *The Process of Forgiveness.* (New York: Continuum International, 2004).

123 Matthews, Dale. *The Faith Factor: Proof of the Healing Power of Prayer.* (New York: Penguin, 1998).

124 Rahner, Karl. *On Prayer.* (Collegeville, MN: Liturgical Press, 1967).

ENDNOTES

125 Kripal, Jeffrey. *Comparing Religions*. (Chichester: Wiley & Sons, 2014).
126 Levy, David. *Gray Matter: A Neurosurgeon Discovers the Power of Prayer*. (Carol Stream, IN: Tyndale House, 2011).
127 McNeil, J. A., et al. "American Pain Society Questionnaire of Hospitalized Patients." (*Journal of Pain and Symptom Management* 16, no. 1 [1998]: 29–40).
128 Baldwin, Philip, Boelens, Peter, et al. "Neural Correlates of Healing Prayers, Depression and Traumatic Memories: A Preliminary Study." (*Complementary Therapies in Medicine* 27 [2016]: 123–129).
129 Boelens, Peter, and Boelens, Eleanor. *Released to Soar: A Medical Study Shows the Power of Healing Prayer*. (Pella, IA: Write Place, 2010).
130 Pennington, Basil. *True Self—False Self*. (New York: Crossroad, 2000).

6 – PSYCHOLOGY TO MYSTICISM

131 Credit: Abidal / Dreamstime.com.
132 Keating, Thomas. *The Human Condition*. (Mahwah, NJ: Paulist, 1999).
133 Hackett, Conrad, and McClendon, David. *Christians Remain World's Largest Religious Group, but They Are Declining in Europe*. (Washington, DC: Pew Research Center, 2015).
134 Tsan, Miao. *Living Truth: The Path of Light*. (Houston: Bright Sky Press, 2014).
135 Kennedy, Robert. *Zen Spirit, Christian Spirit*. (New York: Continuum, 1995).
136 Kennedy, Robert. *Zen Gifts to Christians*. (New York: Continuum, 2004).
137 Merton, Thomas. *Mystics and Zen Masters*. (New York: Farrar, Straus and Giroux, 1967).
138 Hawking, Stephen. *Brief Answers to the Big Questions*. (New York: Bantam, 2018), 37–38.
139 Matt, Daniel C., trans. *Zohar*. (Woodstock, VT: Skylight Paths, 2007).
140 Matt, Daniel. *The Essential Kabbalah*. (New York: Harper One, 1979).
141 Kushner, Lawrence. *Honey from the Rock: An Introduction to Jewish Mysticism*. (New York: Harper & Row, 2000).
142 Barks, Coleman, trans. *The Essential Rumi*. (San Francisco: Harper, 1995).
143 Howe, Mary. *Sitting with Sufis: A Christian Experience of Learning Sufism*. (Brewster, MA: Paraclete Press, 2005).
144 Gulen, Fethullah. *Key Concepts in the Practice of Sufism*. (Fairfax, VA: The Fountain, 1999).
145 Suzuki, D. T. *The Zen Doctrine of No-Mind*. (Boston: Weiser Books, 1969).
146 Therese of Lisieux. *The Autobiography of Saint Therese of Lisieux: The Story of a Soul*. (New York: Doubleday, 1957).

147 Keating, Thomas. *Intimacy with God*. (New York: Crossroad, 1994).
148 Cassian, John. *The Conferences*. (New York: Newman Press, 1997).
149 Chittister, Joan. *The Rule of Benedict*. (New York: Crossroad, 2003).
150 Johnston, William K., ed. *The Cloud of Unknowing*. (New York: Doubleday, 1973).
151 Meninger, William. *The Loving Search for God: Contemplative Prayer and the Cloud of Unknowing*. (New York: Continuum, 1995).
152 Ganss, George, trans. *The Spiritual Exercises of Saint Ignatius*. (Chicago: Loyola Press, 1992).
153 Merton, Thomas. *New Seeds of Contemplation*. (New York: New Directions, 1961).
154 Pennington, Basil M. *Centering Prayer: Reviewing an Ancient Christian Prayer Form*. (New York: Doubleday, 1980).
155 Funk, Mary. *Thoughts Matter: The Practice of the Spiritual Life*. (New York: Continuum, 2002).
156 Therese of Lisieux. *The Autobiography of Saint Therese of Lisieux: The Story of a Soul*. (New York: Doubleday, 1957).
157 Krummel, Richard. *Fear, Control, and Letting Go: How Psychological Principles and Spiritual Faith Can Help Us Recover from Our Fears*. (Bloomington, IN: WestBow, 2013).
158 Keating, Thomas. *Reflections on the Unknowable*. (Brooklyn: Lantern Books, 2014).
159 Kripal, Jeffrey. *Roads of Excess, Palaces of Wisdom*. (Chicago: University of Chicago, 2001).
160 McGinn, Bernard. *Christian Mysticism*. (New York: Random House, 2006).
161 Inge, W. R. *Christian Mysticism*. (New York: Meridian, 1956).
162 McGinn, Bernard, and McGinn, Patricia. *Early Christian Mystics*. (New York: Crossroad, 2003).
163 Moody, Raymond. *Life after Life*. (New York: Doubleday Dell, 1975).
164 Morse, Melvin, and Perry, Paul. *Closer to the Light: Learning from the Near-Death Experiences of Children*. (New York: Ivy Books, 1990).
165 Price, John. *Revealing Heaven*. (New York: HarperCollins, 2013).
166 Alexander, Eben. *Proof of Heaven: A Neurosurgeon's Journey into the Afterlife*. (New York: Simon & Schuster, 2012), 81.
167 Neal, Mary. *To Heaven and Back: A Doctor's Extraordinary Account of Her Death, Heaven, Angels, and Life Again*. (Colorado Springs: WaterBrook, 2012).
168 Cannato, Judy. *Radical Amazement: Contemplative Lessons from Black Holes, Supernovas, and Other Wonders of the Universe*. (Notre Dame, IN: Sorin Books, 2006).
169 Beauregard, Mario, Courtemanche, Jerome, and Paquette, Vincent. "Brain Activity in Near-Death Experiences during a Meditative State." (*Resuscitation Journal* 80, 2009: 1006–1010).

170 James, William. *The Varieties of Religious Experience: A Study in Human Nature.* (1902; USA: Seven Treasures, 2009).
171 Ornstein, Robert. *The Psychology of Consciousness.* (New York: Penguin, 1972).
172 Newberg, Andrew. *Neurotheology.* (New York: Columbia University Press, 2018).
173 Nelson, Kevin. *The Spiritual Doorway in the Brain.* (New York: Penguin Group, 2011).
174 Kelly, Edward, Crabtree, Adam, and Marshall, Paul. *Beyond Physicalism: Toward Reconciliation of Science and Spirituality.* (Lanham, MD: Rowman & Littlefield, 2015).
175 Wilson, Ken. *Mystically Wired: Exploring New Realms in Prayer.* (Nashville: Thomas Nelson, 2009).
176 Goleman, Daniel, and Davidson, Richard. *Altered Traits: Science Reveals How Meditation Changes Your Mind, Brain, and Body.* (New York: Penguin Random House, 2017).
177 Newberg, Andrew, and Waldman, Mark. *How God Changes Your Brain.* (New York: Bantam, 2009).
178 O'Leary, Denyse, and Beauregard, Mario. *The Spiritual Brain: A Neuroscientist's Case for the Existence of the Soul.* (New York: HarperCollins, 2007).
179 D'Aquili, Eugene, and Newberg, Andrew. *The Mystical Mind: Probing the Biology of Mystical Experience.* (Minneapolis: Fortress, 1999).
180 Goldin, Stan. "The Human Soul: Can It Survive in an Age of Neuroscience?" (Harvard Medical School, Cognitive Rhythms Collaborative, For the November 19, 2014 Cambridge Roundtable).
181 Bao, Ning, et al. *Traversable Wormholes as Quantum Channels: Exploring CFT Entanglement Structure and Channel in Holography.* (University of California–Berkeley: arXiv:180.05963v2 [hep-th], November 12, 2018).
182 Kripal, Jeff. *The Flip.* (New York: Bellevue Literary Press, 2019).
183 Sheldrake, Rupert. *Morphic Resonance: The Nature of Formative Causation.* (Rochester, VT: Inner Traditions International, 2009).
184 Teilhard de Chardin, Pierre. *The Phenomenon of Man.* (New York: Harper & Row, 1975).
185 Teilhard de Chardin, Pierre. *The Phenomenon of Man.* (New York: Harper & Row, 1975).
186 Eckhart, Meister. *Sermons and Treatises.* (London: Element Books, 1992).
187 Keating, Thomas. *Reflections on the Unknowable.* (Brooklyn: Lantern Books, 2014).
188 Barks, Coleman, trans. *The Essential Rumi.* (San Francisco: Harper, 1995).
189 Keating, Thomas. *That All May Be One: Christian Non-Duality.* (West Milford, NJ: Contemplative Outreach Publication, 2019).

7 – CALLED TO SERVE

190 Theophane the Monk. *Tales of a Magic Monastery*. (New York: Crossroad, 2001).

EPILOGUE

191 Keating, Thomas. *Awakenings*. (New York: Crossroad, 1990).
192 Rohr, Richard. *Falling Upward: A Spirituality for the Two Halves of Life*. (San Francisco: Jossey-Bass, 2011).
193 Keating, Thomas. *Awakenings*. (New York: Crossroad, 1990).
194 Keating, Thomas. *Reawakenings*. (New York: Crossroad, 1992).
195 Keating, Thomas. *The Parables of Jesus*. (New York: Crossroad, 2010).
196 Eckart, Fred. *Locked Up and Free*. (Houston: Contemplative Network, 1988, http://www.contemplative.net/documents/locked_up_and_free.pdf).
197 Leonardini, Ray. *Toxic Shame and Contemplative Prayer: From Hiding to Healing*. (Folsom, CA: Prison Contemplative Fellowship, 2019).
198 Freeman, Laurence. *Jesus the Teacher Within*. (New York: Continuum, 2000).
199 Penrose, Roger. *Fashion, Faith, and Fantasy*. (Princeton, NJ: Princeton University Press, 2016).
200 Rosenblum, Bruce, and Kuttner, Fred. *Quantum Enigma: Physics Encounters Consciousness*. (New York: Oxford University Press, 2011).
201 *Texas Catholic Herald*. "Houston Deacon Presents Healthy Benefits of Prayer." February 21, 2016.
202 Baer, Ruth A., ed. *Mindfulness-Based Treatment Approaches*. (San Diego: Academic Press, 2006).
203 Dalai Lama. *The Universe in a Single Atom: The Convergence of Science and Spirituality*. (New York: Morgan Road, 2005).

APPENDIX

204 Komonchak, J., Collins, M., and Land, D., eds. *The New Dictionary of Theology*. (Collegeville, MN: Liturgical Press, 1990).
205 Grun, Bernard. *The Timetables of History*. (New York: Simon & Schuster, 1991).
206 Credit: Spencer Sutton / Science Source Faith.